AF653442

RELIGIOUS MUSIC

RELIGIOUS MUSIC

Praveen Patnaik

Commonwealth

Religious Music

© Reserved

First Published : 2026

ISBN 81-311-0000-6

Published by :
COMMONWEALTH PUBLISHERS (P) LTD.
4831/24, Govind Lane,
Ansari Road, Darya Ganj,
New Delhi - 110002
Ph. : 23272541, 23242541
e-mail : commonwealthpublishers2016@gmail.com

Distributed by :
ARJUN PUBLISHING HOUSE
4831/24, Govind Lane,
Ansari Road, Darya Ganj,
New Delhi - 110002
Ph. : 23272541, 23242541
e-mail : arjunbooks2001@gmail.com

Laser Typesetting by :
Dimple Computers
Delhi

Printed at :
Milan Enterprises
Delhi

Preface

Music is verily the finest art which also happens to be the ideal and pleasant medium of getting into communion with the Infinite, from the time immemorial. The three-fold concentration of mind, body and speech is easily attained through music. When a true devotee sings, he forgets the mundane existence and submerges himself in the integration of *bhava, raga* and *laya*, with the result his soul is elevated to great spiritual heights and is led to the door of the Divine.

The genre of music composed for performance as part of religious ceremonies, is called as religious music. A lot of music has been composed to complement religion, and many composers have derived some inspiration from their religions. Many forms of traditional music have been adapted to fit religions purposes or descended from religious music.

Sometimes religious music changes to fit the times; contemporary Christian music, for example, uses idioms from various popular music styles, with religious lyrics. Gospel music has always done this, for example incorporating funk, and continues to do so. One could contrast the western concepts of monotheism and tonality, all tones relating and resolving to a tonic, with eastern concepts of poly or pantheism and sound, a single pitch containing many.

The present volume analyses the organisational concept of religious music comprehensively. Besides religious and professional musicians, students, teachers, researchers and lovers of music will find this work informative and useful.

Praveen Patnaik

Contents

1

Religious Music

Shahnai/Nagswaram in temples, Piano in churches, harmonium in gurudwaras prove the importance of music in religions. However Music is beyond the religions. It has a tremendous capacity to bring different religions together. We have Hindu musicians singing compositions of Muslim ustads. We have Muslim musicians singing compositions in praise of Krishna, Rama, Shankar, Ganesh, Saraswati etc. Pandit Lalji Gokhale (Disciple of Ustad Ahmad Jan Thirakwa) who went beyond their religions and proved that Music itself is a religion.

Music and religion is highly significant that in India, art is considered as religioun and artistes as messengers of God. Everything Indian for that matter, has its basis in spirituality and particularly so is music. The art of music is never regarded here as a mere system of harmonious sounds, pleasing and appealing to the sensuous part of man. It has all along been held as a divine thing and as an outward representation of the Omnipresent Pranava, OM and has essentially been a prime mode of spiritual pursuit. The sapta svaras are said to have emanated from the Pranava and are capable of evoking 'Vairaghya' (detachment) in the nada upasaka. Our composers have always been mystics, saints, philosophers and agents of religion. And religion had been the constant source of inspiration providing phenomenal food for their thoughts and artistic expression down the corridors of time.

There is much truth in the statement that the highest art is always the most religious and the greatest artist is always a devout man, and nowhere is the truth better illustrated and expounded than in the noble and spiritual lives of our great composers such as the Nayanmars, Alwars, Andal, Jayadeva, Purandara dasa, Narayana Tirtha, Muthu Tandavar, the Musical Trinity, Sadasiva Brahmendra, Mira Bai, Gopalakrishna Bhratiyar and many other devotees of the nadamaya form of God.

Music is verily the finest art which happens to be also the ideal and pleasant medium of getting into communion with the Infinite. The three fold concentration of of mind, body and speech is easily attained through music. When a true devotee sings, he forgets the mundane existence and submerges himself in the integration of bhava, raga and laya, with the result his soul is elevated to great spiritual heights and is led to the door of the Divine. The Indian conception of God as Nada Brahma is most pleasant as it is unique. It is well known that ragas are beautiful tonal forms and each raga gives us a glimpse of the Divine personality in Sound-Nada Brahma.

Just as the presence of God can be felt and experienced by persevering devotion on the part of the devotee, so also the personality of the raga is revealed to one who seeks and enters into the soul of the raga with sensitiveness and depth of devotion. The aesthetic joy that one is able to derive after rendering the alapa of a raga for a considerable duration can only be identified with the religious experience of a devotee after tasting the Divine Bliss. Saint Tyagaraja addresses the mind to delight in the nectar of raga rasa which gives the blessings of Yoga, Yaga, Tyaga and Bhoga in his kriti "raga sudharasa."

The history of Indian Music presents a wonderful galaxy of sterling devotees who worshipped the Lord ceaselessly with the garland of songs. The astonishing output of musical compositions on the subject of the Divine stands as a living testimony to this fact. Sankirtanam or singing the glories of God and bhakti are inseparables. Music forms an integral part of bhakti yoga, and bhakti or devotion forms the very breath of Sangita. Bhakti or higher devotion is parama prema or intense love to God. And it is the highest sentiment that the human soul is capable of.

According to Narada, the indefatigable exponent of bhakti and sangita, the path of devotion is easier and more sweet than the jnana and karma margas, as it fills the mind of the devotee with indescribable peace leading to bliss. The single emotion of bhakti takes manifold forms for its expression viz. sravanam (listening), kirtana (singing the glories of the Lord), vandana (worshipping), smarana (remembering), padasevana (doing Namaskaram or worshipping by falling at the feet of the Lord), archana (worshipping with flowers or kumkum), dasya and sakhya (considering one self as the servant and as a friend respectively), vatsalya (affection of a mother) and kantasakti (by loving Him).

The name, form and attributes of God coupled with the moving melody are effective aids in concentration. This nama sankirtana marga has found great favour with the devotees, as it is the most convenient channel for attainment of trikarana aikya. This cult of kirtana found an ideal home in the banks of the Kavery as early as the period of the Saivite Nayanmars who integrated Tamil with music and offered it as an ardent offering to the Lord. Through music, the glory of the Tamil language was popularised, and bhakti was inculcated in the minds of the listeners.

The Saivite saints like the later composers preached through their devotional hymns a religion of hope and love, a religion of hope and love, a religion of communion and social service. Rightly the hymns of the Nayanmars have become part of the temple rituals since the period of the Cholas. Indian Music has grown and has been kept alive by its intrinsic devotional character. Singing the glories of God and his kalyanagunas with a heart over flowing with ardent devotion and in conformity to scientific tradition (sampradaya) is the religion of the devotees of the nadamaya rupa of the Lord.

Music and Religion in Africa

Music and religion in Africa act as a singular enterprise. Between the two, there is no separation of sacred, secular, music, vocals, or instruments. Often, religious music incorporates call and response patterns as well as improvisation. Spirit possession commonly occurs during a sacred song while at the same time dancing becomes trance-like. Drums play a central role in the both the song and dance. Music reflects the beliefs of the community, sends prayers to particular gods of worship and calls on spirits to influence personal actions. Religion establishes a code of African ethics to define the community and its actions.

Gullah provides one of the clearest examples of African American syncretism and an original interpretation of religion with the combination of spirituality with communal harmony, solidarity, and accountability. Methodist missionaries were the first to introduce Christianity to

African Americans during slavery. Gullahs converted Christianity into their African world view and used the new religion to justify oppressive forces, stimulate the community culture, and focus the vision of freedom. Methodist influences continued through 1844 and then Baptist faith took over as the main contributor to Gullah religion.

Preaching and praying done in plantation houses led to the development of praise houses. Praise houses function both as a place of worship and as a meeting area. Spirituals began in the praise houses. In Africa, spirituals were a means to continue the oral history., and spirituals developed within the Gullah culture as a confirmation of acceptance in Christian churches. Through the singing of spirituals, slaves found an avenue to release feelings of joy, hardship, and hope. Spirituals often had double meanings, and much like the transmission of oral histories in Africa, they acted as ways for slaves to communicate with each other.

Spirituals vary widely from region to region but the basic structure remains the same regardless of the geographic location. Along with spirituals, *shouts* also emerged in the Praise Houses. Shouts begin slowly with the shuffling of feet and clapping of hands (but the feet never cross because that was seen as dancing, which was forbidden within the church). Then the tempo picks up and during the dance, the shouters often become possessed and drop to the floor in exhaustion.

Since most Christian churches forbade the use of drumming, slaves incorporated the use of hand clapping and feet stomping in order to keep musical time. This often intricate hand clapping and stomping distinguishes Gullah music and laid the roots for modern African American music.

At the end of slavery, African Americans made an effort to sever ties with the white churches, and new churches began to develop in Charleston, including the Morris Brown A.M.E. At this time, Baptist and Methodist religions were the most popular among African Americans. It is in these churches that the influence of hymn-lining continues. The hymn-liners compose as they go and hold the responsibility for the creation of spirituals that exist today. At this time of movement, hymns began emphasis social concerns, combining past slave spirituals with the songs developing out of freedom and its own hardships.

Following emancipation some people refused to sing spirituals because they reminded them of slavery. Spirituals became more accepted after they began to more closely resemble European music. The new spirituals were neither African or European. When the spirituals began to lose their authentic form, and became more like anthems, and concert pieces. Spirituals became more refined to be sung in large concert audiences. While the authentic spiritual did not disappear it lost its influence to the more mainstream form of music and religious song.

Music and Inner Life

Every culture lives within the interplay of two movements, an outer movement of performing the activities necessary for the continuation of physical life and an inner movement towards relating to forces, being and intelligence beyond and above that life. The music of a culture is a measure of the relationship and balance between these two movements.

There is a music, nowadays practiced mainly in certain places where the traditional spirit has not completely given way to modernity, that uses its power over the feelings to cut through the self-absorption of everyday life and bring one to an experience of communion, the sense of being part of the vast play of forces that encompass and connect all beings. In Africa music and dance evoke a sense of communion on many levels in a rich tapestry that includes spiritual aspiration, religious experience, evocation of deity, psychic and physical empowerment, enactment of myth and history, teaching, healing, courtship, cultural assimilation and solidarization, mutual criticism, celebration, entertainment and exercise.

Traditional Africa maintains a distinction between religious music and social music. This distinction corresponds to the widespread understanding that spiritual life and material life are on different levels. While many processes of a secular nature may take place in a religious context and vice versa, this is felt as part of the unique drama of each situation, not as an undesirable contradiction. In effect, this ambiguity represents an affirmation that spiritual life and material life are inseparably united as constant reciprocal movements of the human spirit.

In Africa, as in many other traditional cultures, religious music and dance play the central role of invoking possession-trance. In possession, the person loses consciousness of himself as an individual and becomes the vehicle or mouthpiece of a "deity," a personification of one of the great forces of the inner or the outer world. The actions and speech of the person possessed are regarded as those of the deity and are looked to for advice, healing, prophecy, and magical power.

The deities in whose service music and dance are performed are traditionally understood not as being divine in themselves-rather, their divinity is a particle of the Divinity of a higher principle, the creative principle behind the Universe. But this principle is already always everywhere and in everything and hence needs no service to call its presence. No special temporal material condition, such as a temple, ceremony, or artifact, can concentrate its force. Its action at our level is non-action. Its symbol is silence. In music, it is expressed by the rhythmic pulses that are heard innerly though the instrument is not played; through their silence, these pulses give shape and meaning to the rhythm that is heard outerly.

The Great Principle is too far above the level of man for him to relate to It directly. The deities are necessary intermediaries through whom man and God address each other. In some traditions the drums themselves are also specially invested as divine intermediaries. The Dogon say that Drum is the ear of God and one must beat it with the attitude that one is speaking to God on behalf of mankind. This attitude requires respect, but also great force. In the words of a religious song of the Blekete cycle (Blekete is the name of a deity of the Ewe people of Ghana and also the name of the principal drum that is used in this cycle): "A feeble effort will not fulfill the self."

Possession is a magic door to religious experience, but it alone does not constitute a complete relationship with the divine. To have this, to make available to oneself the powers and knowledge that are the property of a divinity, requires a further payment-to make oneself morally divine, to conduct one's life in a way that is pleasing to the divinity. Many obligations and prohibitions corresponding to each deity are known in tradition; however, detailed observances are less important than the prime moral law. This law is the sacredness of Life, which includes the need to understand the particular place and way of each living being. Through the experience of dance, song, and music the law is conveyed and received collectively and individually.

Traditional African music is, first of all, participatory. All the activities of daily life may be-and often are-accompanied by music, song, and rhythm. And every day, there may be a special event in which music and dance is the central activity. Almost everyone present will be actively involved in several different ways at once, playing instruments, dancing, singing, hand-clapping, observing, commenting, being commented upon.

Subtle verbal expressions may be encoded in drum language. Almost everybody can understand this language at a basic level; often there will be other levels of meaning woven in which can be understood only by drumming initiates of a certain level of experience. This is the source of the concept of the "talking drum." Drum language may be used for reciting history and myth, for praising kings and patrons, for topical social commentary, for long-distance communication.

In Africa, music touches everything. The traditional musician acts in extra-musical roles that vary from culture to culture within Africa. Among the Senufo, he may be healer and sorcerer. Among the Mandingo, there is a special caste of musicians who serve as historians, having memorized vast repertories of songs and narratives commemorating past events and genealogies. In several nations, there are styles of drumming closely associated with the chieftancy, the king himself being the master drummer among masters (as for example with the Watusi and the Dagomba). Each craft or occupational tradition, such as weaving, blacksmithing, the military, farming, or hunting, has its music and its musicians who play before, during, and after every major activity; this music plays an important role in preparing for and regulating the performance of these activities.

Within this context, a very special role is played by the master musician, who must be not only a consummate artist, but also wise and roundly educated and capable of exercising his power of influence with great responsibility. He must be deeply experienced concerning human nature and its manifestations in relation to the experiences which music can induce. He must develop and constantly exercise an extraordinary alertness and perceptiveness. There is a saying that a master drummer must have seven eyes, and that with these eyes he can see the skeleton inside people. In order to be able to fulfill this role, an individual is carefully selected and intensively trained, often from a very early age.

The training of musicians is a complex matter, differing from tribe to tribe, and even for different types of musicians within one tribe. One theme is apprenticeship, a special relationship to an elder musician who becomes the student's musical father. In the frequent case of family transmission, this mentor would be his actual father. Another theme is initiation. There are numerous secret societies with special music associated with particular rites. Certain music may be played only by initiates of a certain grade. A third theme is a kind of musical scholarship which is an age-old tradition in Africa. Some musicians aspire to know well not only the music of their own community but also that of others, and spend years traveling widely to learn and to carry local music to distant places. Under the conditions prevailing in Africa of numerous coexisting independent but culturally related ethnic groups, this exchange has contributed to the development of a very complex and mature musical culture.

The body of knowledgeable musicians exercises a sophisticated critical influence which plays an important role in musical training, since every player is always being judged by a large number of knowledgeable peers. This tradition supports a system of incentive for personal effort and accomplishment quite separate from the incentives arising from biological imperatives and from economic life.

Structure of African Percussion Music

The foundation of African music is the complex of rhythmical structures expressed by the percussion ensemble. The sound is built up in a series of layers of parts that correspond to a hierarchy among the ensemble members. The simpler, more basic parts are played by less experienced players while the lead part is played by the most experienced musician present. Ideally a "master drummer" fills the role of ensemble lead. His qualifications include a complete understanding of the way all the parts fit together and a developed sense of performance values which enables him to manage the ensemble. He assigns parts and often decides what parts must be omitted or simplified, based on the skills of the performers. When necessary in order to transmit his understanding to ensemble members, he can demonstrate all necessary refinements of any part and can himself play enough parts simultaneously to create an impression of the full texture of the composition.

While no one is allowed to play a part he is not qualified to play well enough to contribute to the ensemble, the hierarchy is not completely rigid; a highly accomplished musician might for example take one of the simplest parts. His experienced touch allows him to obtain a finer quality of sound than a lesser player. His rhythmic understanding and more developed sense of time would enable him to reveal hidden depths in that part, providing example and encouragement to the student. The full expression of the music requires the material support of very fine playing of the most basic parts to provide the foundation and rhythmic energy upon which the higher parts can play. The fullest expression of the music requires the material support of very fine playing of the basic parts, in the same way that a developed sensitivity of the body is the necessary material support for development of the feelings and the mind.

The master drummer may use rhythmic dialog to invite or challenge certain individuals to play lead parts of their own. He may then expand or comment upon their ideas by his response. This is one of the many ways that the master, when he is present, uses the ensemble context as a vehicle for aiding the development of the players for whom he is responsible and for propagating the tradition.

Polyrhythm

The relationship among layers of rhythm within a composition is articulated by the principle of polyrhythm: the simultaneous playing of two or more rhythms having different starting points. This technique is at the heart of African music. While Western composers occasionally make use of polyrhythmic ideas, this technique is much more pervasive and highly developed in Africa.

The basic problem that faces the composer using polyrhythms is how to allow each part to have its own character and at the same time to give the whole ensemble an integrated texture of sound. In African music, which is almost always for dance or for accompaniment of repetitive motions of daily work, there is the additional requirement that the overall sound must evoke and be grounded in the sense of movement of the human body.

The different layers of an African polyrhythmic composition represent different voices in dialog with each other. This is known as "call and response." The vcice expressed by each rhythm has periods when it is speaking alternating with periods when it is either silent or just softly keeping time, listening as it were to the response of another voice, to which it responds in turn. There may be moments of overlap, when a voice begins its response before the preceding voice finishes speaking.

One or more of the simultaneous rhythms may repeat in a cycle whose duration is not a multiple of the fundamental meter. This has been called "polymeter" by some Western observers. However, trained African musicians insist that this is a misunderstanding. There is in reality only one meter in effect at one time, and it is the responsibility of each performer and listener constantly to maintain the sense of this meter as the foundation of his hearing and playing.

The Main Beat

The foundation layer of African rhythm is always the "main beat," which expresses the basic meter. There are almost always four main beats which repeat in a cycle. This is the beat to which a musician will keep time with his feet and body while playing. It is also the basis of the main movements of the body in the dancing that is done to the music. Each period from one main beat to the next is subdivided into either three or four subordinate pulses.The tempo of the main beats must be maintained very precisely for the energy of a performance to develop.

The tempo of the main beats is usually rather fast, from about 60 to about 180 per minute. At the upper end of this range, the subordinate pulses occur as fast as twelve per second.

The first beat of each cycle of four main beats is the downbeat. Neither the main beats nor the downbeat imply extra accentuation. There is a principle that there is no distinction of accentuation between any notes played by the same "voice." When distinctions between different notes are required, they are made by differentiating the quality of sound, not the quantity. This differentiation may be between different instruments, or on one instrument by differences in the way it is struck. For example, on the master drum "Atsimevu" of the Ewe drum set, there are nine different strokes employed as distinctive musical events. These nine are precisely defined both in sound and in the way the hand and stick address the drum.

The Bell Pattern

The next layer is highly characteristic of African music. It is a sustained rhythm repeating identically every cycle, often played on bell, rattle. This "bell pattern" outlines the structure of the rhythmic cycle, providing a basic rhythmic feel for the composition. It also functions as metronomic reference allowing performers of different parts to confirm their orientation with respect to the cycle. One bell pattern deserves special examination. This pattern and its variants are so widely used in the whole of sub-Saharan Africa that it has been called "the standard pattern" by ethnomusicologists. This pattern is also found wherever sub-Saharan musical influences have diffused, including a number of distinctive musical traditions in North Africa and in the Americas. This pattern is coordinated with and fits within the meter of four main beats of three pulses each.

It is of some interest that the pattern between strokes in this bell pattern is the same as that of the whole- and half-steps in the diatonic major scale. Here we are comparing patterns in time and pitch, which might be considered apples-to-oranges; but it illustrates the idea that African music is projected upon a richly interconnected rhythmic organization that repeats indefinitely in the dimension of time, analogous to the organization of tonal music in the dimension of pitch, with tonal pitch conceived as repeating in octaves.

The bell pattern can be heard as two distinct sections which connect to each other through the "intervals." This creates a sense of alternation between outward and inward movements, evocative perhaps of breathing or of the two directions of consciousness. The same device is also used at a larger scale. A rhythm may have a "front section" and a "back section" each of which is constructed upon a similar rhythmic idea, but with mutations of weight and syncopation that express movement out and return home.

Upbeats

The next layer of rhythmic architecture is often a figure in which an instrument will play on the "upbeats," the two pulses leading up to but not including each main beat. Sometimes, a more complicated figure is used which still demarcates the upbeat pulses. This pattern is in call-and-response to the main beats. It is often played strongly on a high-pitched instrument, which makes this pattern very prominent in the overall impression of sound, sometimes more prominent than the main beats, which may be played very softly, or very low-pitched, or not played at all. When played with the precise feel, this simple pattern can evoke an intense emotional response. A traditional description of this pattern envisions it as "a baby crying" above the dialog of the other parts.

Middle Parts

The basic parts combined-main beats, bell, and upbeats-outline the rhythmic space in which the music takes place. We only begin to hear actual music when the important layer of "middle parts" is added. These parts repeat in a cycle which is usually a multiple of the downbeat cycle, but there is more room than with the basic parts for individual improvisation. The middle parts further articulate the architecture of the cycle, dividing it into segments of time each of which is occupied by a "voice" sounding a coherent rhythmic motif. The call-and-response between these voices takes on a sense of poetry, of rhyming.

Lead Parts

The foreground layer of the composition consists of a "lead part" or parts in dialog. Working off the energy generated by the basic parts, the lead player introduces musical ideas which develop the polyrhythmic potential latent within the basic rhythmic structure, expressing his creative understanding. These often cut across the other parts in a way that is a challenge to rhythmic perception. This may stretch the mind in an unexpected direction. For example, in the drumming that is a major component of the Haitian Vodou service, unexpected breaks by the lead drummer are recognized as a principal means by which the master drummer induces and controls possession in the dancers. It is the responsibility of the drummer to be aware of the dancer's changing state and degree of preparation for possession in order to know when and how to intensify or calm the energy.

Bringing the Parts Together

Tradition maintains that the main beat in music represents

one's purpose, while the crossing rhythms represent distracting impulses. The profound difficulty of maintaining orientation to the beat is a surprise for most Westerners who undertake serious engagement with the music. Beginners may solve the problem by blocking out rhythms that conflict with the one they are playing, but to go further, and particularly to play crossing rhythms with the correct feel, requires that the student learn to hear immediately each rhythm in its relationship to the main beat. The reward for learning this is to experience these crossing rhythms as subtle and delightful patterns of tension and relaxation.

To play any part requires a concentration of consciousness within oneself at a depth where one can receive and contain an inward flux of rhythmic energies from the other parts and simultaneously can emanate a rhythmic energy that is not a reaction to what is received but is rather a distillation, an expression of one's individual will conditioned into coherence with the ensemble. There is a drummers' proverb: "The bell does the hard work; lead is the easiest part to play." The bell, as the driving engine of the whole machine, cannot react to anything that may happen outside, not even to others' errors. The bell player must emphasize the conscious attitude of an independent source of emanation. The lead part on the other hand serves to tie the other parts together and raise the energy to a new level; the attitude of the lead player emphasizes the aspect of reception and containment.

The quality of sustaining a relationship to the main beat while playing one's own part is called "grounding." This is especially demanding when the rhythm is syncopated. A student may find his grounding criticized by other musicians. He may be told, for example, to let his rhythm "sit down," meaning to allow the playing to be done through hearing all of the main beats and their subordinate pulse, even when they are implied rather than played. The relationship of the rhythm he is playing must appear through contact with an inner sensation rather than through self-assertion, calculating, or trying to direct the hands with the mind. To assist this contact a musician may allow a dance-like movement of his feet and body while playing his instrument. When this movement expresses continuous contact with the earth, it is considered a sign of good rhythmic grounding.

An African ensemble aims at an extraordinary shared precision of timing and rhythmic weight, known as "locking together." When achieved, it is a distinct and specific experience for listeners as well as performers. This precision is not a function of rigorously equal subdivision of time. Subtle delays and anticipations act as colorations within the rhythmic cycle and establish an organic texture that echoes through sensation and movement within the body. This is analogous to "swing" in Jazz (which was influenced by African music). Each different traditional beating has an essential swing characteristic, far more complex and precise than the analogous elements of Western music. Understanding them and being able to maintain their expression in performance is a key to rhythmic grounding and the essence of African musicianship.

As the basic, middle, and lead parts come together, the composition takes on the richness and vitality that characterize the sound of African music. The tempo of the underlying pulsation is too fast to be grasped by the analytical mind, so the impression passes directly to the emotions and to the instinctive movements of the body. We hear the throbbing currents of life processes intersecting with the psychological drama of individual torment and redemption, all pulsating within a mathematically constructed space of cyclically repeating creation and destruction. Then, as new rhythms investigated by the lead are felt in the body in relation to the sensation of the main beat, a channel may be opened relating awareness within the physical organism to organizing principles and forces that lie behind the surface of everyday existence. This can be one of the main purposes of music and dance, something that traditional Africa has known since time immemorial.

Music of Tibetan Bhuddhism

Tibet stands at the influence of three civilization, the Turko-Mongolian, the Chinese and the Indian. Enriched from time to time by influences from these, its own ancient tradition has developed in high isolation from the rest of the civilized world. This tradition embraces a very distinctive way of life and a music all its own. Music plays an important part in Tibetan life and has three aspects:

— the folk-music - found in the daily lives of the people

— an art music - cultivated especially by professional minstrels

— the sacred chant and instrumental music of the Buddhist Liturgy and other rites - centering around the monasteries.

The Lamas say "Religion is sound". The recitation of *mantras*, chanting and the playing of instrumental music are fundamental in their worship. For many ling hours, day after day, year after year, the red-robed monks intone their prayers, sitting cross-legged under the soft light of butter-lamps. Their cerebrations include the services of the regular Liturgy and various extra-liturgical rituals.

The Chant

The liturgical language is Tibetan, though Sanskrit is also

occasionally found. The chants are sometimes free but more usually metrical, in both symmetrical and asymmetrical measures. The voice-style, close-throated or constricted and usually very deep in pitch, is, as the natural voices of the monks show, unnatural; it is deliberately cultivated style.

Tonally speaking, the chanting varies from an inflected monotone to a melodic pattern (oft-repeated with variations) based on a definite mode (varying from three to seven notes, but very often four or five), and is decorated in a variety of ways, especially by glottal slides up to or down to an note, or down from a note. A traditional notation exits for the chants.

The chants may be performed by a single monk in private devotion or by a choir of monks or, where relevant, by laity in services conducted for them by monks. Chanting is sometimes unaccompanied, but is more usually accompanied by na ensemble which amounts to an orchestra (*passim*). This orchestra consists exclusively of wind instruments - always played in pairs - and percussion instruments of indefinite pitch. There are no stringed instruments, which are found only in the secular music.

Wind Instruments:

— *rGaling,* a reed instrument of the shawm class, which plays melodies, both as part of the monastery orchestra, and separately in a repertoire of tunes for special occasions.

— *Dung,* a long metal trumpet, which plays pedal-notes or calls (often centring on one note), either alone, or as part of monastery orchestra.

— *Dung-dkar,* a shell-trumpet made from a conch. Its orchestral role is similar to the one before.

— rKangling, a short horn made from metal, but formerly from human thigh-bone. Its orchestral role is similar to the ones before.

Percussion Instruments of Indefinite Pitch:

— *Drilbu,* a hand-bell, held in the left hand, and played with the hand-drum by the same player. Its pitch may be definite, but is not functional as such.

— *Damaru* (the Indian name by which its usually called among Tibetans), a hand-drum shaped like an hour-glass, and played by rotation of the right hand, so as to make its clappers strike the membranes. Played with the hand-bell by the same player. Made from wood, formerly from human half-crania.

— *R   olmo,* cymbals with broad central bosses, held one above the other and struck by vertical movement.

— *Silnyen,* cymbals with small or no central bosses, struck by horizontal movement.

— rGna, drum supported on a pole or suspended in a frame, and struck with a crooked stick or, occasionally, by drum-sticks.

Percussion Instruments of Definite Pitch:

Apart from instances where the *rGyaling* (shawms) and *dung* (long trumpets) play alone, the only purely instrumental music met with was an orchestral piece which adds two further percussion instruments - this time of definite pitch - not found an any other instance:

— mkar-rnga, *gong*

— Ting-ting, *metal disc.*

— The Ensemble

In services where voices and instruments occur together, sections of full orchestra usually alternate with sections of chant lightly accompanied by cymbals and frame-drum only, while the hand-bell and hand-drum are signals marking off the sections of the service. The orchestral section sometimes employ the full percussion only. To this ensemble the shawms are more usually added, progressive additions being long trumpets, and also occasionally the other wind, i.e. conch-trumpets and short horns.

A *tonal* melody may thus be found with an "accompaniment" which is *atonal* in relation to it. On the hand, we have something comparable with the music of other high oriental civilizations; on the other, something more primitive which cannot be compared within the same reference-frame. This amy reflect, in musical terms, the juxtaposition of Buddhism of Indian origin with the native Tibetan shamanism which, with other influences from surrounding civilizations, have combined to produce Lamaism as we know it. The disposition of instruments also suggests as much, for some may be traced to the Chinese sphere (cymbals); some to the Indian (hand-bell); and some to the Iranian (shawm); but the more distinctive monastery instruments had already progenitors in the Late Stone Age, and of these at least the bone-horn and skull-drum are indigenous to Tibet. The style of the Liturgical music of Tibet must be accounted a major Oriental style which, having emerged and developed i relative isolation under the creative force of Lamaist spiritual life, has retained some very ancient features.

Buddhist monks from China and Taiwan will perform together on a global stage. Beijing, Feb 16 (AFP) - More than 60 monks from China and Taiwan have set off on a tour through Asia, the United States and Canada to showcase traditional Chinese Buddhist music. It is the first time

Buddhist monks from China and Taiwan will perform together on a global stage, indicating a closer cultural relationship, the Xinhua news agency said on its website. The troupe will perform Chinese Buddhist music to religious and secular audiences in Taiwan before moving on to Macau, Hong Kong, Los Angeles, San Francisco and Vancouver.

The troupe will perform Chinese Buddhist music to religious and secular audiences all over the world.

The monks come from prestigious Buddhist temples including Mount Foguangshan in Taiwan, Wutai Temple in north China's Shanxi province and Shaolin Temple in central Henan province. They represent the three branches of Buddhism in China, namely Chinese Buddhism, Tibetan Buddhism and Pali Buddhism.

Buddhist music, which originated in ancient India, found its way into China some 2,000 years ago, and absorbed elements of traditional Chinese folk music, court music and other religious music.

Buddhist music, which originated in India, found its way into China some 2000 years ago.

"The Buddhist music on the Chinese mainland has a more traditional flavour, while that in Taiwan is more appealing to a secular audience," said Tian Qing, an art director of the troupe and professor with the Chinese Art Institute.

Sheng Hui, vice president of the Chinese Buddhism Association and head of the troupe, added: "I hope the joint performance will further enhance ties between Buddhism followers and people across the Taiwan Strait and bring peace and prosperity to the region and the world through Buddhist praying for tolerance, peace and harmony."

Ritual in Buddhist Musical Cultures

Buddhist musical practices accompany, inspire, and guide body postures and prostrations, hand gestures, and breathing rhythms, and also aim at guiding prescribed non-movement in some instances, as in disciplines of establishing stillness of the body. In addition, Buddhist ritual practitioners instrumentalize the body, for example, as they perform throat singing that makes audible the body's resonant chambers, and as they perform instruments made of skulls and bones. Because the aim of this issue is to examine Buddhist practices cross-culturally, the articles here examine the Buddhist practices of diverse cultures, including China, Indonesia, Nepal, Sri Lanka, and Vietnam.

Meaning, Style and Change in Gamalan and Wayang Kulit Banjar Since Their Transplantation from Hindu-Buddhist Java to South Kalimantan

This section examines the origins and development of a syncretic Hindu-Buddhist-Animist musical theatre form known as *wayang kulit* Banjar (Banjarese leather puppet shadow theatre), a complex combination of word, music, drama, stagecraft, movement and mystical ritual. Transplanted with its accompanying *gamalan* music from Java in the fourteenth century, it survives to this day among the Banjarese people of South and East Kalimantan, a mainly Malay society which adopted Islam from the sixteenth century. While Muslim influence in *wayang kulit Banjar* is only superficial, the story lines, puppet characters and texts preserve archaic Buddhist-Hindu-Javanese elements.

Drawing on the literary sources as well as fieldwork interviews and recordings of performances, the author analyses the cosmological association and meaning of elements of *wayang kulit* and *gamalan* musical style.

Transcriptions are included of four excerpts from the author's 1993 recording of a Mahâbhârata-plot based shadow play entitled Terfitnah dalam Kejujuran ("Rumours Destroying Honesty"), led by *senden dalang* Abdullah and accompanied on a *gamalan Banjar.*

Bp Abdullah manipulating the *gunungan* puppet (symbol of the universe) inserted into banana stems and held in front of a coconut oil lamp. A *babun* and a *saron*are pictured in front. Other puppets, inserted in their banana stems, stand at either side.

Wayang Kulit Banjar: The White Monkey (Hanuman), carved in Banjarese style for Ramayana performances. Held in the Museum Negeri Lambung Mangkurat Propinsi Kalimantan Selatan.

Music and Movement in Vietnamese Buddhism

Buddhism is realized by a monastic community of meditators, preachers, and chanters. Introduced to Vietnam in the second century A.D., Buddhism evolved into these three elements only ten centuries later. They coexist, each self-absorbed in its own activities. The chanting school, called ung phu, practices liturgical ceremonies which include a complex system of rituals, chants, and dances. They are performed in over two hundred ceremonies at temples or public places on numerous occasions. This article will attempt to describe and analyze the process of rituals, aspects of the Buddhist chanting dancing rules, and the philosophical meaning of ceremonies.

Ritual performance in Vietnamese Buddhism.

A page of the Mong Son Liturgical Book which illustrates the positions of chanting monks in a Chan Te Ceremony.

The lower part of the page shows a transliteration of a mantra from Sanscrit scripture into both classical Chinese and Vietnamese *quoc ngu* characters. Is the Wind, the Banner, or the Mind Moving? The Concept of Body in Chinese Han Buddhist Ritual Performance and Its Musical PracticesIs the Wind, the Banner, or the Mind Moving? The Concept of Body in Chinese Han Buddhist Ritual Performance and Its Musical Practices

Chinese Buddhist Ritual Music

This section explores various concepts of body and its role in the ritual practices in contemporary Chinese Han Buddhist communities, with particular emphasis on the concepts of "profane body" and "sacred body," "moving" and "unmoving," and individual and group. The physical movements of the actual body and stabilization of the ritual body are discussed, together with a possible classification of Chinese Buddhist ritual music, which attempts to show the inner relationship between musical practices and Buddhist theory. Music, as suggested in this essay, becomes not only the mediator of the ambiguity between the actual and conceptual practices, but also the medium between the profane space and sacred space. Finally, this study illustrates how an ancient term can be interpreted in different ways according to an individual's understanding of "tradition(s)."

Neku Horns, Himalayan Shamanism, and the Transmigration of the Disembodied Spirit

In rituals following a death in the Kathmandu Valley, members of the Buddhist Manandhar (Oil Presser) caste of Newars sound the *neku* buffalo horn, a specially venerated, even deified instrument. The horn is likened to a relic of the dead person through mythical and symbolic identification of the buffalo as a person's incarnation. Many practitioners believe that the neku sound is heard and recognized by the dead person as he or she journeys through the murky stages of death, disembodiment, and re-integration into a new mind-body complex.

It is recognized as a helpful sound heard during previous transmigrations, when *neku* rituals also were performed. The dead person, whose progress toward rebirth may be hindered, follows the sound to find advantageous rebirth, and the living find healing, peace, and religious merit. Its mystical familiarity transcends the usually inscrutable boundaries of death and rebirth, and as Manandhars contemplate it, they reconceptualize their own bodies and actualize Buddhist soteriological beliefs. Newar children performing the *neku* ritual in the Kathmandu Valley.

Jataka Narrations as Multimedial Reconstructive Embodiments of the Mental System Buddha Shakyamuni

This section aims to unify constructivistic-systemic philosophy with Buddhist conceptions of embodiment. Music is analyzed as part of the constructive potential, through which both individual psychic systems and collective, cultural ones are created and maintained. The embodiment of a single psychic system in a sequence of incarnations is constructed in the Jataka tales in two specific ways: a) in the main actors of the stories, who are different persons but in the end one and the same, and b) in the personification of special qualities—like generosity, selflessness or honesty etc.—one of which the main actor of each story embodies, as specified by the narrative.

As the continuity of a cultural system is always an act of memory and depends on the memory-related activities of the participants, the article shows how multimedial performances of Jataka tales preserve, in part, the multimedial network of Theravada Buddhist culture in Sri Lanka today. Music is seen as an important part of this network, and one sensory component in the physical process of transferring the embodied content of the ancient story to the contemporary audience. Description and analysis engage three very different kinds of Jataka performances that exemplify the rich tradition and show continuity despite musical change:

a) the archaic story-teller, who accompanies himself with his rabana, declaiming the Serivavanije Jataka at a Vesak pandal;

b) the verses of the Vessantara Jataka, which are sung or performed as a scenic play at funerals or other sad occasions; and

c) a recent pop/rap version of the Sirisanghabo Jataka, reinterpreted by the male Pop-duo Bathiya & Santush.

Buddhist musicology, in its ethnographic, folkloric, textual, historical, and musicological dimensions, has tremendous and broad-based momentum. It is a rapidly growing field with much to offer, particularly if lingering obstacles separating the many scholarly literatures on Buddhist music can be bridged.

History of Music in Islam

In history of civilizations,Islam stands as a pinacle culturally between the Dark Ages and the Renaisance period.Although "Islamic Civilization" conotes a purely sociological implication, in spite of its pristine religious insularity, Islam spread over a quarter of the then known geographic world, gave rise to a specific mode of lifestyle, and became a cynosure for all observers beyond its boundaries.

The cause was simple: When the Prophet Muhammad's (swas) revalations were heralded to the world in the seventh century of the Christian era, the "message" could not be confined to the Hijaz or the Arabian peninsula. Within three quarters of a century the banner of Islam"s Prophet migrated eastward to ends of Transoxiana, southward to the banks of the Indus river in India, northward to the shores of the Black Sea in Asia Minor, and westward into Spain onto the Pyrenees.

Islam's newly won empire's civilization outshone rest of the world. From Samarkand in Central Asia to Cordova in Spain, famed institutions of learning, the arts, sciences, literature, musical arts, and techinical discoveries, inventions and improvements, brought exciting wonderment to all peoples. Islam's sociological trend was produced with sublime surrender in religion as the basis, and taught universal brotherhood without racial, national, or geographic boundaries.

In Islam's empirical dominions it was inevitable that all other nations would subsume themselves into the culture of their Arabian Muslim conquerors, incorporating an adulterated Arabic, which then became modified and tempered by those cultures. This fusion of cultural ideas gave greater mobility to the newer civilization which still has a vital influence on the western world.

Many of the world's peoples contributed to Islamic civilization: Arab, Turk, Kurd, Persian, Aramean, Syrian, Egyptian, Greek and Goth. "Two lands" culture especially played a prominent role in the music of this new civilization, from the east, and from the west. Greek music was more theoretical, dominated by works of ancient authors centuries deceased.

The visible signs of music and religion in ancient Arabia, confirms that the Arabs of the peninsula had indeed inherited and were conservators of the Mesopotamian cultural heritage. Music was, in practice,was then largely delegated to women, especially in the upper elite class, Those people who were attached to upper class households, were employed as 'qainat'(singing women) for purpose of entertainment. The male 'mughani'(singing men)and 'mitrib"(musicians) and the 'alati' (instrumentalists) were written about by Ibn Musa al-Nasibi (d.circa.860) in his Kitab al-Aghani (book of songs).

In ancient Arabia, the Holy Ka'aba wa a place of pilgrimage. In the Hijaz, mecca was the centers for fairs, where musicians and poets met in contest for being the best in their arts, and treasured poems, like the Mu'allaqat, were sung and recited entire as qasa'id (odes). Ghina (singing) came from huda (cravan song); out of this developed biqa (lamentation), nauh (elegies), and nasb (secular songs), Two types of songs were used, the Himyaria and Hanifiya; all tell of joy in then happy Arabia.

The Gassanids employed singing-girls of Mecca in their capitol al-Hira and Byzantium, who sang with accompaniment of barabat (lute). The reed-pipe came from their region, and the Arabs borrowed it, calling it zambaq, as it was made from sambucus wood. The Arabic harp is called zannaj or wannaj, a loose phonectical prounciation from Syriac-Greek dialect. word for phoenix.

The other great influence to the north-east was Persia, then the font of culture. The origins of Persian music began in misty Mahabad, at the beginning time (Dabistan).

Firdausi is his great epic, the Shaha Nama, tells of rud (resplendent music) and sarwad(singing), strings of chang (harps), tanbur (pandore),barabat or rubab (lutes), ruyin (pipes) and ney (reed-flute), which gave out delightful notes. Processions resounded with blasts of karranay, shaipur, and buq (horns-trumpets), tabira and kus (kettledrums), and the noise from hindi, daray, zang, and sinj (tininabulating throngs), chang (upper-chested harp),von (lower-chested harp), kannar and shisak-cousins of ghoshaka (Sitar Sanscrit instrument), and tumbak, dumbalak (drums). Many of these instruments are shown in reliefs at Taqi Bustan. (A.D.590-628).

The scientific theory of music in those days in Persia was present in treatise on music of pre-Islamic times. Practical theory is evident; in the Dastanat of Barabad, seven modes and 360 melodies are mentioned; relating to the numerical metaphysics of Ancient Mesopotamia. From al-Hira, the capitol of the Lakhmids, Persian musical practices filtered into Arabian lands, and those people were great lovers of musical arts.

At the emergence of Islam in Hijaz, the first year of Hegira-flight, 622 A.D., spiritual newness dawned on the world. The religion of Islam prospered, and nothing else mattered. At first all was aesthic happiness and austerity. When Prophet Muhammad (sws) passed into greater glory year 632 A.D., his Companions sought, like their holy Prophet, to keep the minds of men only, away from the malahi or forbidden pleasures of old, including wine, women, and song.

Although the Quran neither contained nor mentioned specifically any words against music, the purists of Islam began to collect a'hadith (sayings) of the Prophet Muhammad (swas) which supposedly condemned listening and singing to music. Hard-core purist fuqaha legists used these proported sayings of the Prophet with considerable effect. These fuqaha forbade any kind of music save what was tolerated by the Prophet and according to their own specific interpretations. Eventually the four legal schools of Sunni Muslim's thought, Hanbali, Maliki, Shafi, Hanafi,and with the Shia who had their own fuqaha-legists who also decided more or less against listening to music; and the subject developed a controversial literature on permissability. It grew on, and still is a topic of heated debate by conservative fundamentalists on into comtemporary times.

Mustafa Sabri was one of the top Ottoman scholars in the 20th century. He served as a *shaikhulislam* (Highest religious authority) in the Ottoman State. He died in 1954 in Egypt. This translation was prepared by Muaz Özyigit.

> If the head of the family is fond of tambourine,
> It is no wonder why the whole family dances!

Whether it is through natural/physiological means or instruments, or tunes, depending on the kind or the different ways, music may be forbidden or disliked or even allowed according to some Islamic religious edicts. However, it is also known that Islam avoids absolutely accepting or remaining indifferent to the issue of music. It is this latter fact, ie, a sort of position by Islam, of cautioning by not allowing music, or encouraging it without reservation.

It would not do justice at all to compare this position of reservation by Islam with heartsick people who are unable to appreciate the joyful effect of music which is considered by those who are fond of pleasures, as of great spiritual value. Perhaps Islam does not see right to remain indifferent to music because it knows how delightful music is to our nature and how strong it is on our feelings. Islam religion has an exceptionally good view in any case, in discovering the hidden dangers which might be inherent in the sweetest and most pleasurable things. Indeed, a heavenly religion should lead to the truths which are unattainable by man himself, as this is expected in the guiding nature of the religion.

Firstly, music is a useless activity which in fact, is a state of passiveness.

Secondly, the benefit and pleasure taken from music involves a meaning of deep slavery in passion. Since Islam is the only enemy of passiveness and slavery in passion, an important duty of Islam is to search their traces in unexpected hide-outs.

Although it might be difficult for some to realize the fact that music has a sense of passiveness, those with a subtle mind would not hesitate to accept it, as it is not possible to imagine another worldly benefit of music. As for this world, it is useless as in the idiom of "no good for stomach". One should not ask hastily: how could this be claimed while there are many singers, instrument players in the West, for example, making a living or even a fortune? To make a living would not be proper unless it is done in a way which does not harm human dignity since it would not be at ease with conscience otherwise.

The acts of pure entertainment are considered low-level professions in the eyes of unpolluted human nature. You should not take seriously the applause and respect and perhaps requests given to the famous of these kinds of artists. Those who pay respects and make requests do not mind doing so, since they do it, in a way, taking away a crumb of honour from the artist, by hiding this loss from him. Likewise, a lot of respect is usually paid to some ladies in order to take sexual advantage of them.

From such an entertainment point of view, it shows a quite bizarre mentality of some parents who are proud of having taught their daughters how to play an instrument. It is also bizarre to see some people wishing to marry a girl with musical training, in an attempt to imitate Western civilization which, they think, gives the utmost importance to the respect of woman. It might be said that being able to play an instrument is not a shame for a woman as it is her natural duty to make her husband happy with her company. However, such an objection is not valid because happiness and enjoying each other's company in a marriage is a mutual benefit. Then, one can imagine how bizarre and ridiculous it would be for a man to say he is lacking the qualities for marriage just because he does not know how to play an instrument!

Compared to singers and instrument players, although composers look, to some extent, free of the hidden disgrace explained above, the art of composing could not get rid of the pros and cons of singing or playing as they depend on each other. Also, while the waves of pride and dignity rise in teaching knowledge, as opposed to an atmosphere of of frivolity spreading from the classes of composers. Of course, we all appreciate the meaning of "playing music after forty years of age". That is why it would be quite offensive to ask a man of high rank in a government to sing a song no matter how good it is as it would be an affront to his dignity. As opposed to this, teaching knowledge regardless of rank is considered a means of increasing honour and pride.

An attempt to cover up the problem above, by claiming that a composer can concentrate on teaching music without having to put himself in a frivolous and disgraceful position by shouting or singing before students would, in fact, mean to admit our claim, let alone being an argument against it. All these problems we have tried to expose above are about those who make a living through music. As for those who see it as a hobby, playing only for friends, the passiveness and the waste of time for both player and listeners are pretty obvious, not needing a special attempt to expose it.

During listening to music, people would not be doing anything for the good of humanity. They would cause, instead, a lot of money to change hands. And, in return for the money, what do these people get? Nothing! Consider this: Suppose a shoemaker sells you a shoe. And you wear it and walk to your shop. Let us say you sell books in your shop. You both make a profit and help knowledge and science spread in your country. This way you would serve in a chain of benefits in the society by making other people too to benefit, such as those who print or write books, and the manufacturers of paper or the cotton farmers and on the other hand, there are the craftsmen who process leather for shoes and the farmers who raise animals to provide leather. When it comes to music, although those who manufacture instruments and those who offer their skills for your hearing appreciation, by playing them certainly benefit, this chain of benefits ceases at you!

Paying for music is not the same as hiring a horse-and-cart to go out for a picnic, because this way you could contribute more to your work of being a complementary part of the chain of human needs by benefitting your health in addition to helping the cart driver make a living. Besides, those carts are used for transportation at other times than those of picnic. In short, picnic is one thing and music is another. Of course, nothing could be said against music when it is a medical necessity for a patient like clean air being one of the most important necessities in treating patients. Nevertheless, it is not known yet that music is prescribed by physicians despite the fact that treatment with music has recently become a familiar term.

Another face of musical pleasures, the one involving a deep indulgence in passion: Under what kind of influence are the feelings of those who are in an atmosphere which is full of emotional temptations caused by music? The effect of music can have various ways: with music, a lonely person feels his loneliness more, an orphan feels more the loss of his parents, a patient feels more sorrowful of his situation, and an aged person feels sorrier that the most of his life has already gone. Yet again, with music, a lucky person with wealth and a high ranking position feels happy more than he usually is. In short, music paints the reality in darker colours by increasing the sorrow of the the sorrowful and the happiness of the happy. And this way, the effect of music resembles that of alcohol, causing people to perceive the reality in a more stretched way than it really is. Above all of these, music has a tremendous effect in agitating the feelings of romance and love. That is why a banquet with music is usually accompanied with pretty women and alcoholic beverages.

Therefore, the most intimate secrets of love are exposed first by poems, then, under the disguise of music, in a similar manner to some women making themselves more attractive under the disguise of the hijab. Or, the words that cannot be normally said by lovers can be uttered by means of music and poetry. That is why it is not considered rude, if a person who is too shy to say "I'm dying for her, I'm crazy for her" shouts the same words before others by music and poetry. Furthermore, how parents who would like to raise their daughters in chastity and modesty with wisdom allow them to sing the most intimate words of love, considering this a good quality for a girl at the age of marriage despite the fact that it is shameful (in our society) for girls to utter even the word of marriage which is lawful in Islam. If the opinion of some thinkers of this century, who said "if women are not kept busy, they would think of some other things do to", is to be taken, then women who are fond of playing instruments would have found even an irresistible guide to those kind of thoughts.

However, is dreaming love and romance a bad thing? What else is like love that makes man feel angelic and gives compassionate and elevated feelings? Love is so strong that it is not possible to remain indifferent to the whining of the lovelorn and suffering hearts. Yes, this is quite true. However, there is no other issue, as delicate as this, vulnerable to abuse. Indeed, it was not an exaggeration when Hoja Nasruddin (Juha), when asked if he ever had a love affair, said: Yes, I was just getting involved once, but we were surprised!. Although love cannot be but mutual, it seems shameful for women in particular. And a man esteems a woman who only loves him. Besides, he would not excuse other women being in love with other men. And the woman he loves has no importance attached to her by others.

Having said these considerations about music, it has become easier to express an opinion about love odes which form the most elegant kind of poetry. As for the poetry of eulogy or satire they are not usually commendable as the former is a kind of flattery and the latter is fault-finding. As for the poetry to uphold the moral values we have no objection. Islam's position can be summarized as accepting the good poetry and rejecting its bad kind, anyway. Although poetry is perhaps the best of the literal arts, Islam's uneasiness about poetry is because it does more harm than good. Even a student's obsession of poetry is considered a sign of going astray, leaning towards laziness even by scholars of the modern times. What consists of the capital of poetry is confessed by poets themselves:

> "The material of poets never runs out
> No end to lies even to an end this world is brought"

In ancient times when poets never made such confessions (out of their pride), the nature of their poetry was exposed by the Holy Quran:

> As for poets, the erring follow them. Hast thou not seen how they stray in every valley, And how they say that which they do not?

However, poetry is far more important than music as poetry sharpens the mind and can be informative. Before we finish the topic of music, let us add that, if the effect of music on feelings must indeed be an important need for the soul, the recitation of the Quran serves that need in a much more dignified way. This is also shown by the fact that harmonious recitation of the Quran is recommended in Islam. However, it should also be noted that a musical tune accompanying the recitation is not proper. In other words, a harmonious recitation is recommended in some hadiths of the prophet (pbuh), yet the scholars are against the musical recitation of the Quran. The reason of these two seemingly conflicting opinions can be understood by making a distinction between the two concepts of music:

If music is to be applied with its rules and techniques to the recitation it would violate the rules of tajweed . So, this kind of music with notes and rules, like composed pieces, is not allowed in the recitation. However, if a person recites the Quran, associated with the beauty of his natural tunes, this is commendable. This way is very reasonable considering the fact that an abuse of the Quran with music must be avoided. That is why a piece of music is listened to for appreciation of its musical value, without necessarily understanding its words, for the most part. Although the meaning of the words in some pieces of music can be realized to some extent, the composers usually have to fill the gaps with "la la"s to balance the piece of music. Obviously, such a practice in the Quranic recitation is out of the question.

Besides, nobody wants to listen to the music of a person with no talent for it. As for the talented, their natural tunes are more pleasant and impressive than their musical skills acquired through musical training. We have witnessed the loss of purity and sweetness in the recitation of once famous Quran reciters, after being exposed to musical education. Therefore, natural music should be superior to the acquired musical skills, as the former is an extempore act while the latter consists of repeating composed and used tunes. At this point we have got one more claim: It is known that one nation may not enjoy the music of another. So it means that the effect of music is in proportion to its locality. Therefore, a person's natural music should be superior, as being his personal music, to his national music.

In recent years, certain developments have taken place which has brought the subject of music as an extremely significant issue. Music has spread to such an extent that it is afflicting every muslim in this modern era. Today, individuals are being confronted by a situation where one is forced to listen to music whether by choice or without. Music is played in nearly all department stores and super markets. Even whilst walking in the streets, we find cars blaring with music. No matter which direction we go, we are blasted with music. The increasing popularity of music, which is prevalent in our society poses a tremendous danger for muslims.

Music is Haraam

References within the context of the Holy Qur'aan along with the Hadith of the Prophet confirm that music is haraam. Interpreters of the Qur'aan have defined the term 'lahwal hadith' which is mentioned in the Qur'aan as:

1) Singing and listening to songs.
2) Purchasing of male and female singers.
3) Purchase of instruments of fun and amusement.

When Sayyidana Abdullah Ibne Mas'ood , a very close companion of our Prophet was asked about the meaning of the term 'lahwal hadith', he replied

> "I swear by Him besides whom there is no other God,that it refers to ghinaa (singing)."

This statement, he repeated three times. This view is unanimously supported by the four Khalifas, the eminent Sahabaah, Tabi'een, the four Imaams and other reliable Islaamic scholars and authorities.

One hadith from the Bukhari Shareef, the most authentic Book of Hadith, further confirms unlawfulness of music and singing:

> 'There will be people of my Ummah who will seek to make lawful; fornication, wine-drinking and the use of ma'aazif (musical instruments).'

Detailed analysis of the arabic word 'ma'aazif shows that it refers to musical instruments, the sounds of those musical instruments and singing with the accompaniment of instruments.

Closer analysis of the wordings of the Hadith establishes the prohibition of music. Firstly, the words 'seek to make lawful ' shows that music is not permissible, as logically one can only seek to make lawful that which is not allowed. Secondly, if music was not prohibited, then it would not have been brought within the same context as fornication and wine-drinking.

Effects of Music

Muslims are aware that nothing has been prohibited by Allah except that which is harmful to the welfare of a Muslim individual and the society as a whole. The divine attribute behind the prohibition of music can be comprehended by looking into the diverse influence music can have.

Experiments carried out by doctors and professors have confirmed that the music of today is such that it does not only affect the brain, but each and every organ of one's body. There is a close relationship between music and bodily movements. People listening to music automatically start tapping their fingers and feet, as if the music is permeating in their blood.

It is also proved that music affect's one's emotions, increases arousal in terms of alertness and excitement and also leads to various physiological changes in the person. In a psychology experiment, it was found that listening to moderate type of music increased one's normal heart beat, whilst listening to rock music the heart beat increased even further, yet people claim that music has no effect.

It is a very ignorant and misguided attitude to percieve music as a form of pleasure and passing of time, since the messages of today's music follow a general theme of love, fornication, drugs and freedom.

We find that the whole world is obsessed with the kufr idea of freedom, i.e. freedom of speech, freedom of movement, etc. In western schools and universities, we observe independence, free expression and secular thinking being encouraged. This idea of freedom, " It's my life, I'll do what I want" is a predominant, underlying theme of today's music. It is being used as a means for drilling western ideologies, which are totally contrary to Islamic Shariah and values, into the minds of Muslims.

One should abstain from evil audacities such as listening to music and encourage others to do the same too.

Music is something unique to every culture and group of people. It defines their experiences and can provide a powerful means of bring people to Islam as seen through the works of Yusuf Islam, Dawood Warnsby Ali, MYNA tapes, Sons of the Crescent and others (all have used musical instruments and sounds in one way or the other). Allah says: "Say: who has prohibited Allah's beautiful things which He created for His servants and good provisions?" Music can be a powerful tool if used correctly. There is no doubt that music and songs about haram activities is not allowed in Islam. But before we make a judgment on singing and instruments for Islamic purposes one must look at the arguments for and against the use of Instruments.

There is a general rule in Shariah that states that everything is lawful unless proven unlawful. There is not substantial proof in this hadîths because of the following reasons:

Sheikh Muhammad Al-Hanuti stated: "The Hadith referred to in saying that it is haram as narrated by al Bukhari is not fulfilling the requirements of the Sahih in al Bukhari's collection.

1) Al Bukhari in Hadith al Ma'azif himself narrated the Hadith to be of a broken chain of narrators in which there is a gap between al Bukhari and the second

narrator, so he drops the first narrator in his chain. That is called Mu'allaq. Some scholars tried to connect the chain through other means like whan ibn Hajar did in his dissertation (connecting what is disconnected) in which he connected the Isnad of this Hadith. But still, one of the main narrators whose name is Hisham ibn Ammar as profiled in Tahthib at-Tahthib by ibn Hajar is not reliable enough for some scholars to be a source of a narration that depends on somebody like him.

2) Even when we said the Hadith is Sahih, there are questions that would emerge when we study the version of the Hadith when it says, "People will make adultery, pure silk, liquor and Ma'azif into Halal." We know that adultery is Haram by another proof and it is a unanimous Hukum. Pure silk is not of consensus Hukum. If a Muslim says Zina is Halal deliberately, then they are considered a kafir. However, if a Muslim says pure silk is not Haram, he is not a kafir. We know that liquor is Haram as it is in the Qur'an, but where do we find an authentic hadith or Qur'an to tell us that Ma'azif are Haram other than this source. The last point is to get the clear meaning of Ma'azif in arabic dictionaries because there are more than one meaning for Ma'azif. It is acceptable for a Muslim to hear somebody says Makruh but not Haram because Haram is in need of clear-cut meaning and certain narration."

Music Art and Science

It is an exact science of sounds, rythums, tones,forms and beats. It is the Divine created, melody and harmony of life itself. Allah created the universe, the carth and all its in habitants therein, andd all for Allah's own pleasures! As we humankind read and know before there was anything in existance, there was absolutely Nothing...NO...Light, dark, sound,ojects nor any movements...Like complete blank void! Then Allah spoke in many actions and so commanded...BE! And all things came into existance! AWESOME!

There was not one part of this great universal creation that is not an symphonic orchestra nor is without sound, motion, rythum, tones, beats and forms. All of them are syncronized for perfect melodious harmony in unison, pricisely, and perfectly composed, directed, and conducted by its Creator Almighty Allahu! The beautiful, melodious symphony of new birth of life, was entirely composed by its Creator Allah,and with many sounds, movements, rythums, and beats in specific arrangements in the various forms of nature, and the sounds are melodious harmonies which soothes one's soul. Music transcends; it does not shut out the very essence of Allahu's spirit-(dhat) The-Light-(en-Nur!) As The "Creator-Allahu" most infinite and very eternal existence.It is The Most Magnificent of any musical compositions,and is composed as a gift of Allahu's Great Love for mankind from Allahu Most Generous.

During the holy prophet Muhammad's (sws) time and after his death, there developed new Islamic art of musical styles in the Hijaz in the holy cities of Mecca and Medina, which were the centers of Islamic religious and political power. The activities of a rich art and musical foundation in regligious and secular life came into being, a tradition associated with celebrating life and it's given religious,and spiritual mystical dimensions. This occurred despite vehement attacks from strict " puritanical theologians". Envisage the transformation of explicit and systematic inference of the Great Traditions, as applicable to urban and non-urban cultures, emerging and meeting in new centers under new religion of Islam during prophet Muhammad's (sws)time and the succeeding caliphs. This synthesis, effected in sprited compromise, it resulted in an agreed successful arrangement of old and new, a representative of orthogenesis. A most important manifestation was a quest for linguistic purity, a concern shared equally by all reciters and chanters of the Holy Quran, grammarians,poets, and musicians alike,all for proper recitation of Quranic verses (suras) and stanzas (ayats).

The necessity of explaining the sacred Quranic text gave birth to the art of music science of grammar, musical modes,styles and lexicography. Philogists actually discovered that the best material was found in Islamic poetry; the same was found by musicians,poets, and specialist reciters-chanters (qir'at) of Quran, they made rules of solemn recitation-cantillation based on poetic musical language and its renditions. The ruling-authorities-(Alemas)accepted these musical recitations-cantillations. The poetic rythumic modes of phonic and tonal accentuation, and intensity of equlibrium between emotional values, became the models for both experts in Quranic cantillation (talhin), and also for the composers of poetic songs(gazels). They underlined the expressive , artistic manner of rythumic speech in many ways as a chant "combined recitation-cantillation" and emotional exression of song, sacred music and rhetoric.

No legist nor religious authority can either prohibit or authorize something a priori by a persoanl decision; as all or any authority are obligated to base arguments but, only from direct references in sacred writings, or by closely reasoned analogy. The first most sacred source is the Quran both for those opposed to music and those who are not. Although nothing specific in Quran is concerning music explicitly. Holy prophet Muhammad (sws) who liked to listened to his young wife Aisha(ra) and her friends while playing music and singing, he did favor some music, and he twice rebuked the reactions of his young wife's father Abu Bakr in two incidences. The holy prophet (sws) then declared that art, music, singing and playing of some specific instruments were permissable on occaisions of: birth, marriages, cultural folk festivites, funerals, and most of all for religious,spiritual occaisons. (Transmitted by hazret Aisha(ra) in the "Sahih" collection of al-Bukhari).

There were three things the prophet Muhammad (sws) did not like or approve of at all: (1) was clapping of hands in public performances, of either religious or secular nature; however, (2) He dissaproved of the "sensual" singing which was combined with "sensual" dancing in public taverns, by males and females alike.(Ahadith-"Sahih" collection of al-Bukhari and Muslim).(3) Holy prophet (sws) also declared that the selling , buying or teaching of performing girls (qaynat) is also unlawfull:-(transmitted by hazret Aisha(ra) in the("Sahih collection of al-Bukhari).The great theologian Abu Hamid al-Ghazali , stated that : "those particular ahadith refers only to the girls dancing and singing in the taverns." Whereas, the traditional ahadith of the holy prophet Muhammad(sws)did approve of singing in one of his pertinent sayings: "Allah has not sent me as prophet except with a beautiful voice, and Allah listens more intently to one with a beautiful voice reciting Quran as dose the master of a singing girl (qayna) listens to her beautiful singing voice." Transmitted from ("Sahih" collections of al-Bhukari).

The Importance of correct, careful and solemn recitation-(Qir'a)of Quran, from Islamic teachings established were of an urgent task. The term for ebellishment (tajwid) in recitation of Quran became the art of music science. A remarkable system regulated cantillation (talhin) with respect to the law of phonetics and prefered diction of musical aspects in recitation-(Qir'a) of sacred texts. Prophet Muhammad (sws) recommended reciting/ cantillation of Quran in musical melodies of the the people from Nejd reagion of Arabia,as he prefered the pre-Islamic simple musical forms of huda and rakbani, with pauses which became a major trait of Quranic cantillation (talhin). Holy prophet(sws) had recourse to old Arabic tunes used in classical recitation/cantillation of poetry,together with classical poetic rules of parosody which was a transvaluation expressed by Ibn al-Arabi: "The prophet Muhammad (sws) wanted Quran to be an exclusive passion to replace styles that all chanters were accustomed to singing during that period in time.

The call to prayer (adhan-azan), was instituted by prophet Muhammad himself between, and the first muezzin who was Bilal an Abyssinian maula, also one of the first martyrs in Islam. Originally the call to prayer (adhan-azan) was a simple anouncement in the streets or from roof tops. It quickly grew ornate, as a moving chant issued five times per day from height of a mineret of a mosque. Call to prayer (adhan-azan) was composed of short phrases sung in chanting tunes that varied in all countries, and in some regions the melodic tunes beacame archlike, with maximum densities at its peak. These two types of musical cantillation (talhin) effectively made it known as "compulsory" religious mosque music known as hymns. Many hymns were and are used on festive occaisons and one in particular on celebration of : "Maulid-en Nabavi/Milad-en Nabi", the birthday aniversry of holy prophet(sws). All mysitcal dimensions in art and music stem from sacred Quranic spiritual mysticism, which was adhered too and are follwed by many mystical orders-(tariqats)which was instituted originally by prophet Muhammad (sws) to his companions (awliya), and was used and known at that period in time as spiritual mystical devotional music.

In Islam's art of music sciences, include some aspects in Islam which are in accordance with the teachings of a great theologian Abu Hamid al-Ghazali, an exceptional religious reformer, and a devout spiritual mystic. In his great authoritative work: "The Rivival of Religious Sciences"-"Ihya ulum al -Din", he integrated mystical Sufism and Orthodoxy. Ghazali's importance dealing with laws of "listening- Sama/Sema" and the music of ecstasy analysed the main cruz of controversiality. Ghazali came to an important conclusion that both statuatory and analgous evidence indicatively shows the admissability of art and music science in Islam. A major point in Ghazali's findings is that music and singing are a spiritual evoking of the truth in one's heart and soul. It influences the heart and soul which reveals itself and its contents to only Allah. This elaboration was also a prouncement made by another famous authority also a devout spiritual mystic al-Darani who said: "Music does not provoke in the heart or soul that which is not there." In those words the nature of music's influence on mankind very much depends on the basic intentions of the listener, and the purpose for which music is used. Ghazali clearly defines seven purposes for which music is allowed-(halal)and five cases in which it is forbidden-(haram) as follows:

Music allowed-Halal

1) To evoke and invoke the love of Allah.
2) To elicit love and longing for Allah in circumatances that permit singing, playing of permittied instruments
3) To evoke lamentation and sorrow-the latter being of two kinds: (a) blameworthy (b) praisworthy.

4) to arouse joy.
5) To encourage pilgrimage, and only for those it is permissable
6) To incite for battle
7) To inspire courage on the day of battle

Music forbidden-Haram

1) When music is produced by singing and dancing of men and women in taverns and in other public places.
2) If certain instruments are used for only"secular" purposes, they are strictly forbidden for use for only"religious" purposes.
3) When the song's contents are not compatible with spiritual concepts and precepts of religion.
4) When the listener is ruled by thoughts of lust and lustful actions.
5) When a person listens to music for inviting sensuality for sexual reasons only.

The relations in dicussion between music and religious doctrine in the course of those controversies an ideological system or systems evolved, and has been the focus of numerous debates on technicalities of lexicography in texts. Music and religious doctrine consider the fact of concept of art and music are integrated into relavant system of thought. The inference is that music does not act independantly of its own fundamentals, nor is art and music to pursue the dictates of imagination. Religous art and music are subordinate too, and interacts with legitimate mankind's orientation to the universe of The Creator and to various wordly goals in life.

For the first time in Islamic history, the language , sound, and form was known as music art science, and it became its vehicle as Islamic music art science which was born in Arabia, and became an universal art, and has an intrinsic persona of its own esthetics. The sciences of art and beautiful music, did not exist in Orthodox Islam's concepts. The main reason was that ancient legists-puritan believers put great trust in the doctrine of influence (tahir)instead of Allah's creation. In the musical dogma of art and music,so theses beliefs is in an acretion of anthrophorphism which is supreme. Music is a part of the macrocosmic system of creation accepted by many Islamic philosophers, astronomers, mathematicians, and physcians. And by metaphysical reasoning melodic modes -(maqmat) and rythumic modes (iqa'at) were closely linked to the universe and so recognized by the holy prophet Muhammad(sws)himself.

The that was music practiced in religious ceremonials in ancient Arabia were practiced by believers who where encirling the (Ka'ba)"house of worship" and the "Black Stone"-"Seat Of Mankind" housed therein, and chanted a musical cantillation (talhin) as used a transmitted-(talbiyya) from Adam and Noah. These modes of musical chant were practiced during pilgrimage-(hajj) accompanied with fife/ flute (shahin) and drum (bandir/tablah) during circumnabulation (raqs) around the "Ka'ba" and the "Black Stone" therein. Islam thus has its own specific religious art of music, incomparable to the smililarity of Christianity's church chants which have originally been borrowed from the religious chants of Islam's music art sciences.

The music hymns are in forms called praises (Illahis-nasha'ids) and has its place both inside and outside mosques, and along with recitation (Qira'a) of Quran and cantillation (talhin) , call to prayer (adhan-azan),and listening -(Sama/Sema) music of the Sufi-Dervishes fraternal/Maternal orders-(tariqats) with their many varied spiritual religious chants and ecstatic spiritual dances. The mode of recitation (Qir'a) and cantillation (talhin) lent itself to Quran because of its prosodic structure, it's content consists of rhymed prose (saj-gazal) making the voice modulate in recitation and cantillation-(talhin). Ibn Qutaiba relates of an early chanter who practiced melodies for 'call to prayer'-(adhan-azan) as related by Ubaidallah b.Abu Bakr Defitions of modes of Islamic art and music sciences: Cantillation was (lahn)- a dirge-like melody,and the lamentation is incomparable to any ordinary secular singing (ghina).

The "puritan legists"(fuqaha) who were in opposition to any music and looked upon all chanters and singers as "improper"- "(makruh)," so they discriminated between holy Quran's "cantillation (talhin)"religious chants, and the "secular" singng voice-(ghina), and so banned all music of that period in time. However, by the 9th.,century many melodies of popular ballads were being used in recitation-(Qir'a) and cantillation-(talhin)of Quran, despite the vehement opposition of some of the "puritan- legists." Recitation (Qir'a)and cantillation-(talhin) of Quran became one of Islam's most elite art of music science, and the greatest religious and cultural accomplishments, in its prosodic vocalization, perfect grammar, punctuation, with strictly governed rules laid down by Ibn al-Jazari. Cantillation (talhin) was not confined to any fixed melodic sounds , it is found from Morroco to the Oxus, with many patterns and syles as there are mosques in the world.

During the time of the Orthodox Caliphs (A.D.632-61) at the close of the reign of caliph Othman, male musicians (mughanis) and instrumentalists (mitribs) came to the forefront in the person of one man Tuwais, who was acclaimed the first male musician under the banner of Islam. This musician copied from Nasht a Persian musician, who was compelled to include Arabian melodies in their music repertory. The Arabian music became well known, and a century later Ibahim al-Mausil an Arabian musician came to Persia, and he studied Persian styles of music there.

When the incomparable Zitiab peformed before Abd al-Rashman II, all who had proceeded him went into oblivion. There never was another male musician performer more admired. The Arabian school of music flourished in forms created by Ibn Mishah and Ishaq al-Masuli.The last periods of the Caliphate(1045-1258) heralded the decline of greatness. Political control went to the Turkish Seljuqs in (1037)and then Ottomans in(1453),and they became the new masters and brought a fresh cultural environment into the aforementioned lands.

Islamic art and music were born in Arabia, and was nurtured under Persian, Syrian, Turkish and Greek tuteledge and became a universal art of music science. Its intrinsic persona was changed by Safi al-Din who composed the Korasani scale of music, under Mughal and Turkish influences, which were followed into the 14th., century by the Pyhthagorean music scale which then spread elsewhere in the world. Finally with the adoption of the modern scales from period of Islam's "Goldenage," and al-Andalus into the West,and there where those who did preserve their art and music, which is still played in Morroco and other parts of North Africa -(al-Magrib,) and farther on into the modern contemporary world times.

Music in Sufi

"Sufi Dervishes" utilization and conception of music, song,trance,dance is an intrinscic aid to their religious lifestyle. It is of the utmost importance to the developemnt of the soul in two ways:(1) physically on account of musical structure (2) spiritually, in structural similarity to the soul. Sufi masters such as al-Hujwiri and al-Ghazali separated people influenced by music into two groups: (a) those who hear material sounds,(b)those who hear spiritual meaning. Sufis doctrine per sae does not hear notes or beats, melodies or rythums of music. Hujwiri quotes prophet Muhammad's (sws) saying: "O Allah, let us see things as they are." The "listening (sema-sama)" to music only,and alone will acconplish that requirement.

Thus Sufis teachings reaveals the meaning of music in the Schopenhaurian sense as eternal will itself. The great Arab mystic, Abu Sa'id ibn al-Arabi believed ultimate truth could be caught only through Divine ecstasy, as the lifting of a curtain-veil, and witnessing the Watcher Allahu. An epitome of potent means for attainment of ecstasy to achieve is "listening (sema-sama)" of sacred music. Dhu'l-en Nun Misiri, the Egyptian mystic said: "We have in this "listening (sema-sama)" a power that creates a Divine influence which stirs the heart to seek Allah, and leads one to find the existence of the Truth behind the spiritual curtain-veil", as did Abu'l-Husein al-Darraj who also having previously testified.

It was from these strong beliefs and practices that spiritually sprang the numerous Sufi Dervish orders (tariqats), with which music and dancing are used to create a spiritual hypnosis-trance for attainment of higher religious sublimation to Allah. Almost all these Sufi religious orders (tarlqats) have set laws and rules governing their particular order (tariqat) or "pathways",they have their chosen Sufi masters they follow, who passed down their succession (Khalifat) the teachings to the various seekers of the Truth, those who have not been taught the aesthetic, spiritual esoteric ways, thus perpetuating lines (silsilas) of succession of their particular "Sufi orders (tariqats)."

Religious sacred music in Islam does not begin nor end in pious edifices as such, since in every Islamic land, religious cantillation(talhins) has been an integeral part of social life. Muslims in their Islamic festivals religious, and also social events all recieve the pleasure in religious music. Where ever one travels in Muslim lands, the universality of hymns (nasha'ids-Illahis) and cantillation (talhin) is very apparent indeed. In some regions it has been a part of formal education, and has prevailed in spite of the vehement opposition of some powerful legal patriarchs. Music at that time was considered a diversion,and was taken as unpraisworthy, and "frowned upon (makruh)" by some legist-puritans,as with some others strenously with constancy did oppose music in any form as being sinful and "not allowed" (haram) because of their own specific puritan interpretations.

Sufi Dervishes-Sema/Sama:- Music, Trance, Dance, Ecstasy

Prophet Muhammad (sws) announced: "In Islam their is no monkery" in Quran V:89. In 632 C.E. Higra, forty-five men during the time of holy prophet (sws) in Mecca joined themselves to as many in Medina, and took oath of fidelity from the Holy prophet Muhammad (sws)himself,and pledged too his teachings, thusly forming the very first Islamic Sufi paternal- fraternal order. This fist Sufi order intended was to establish community property, and reform daily religious practices through penitence with patience. These initial members of the newly formed fraternity wore rough wool clothes for more penitence with patience,kept in honor for their master prophet Muhammad (sws),they called themselves Sufis from a word "Suf" meaning wool.

This word also meant wise, pure, purity as well as refering to the suffah, the platform on which the Holy prophet (sws) and his companions all sat upon discoursed,recited spiritual meditative prayers and sang sacred songs together.

Abu Bakr father in-law, and Ali ibn Talib son-inlaw of prophet Muhammad (sws) also established assemblies (jama'at-majalis) wherein vows were taken with religious excersises were practiced. In 657 C.E Uwais Qarani established the second Sufi paternal/fraternal religious order (tariqat) in honor of prophet Muhammad (sws). The holy Prophet had lost several teeth in battle of Uhud, and Uwais broke out his own front teeth, and he also required his followers to do the same. The very first "House of Unity (tekke-kanegah-dergah)" was built by Syrian Zahid to provide a house for any and all those Sufi dervishes who followed the Holy Prophet's (sws)given Sufi doctrine(tassawuf),and as a place of sanctury for those weary dervish travelers,for the impoverished, hungry,and also for the unwanted, forgotten, dregs of societal misfortune, for all to come and be safe, and rest in Allah's Light(Nur),and learn to recite the 99 names of Almighy Allahu in Rememberance-Ziker-Dhiker.

Sufis Creed

Sufis believe souls differ in degree but not in kind from Divine spirit, their particles ultimately will be absorbed, the spirit of Allah pervades the universe, ever Omnipresent Allahu alone is the Perfect Benevolence, Perfect Truth, Perfect Beauty, Perfect True Love (eshq-en-haqqiqa). The material love is objectivity, an illusory love (eshq-en-majazi). All beauties of nature are faint resemblences, images in a mirror of The Divine charms, eternity without end, supreme bestowed happiness. All humankind can attain to this only by performing their part in the primal covenent between themselves and The One Creator. Nothing is pure or has absolute existence but with mind and spirit. Material substances are no more than lovely pictures sent to the mind by the Semiternal Artist.

Beware of attachments, except that to Allahu exclusively, soley and truly. Remain in a forlorn state of Remeberance of Allahu. Sweetest music with gentle dance, glorious singing are as myriad fragrant flowers, perpetually refreshing a fading memory, melting them with tender affections that cherish the flames of love by abstracting their souls from all vanity. Proximity to Allahu's Essence (Dhat) in final union too and from Allahu who will form their supreme spiritual beatitude.

Sufis Rememberance-(Zikr-Dhikr) Allahu

The statutes of nearly all the orders (tariqats) require them to repeat the following names of Allah on daily basis praising with reciting in remembrance as follows:

Bismillah ir Rahman ir Rahim

(In the name of Allah the Most Merciful, Most Compassionate)

La ilaha ill Allah!

(No god but The One God)

Ya Allah (O God)

Ya Hu (O Presence)

Ya Nur (O Light)

Ya Hayy (O Living)

Ya Haqq (O Truth)

Ya Kerim (O Genrous One)

Ya Gafoor (O Forgiving)

Ya Qayyum (O Self-Subisting)

Ya Majid (O Glorious)

Ya Wudud (O Loving)

Ya Quddus(O Holy One)

Ya Sabur (O Patient

Ya Samad (O Eternal)

Ya Qahar (O Dominant)

These exercises of awe-filled contemplation (muraqibah) and Divine Unity (tawhid) are practised as follows:

(1) The Sufi dervishes kneeling sit back on their heels, elbows touching lightly in a circle with simultaneous movement carefully balanced, slowly turning heads first to right shoulder, with head pause in center,and then to left shoulder with head return to center.

(2) All seated as they begin these motions in measured cadence, with fixed countenance, eyes are closed or fixed looking downward to the ground or floor, then slowly stand up on their feet raising eyes up to sky or ceiling, and heads comes back down in bowed position as they sit back down again.

(3) The Sufi dervishes,sit nine to thirteen in number in circles or in one big circle, all are sitting on sheepskin/ rugs on the floor at equal distances from eachother, for half an hour arms folded on chest, eyes closed, heads bowed,in this position they will remain in an motionless, and quiet, absolute, profound, reverent meditation.

The Sheykhs/Sheykhas, are sitting at their head of circle, they sit on red or black wool rug or a small carpet,and will break the silence with a hymn (nasha'id) in honor of Allahu,then they invite the assembly (majalis) to recite with with him/her the first Verse (Sura) of Quran. After that the respective sheikhs/sheikhas chant (qi'ra) paying honor to Allahu, to all the prophets, especially Muhammad (sws) and his family, to his first wife Khadijah, his daugher Fatimah, his grandsons Hassan and Hussein, all his other wives and departed kin, all of Allah's followers,and the prophet's (sws) companions-(awliya). To all the holy women and men saints of Islam, to the founder/s of the order/s, to all the many Sheykhs/sheykhas past and present, their long line of successors-(sililas), to all Sufi dervishes and seekers of "pathway of Truth" (tariqat), for Islam and all it's adherents,for prosperity, peace, and compassionate mercy for all the non-believers from every cultural society upon this earth.

The Sufi muscians (mitribs) now start to play their sacred lilting music with vibrancy and sweetness, dipicting The Most Beloved Allahu. The sounds of the instruments escalate in volume, and the throbing of drums keeping steady rythum simulating heart-beats, as the rest of the instruments used play in perfect harmony, making all the many participants in this sacred, spiritual, dance, ecstatic trance of the Sufi dervishes sway, and turn smoothly in unison in time with the lilting, spiritual music, and with this loving ecstatic experience unlocking the very Essence (Dhat) of Allahu's presence in their minds, hearts,and souls, oblivious to all who are present. Now the sacred, spiritual Divine ecstacy dance ceremony starts as follows:

All the Sufi dervishes stand in line to the Sheykhs/ Sheykhas left side, with arms folded on chest, head bowed, and slowly approach the right side of Sheykhs/Sheykhas and bow in salute, then with two steps foward stand opposite facing the right side of sheikhs/sheikhas, once again turning to them and bowing in salute. The rotary/turn dance (daur-raqs) now begins. The sacred dance consists in turning on left heel to toe, simultaneously followed by the right foot, then rotating around the hall or courtyard with eyes closed, arms stetched outward on each side of their body, hands held open with right palm facing up and left palm facing down so the blessings of Allahu flow trough them while they rotate/turn (daur-raqs).

The dervishes intermittantly stop their turns (raqs), stand still for short pauses, while their repective Sheykhs/Sheykhas recite more prayers (duas) as the dance of Divine ecstasy lasts about two hours. Then returning to their seats the Sheykhs/sheykhas recites (qi'ra)the first Verse (Sura) of Quran with more short prayers (duas). The dance is now concluded all dervishes leave in single file for the dining hall into "House of Unity"(tekke-kanegah-dergah)for refreshments and light socializing. The Sufi dervishes then depart to their repective duties in life until the next sacred, spiritual, session of "listening (sema-sama)" with the blessings of Almighty Allahu carried within their minds, hearts and souls.

The Sufi musicians (mitribs) their task well done, now leave carrying their instruments as the assembly disperses, where each listener holds within them the fullness of a world of sacred tunes of spiriutal melody of sounds heard, that still lingers over the now silent hall/courtyard. With this Divine Essence (Dhat) power of The Divine love (eshq), permeating sounds of spiritual music speaks, is most welcome sound to all ears with a familiar sweet message, while revealing to the "seekers of the Truth " of the realms beyond their human knowledge,leading them each on their own personal spiritual pathway, and yet joining all together in revered fervor of shared sacred, spiritual, mystical music experience. May The Great One Creator Omnipresence of Ya HU!, bring all participants the many countless,sweet, enlightened blessings,and to all who those who seek the pathway of Truth!

MUSIC INSTRUMENTS

BUZUQ-SAZ-stringed instrument, the name of it comes from Turkish meaning "bashi" name given to the Ottoman troops literally meaning "burnt head or uprooted." This instrument is an essential one in Rakbani style of religious music, it is a hybrid instrument of it's larger relative the deeper-toned saz, and is compared to as viola/violin in modern Western instruments. A long-necked fretted string instrument, the buzuq-saz is made with two metal strings which are played with a plectrum-pick, having an metallic lyrical resonance of sounds.

MIZAR-DAFF-a name for a type of popular instrument called a tamborine. It consists of round wooden frame, covered on one side with tight fitting goat or fish skin. Pairs of brass metal discs that are set into niches carved in frame, to provide the jingle sound when struck by hand, The sounds of this percussion instrument set the rythum of the music, particularly in the religious performances of Islamic classical styles of Islamic religious music.

KANUN-QANUN is a decendent of old Egyptian harp and has played an integral part in Islamic religious music since 10th.,century. A kind of zither-dulcimer, its Arabic name which means 'rule' or 'law'. The qanun-kanun was introduced to Europe by the 12th., century and came to be known during 14th-16th., century as a psaltry. The form of a qanun-kanun consists of a trapezoid-shaped flat board, over it spread 81 strings which are attached in groups of three with 25 treble chords to each note. The instrument is placed flat on knees or small table in front of musician the strings are plucked with finger-plectra-picks, one plectrum attached to the forefinger of each hand. More than any other type of instruments of Islamic music, qanun-kanun is suitable for display of virtuosity, and execution of fioture and rapid scales. this traditional instrument had been replaced by less complex harpsichord, exchanged with zither's plectra-picks with hammers which grew into the piano a percussion instrument.

HARMONIUM- are hand made musical instruments of stained, polished wood akin to the early pump-organ with keyboard and is played with right or left hand fingers while pumping bellows with the other hand. These instruments give amazing good sound. Their mellow, warm sounding tones blend well with human voices. These wood hand-crafted instruments come in varied sizes, and with its own unique sounds and styles, with differences in volumes, tonations, playing charecteristics, and each has its own individual scales, stops, bellows, and octave couplers, and these instruments are also prized for thier harmonious blends of graduated sounds in Islamic devotional music.

BANDIR-TAR-is framed wood hand drum with goat skin stretched over one side,this drum has great resonance of graded sounds, loudest being close too rim of drum,with progression toward center of drum being dullest sound like a beating heart. Drums are various sizes,having niches cut into one side of wood-frame as tumb-rest,some have small hole for thumb-rest insert. One hand holds drum resting in palm of hand, leaving four fingers for secondary beats on surface of rim. The main beats come with other hand beating surface of drum. Each hand-beat on surface of drum keep tones simulating rythumic heart-beats in Islamic religous spiritual music.

OUD-UD-literally means 'branch of wood" from the sambucus tree, it wa used between 6th-10th.,centuries, the instrument had only four strings; a fifth was added by Zitiab a famous musician, a 6th, string was added later in 15th., century. Shaped like a half pear with a short neck, oud-ud is 6 sets of 2 stringed instrument played with a plectrum-pick, often a trimmed eagle's feather, producing a deep and mellow sound.Used by Virtuosos all across the Islamic countries. And is referred to as the 'king' of all fretted instruments in Islamic religious music. The English word for oud-ud is lute which is derived from Spanish word 'laud'. which originally came from the Arabic word al-oud.

DURNEY-which literally means 'dual' in Arabic, is a double pipe-reed later became an clarinet which was popular instrument used in Islamic religious music, and its equivalent is known as the North African maqrum. NEY-is a single reed-pipe with rich long mournfull sound,and comes in many lengths with octaves higher/lower, and are simple hand-made instruments by the Lakmids-Persians. Both these instruments are played by blowing gently through a circular opening at one end, and by manipulating the holes down front of pipe tubes in order to produce specific sounds. In good performance the sounds are well reflected by the musical dialogue between moods of modes. Another similar relative is the minjarah, an open-ended small reed-flute played in the same manner as these reed-pipes.

DUMBEK-TABLAH is a membranaphone with goat or fish skin stretched over top of a vase shaped form with hollow opening in smaller end, it is usually made of baked ceramic or metal with intricate designs or plain. When played it is put bewtween the legs or hung with strap to shoulder leaving both hands free to beat top of skin on drum. The hands beat the rythum with hard short with inbetween beats which keeps well blended in the Islamic spiritual music hymns. A is smaller version which is long and slender that is placed on top of shoulder and played with one hand.

Many instruments used by Arabs, Persian and Turks were made in then Muslim Spain, were there were large factories that prided in craftmanship as works of art, as noted by Ibn Sa'id al-Maghribi. The many instruments made and used by religious and non-religious musicians entailed myriad variety. All these instruments shown here, were used for religious music only, were in use during prophet Muahmmad's (s.w.s) time and after as well. Some instruments utilized were from regional cultures.However, some other instruments were not permissable for religious music ceremonies, and are not listed here as those instruments are specifically used for only secular music.

2

Spiritual Practices in Music

Christian Mantras And Meditation

Chanting of mantras and the practice of meditation are time-honoured traditions in oriental religions like Hinduism and Buddhism. Christians use the concept of chanting in a variety of ways in their prayer. The Divine Office or Prayer of the Church is a rhythmic recitation or singing of the Psalms in monastic communities. For a Christian the practice of meditation is the practice of an 'awareness' of God in Christ. Equally, at the heart of the practice of Christian meditation is the essential onslaught on the 'ego' so that we may be completely free from its domination. Prophet Isaiah says : "In conversion and tranquillity lies your salvation". Chanting, Christian Mantras, Spiritual practice, Spiritual practices, Meditation, Christopher Mendonca.

Chanting of mantras and the practice of meditation are time-honoured traditions in oriental religions like Hinduism and Buddhism. But because of the universal validity of this practice, the Desert Fathers adopted it and made this the starting point for the "tradition of pure prayer" which they handed down within the Christian context.

Christians use the concept of chanting in a variety of ways in their prayer. The Divine Office or Prayer of the Church is a rhythmic recitation or singing of the Psalms in monastic communities. The Rosary is the successive repetition of the 'Hail Mary'. But perhaps the most popular mantra used by Christians is "Lord Jesus Christ, have mercy on me". The Way of the Pilgrim is the story of a Russian pilgrim who learned the practice of the presence of God through the constant use of this mantra.

Eastern tradition of meditation helps the mind turn away from thoughts and images, to help achieve liberation. Similarly, the Christian tradition of pure prayer seeks to protect us from distraction, taking us to the inner silence of the heart where Christ prays in us through the Spirit. For a Christian the practice of meditation is the practice of an 'awareness' of God in Christ. Equally, at the heart of the practice of Christian meditation is the essential onslaught on the 'ego' so that we may be completely free from its domination. Prophet Isaiah says: "In conversion and tranquillity lies your salvation".

Conversion and inner silence are the essential ingredients of Christian meditation. Solitude is the place of conversion. It is not a private therapeutic place. Rather it is the place where the old self dies and the new self is born. It is in Christian terms a death-resurrection experience, a participation in the Death and Resurrection of Jesus. Meditation helps us get free of the domination of the ego.

The practice of Christian meditation is very simple. You say your word - from the scripture, or a short devotional phrase. As you recite it you also begin to internally "listen" to it. The word recommended is Ma-ra-na-tha (meaning the Lord comes!). When you sit down to meditate, you close your eyes gently and sit upright and then in the deepening silence within you, you repeat the word, the mantra, "Maranatha", for the entire time of your meditation. That is all.

You listen to the mantra as you repeat it and you do not think about yourself - and that is the power of the mantra. All your attention is deflected from yourself to the word. We have to turn the light around, away from ourselves, beyond ourselves or perhaps through ourselves. In other words, the only way to transcend the ego is to ignore it. This is what the mantra enables us to do. It is not so much a matter of 'intention' or an exercise of the will. We all experience our utter failure in this regard. Rather it is a matter of 'attention'.

Silence is a presence and at the heart of it is God. It is the late John Main, a Benedictine monk (OSB) who in recent years rediscovered the lost tradition of Christian meditation. His disciple and successor Laurence Freeman OSB has continued his good work establishing what is now known as the 2012 Community for Christian Meditation (WCCM) in London . He is active in the contemplative meeting of the different faiths and led the "Way of Peace" initiative with His Holiness the Dalai Lama.

Acoustics in Hinduism

Acoustics has played important roles in all cultures and religions of the world. This is natural as acoustics deals with sound, one of the senses of perception. In Hinduism, acoustics is of major importance in various aspects of life, namely spirituality, religion, culture, science, art, *etc*. There are four aspects of acoustics in Hinduism. They are:

1) Chanting of mantras from the Vedas,

2) Sounds from conch-shells,

3) Music (percussion instrument) and

4) Musical tones from pillars.

Vedas, the revealed literature of Hinduism, is an infinitely large collection of mantras (chants). These mantras describe the various facets of knowledge dealing with life and cosmos. It is through precise oral tradition from antiquity to present times that these mantras are taught by teachers (Vedic pundits) to disciples. This transfer of knowledge through recitation requires a pure mind with precision in intonation and pronunciation for both teacher and disciples.

Chandas

The language of Veda mantras is called Chandas and is quite similar to current Sanskrit language with some differences in grammar. Sounds of the Veda mantras carry the listeners to spiritual experiences. The acoustical characteristics, in addition to the clear phonetic articulation of chants, have deep impact on the listeners. The intrinsic pitch difference effects can be overridden in Vedic chanting. The video clip attached below is from a Vedic school "Sri Sarvaraya Ved Pathasala" in Kapileswaram, Andhra Pradesh, India. In the segment shown, both teachers and disciples are chanting in a practice session. The sitting arrangement is in two rows to facilitate alternate chanting.

The chants from Vedas are extensively used in worship and sacrament rituals at homes and temples. In Hindu temples, sounds from conch-shells, bells and musical instruments are used along with worship rituals. It is interesting to note that sound from a conch-shell has a sharp tonal quality that can be recognized while listening. It has a very high Q-factor. The video clip below shows the ending of a ritual in which a lamp is waved as an offering to the deity and then brought to devotees to receive the light of

God. The conch-shells are blown and bells are rung in addition to the chanting by priests during the waving of a lamp. This video clip is from the Hindu Temple and Cultural Society in Bridgewater, New Jersey.

In addition to communication and entertainment, the Vedic literature emphasizes that speech and music have a spiritual role. Speech connects the abstract thoughts and physical actions. The phonetics and grammar of Sanskrit language bring out the spiritual effects through prayers, chants, etc. The sacred role of speech is emphasized in the unison of thought-speech-action as a spiritual goal. The classical music according to Hinduism has divine origin and is a medium primarily for spiritual experiences. There are two types of classical music of India namely Carnatic and Hindustani. Music is also a driving force for dance. Music transforms the listeners. In the words of yogi-seer Sriranga Sadguru, "Music should become the bridge that takes the listeners from sensual level to spiritual level of Atman".

The classical vocal and instrumental music of Hindu culture synthesize both art and science of acoustics. In particular the sounds from the percussion instruments Mridangam and Tabla are melodious to hear in addition to their rhythms. The Nobel laureate Sir C.V. Raman has shown (in 1920) that the melody in Tabla and Mridangam is due to their special design in achieving harmonic relationship in first five natural frequencies. The video clip attached below is a sample of melodious rhythm played by the maestro Zakir Hussain.

Acoustics plays a very important role in Vedic metaphysics. An evolutionary order is given for the five elements of nature. The Vedic evolutionary order is from the subtle to gross i.e. space, air, fire, water and earth. This order of elements is matched with senses of perception as shown in the table below.

Element	*Senses of Perception*
Space	Sound (hear)
Air	Touch and Sound
Fire	See, Touch and Sound
Water	Taste, See, Touch and Sound
Earth	Smell, Taste, See, Touch and Sound

The Vedic metaphysics emphasizes that sound is the only descriptor of space but also can be used in sensing other four elements. Hence acoustics has received primary importance in Vedic Hinduism. In ancient India, the Hindu temples played important roles in all aspects of life such as for worship, a space for art performance, and for education. The video clip attached below shows a musical performance from granite pillars. This special hall, called Purandhara Mantapa, was built in the 16th century during the time of Vijayanagara Empire in Hampe, Karnataka, India.

Spirituality in PopMusic

Spirituality is hip and was omnipresent in pop music in 1998. From pop to hip-hop, Sanskrit to Scripture, popular culture displayed a renewed spiritual consciousness. At the year's Video Music Awards, Madonna, the former Material Girl, performed "Shanti/Ashtangi," a Sanskrit sloka off her award-winning album, *Ray of Light*. At the Grammy Awards, Lauryn Hill accepted the award for "Album of the Year" by reading a passage from Psalm 40, and adding "Know that God is great and he conquers all."

And the growth in spiritual interest is hardly limited to the universe of music. One could also point to the popularity of the angel-to-the-rescue dramas on TV, the apocalyptic blockbusters in theaters, and the bestsellers on the soul in bookstores. Some cultural analysts have even suggested that the 1990s may well be remembered in the publishing world as "the decade of the soul." Nevertheless, spirituality is going platinum in the music world and it may well portend to a deeper longing in the contemporary consciousness. It is to this possibility that my comments are addressed.

Beat of the Heart

Music has a unique place within youth culture. Even more than fashion or entertainment choices, music is the identity trademark of teens. Historian Garry Wills once wrote, "Show me your leader and you have bared your soul." Likewise, show me your CD collection and you have bared your soul. Tell me what music you most identify with, what posters hang in your dorm room, and you say a lot about the state of your heart. Whether you listen to pop, electronica, metal, Ska, grunge, Goth, hip-hop, country, Phish or the women of Lilith Fair, your choice says something about who you are.

Music, then, is the beat of the heart and explores the most basic questions of identity: "Where do I find security?" and "How do I find significance?" Put differently, teens long to "find a home" and to "make a name" for themselves. In the parlance of hip-hop, identity is about "finding blood" and "getting big." *The New York Times Magazine* editor Charles McGrath, commenting on a photo essay of American teens, observes, "The really powerful feeling here, the emotion animating almost all these pictures in one way or another, is not so much physical desire as simply the wish to connect: to belong, to fit in. It may not be too much to say that all these kids are looking for surrogate families, for people who will take them in and accept them without question, and what's fascinating is how much the process is reduced to symbols and uniforms."

Spirituality is an important theme within pop music and music is an important vehicle through which teenage identity is expressed. We will look now at three frequent themes expressed through pop spirituality: a crisis of meaning, a critique of Christianity, and a celebration of paganism. In the summer of 1996, *Rolling Stone* magazine declared that the "Hot Mood" of 90s youth was confusion. In the article, Will Dana referred to a line in Yeats' poem, "The Second Coming:" "Things fall apart; the center cannot hold." Of contemporary youth culture, he wrote, "We used to think the center couldn't hold. All of a sudden, there doesn't seem to be a center at all." Contemporary music does not simply speak of the loss of meaning, but the loss of the possibility of meaning. Reality doesn't leave many options.

Songs about sex, love, and relationships are essentially spiritual explorations about the meaning of life at heart-level. Listen to Tori Amos' song "Leather," to the poignancy of her questions. There is nothing theoretical or abstract about the fear, loneliness, and finally despair exposed in her music.

The angel's spiritual counsel is that you are, in fact, alone here, and so if you want a solution, you'd best jump far. Many are following Tori Amos' lead by abandoning traditional religious answers for newer forms of spirituality. But in route, a few cheap shots at one's upbringing are standard fare. This is the second theme of pop spirituality—a critique of Christianity.

Pop spirituality is largely spirituality without God, if God is understood as the transcendent God of the Bible. Sarah McLachlan in her 1997 release of "Dear God," writes a cosmic "Dear John" letter blaming God for all the evil and disease in the world. Listen to her musical testimony to the rejection of God. There are many people who may still use "god-talk," but in more and more cases the meaning has changed. The immanent gods of Nature are replacing the historic transcendent Creator God of Christianity.

Celebration of Paganism

With a few notable exceptions, God is largely dead in pop spirituality. Instead we are offered a design-it-yourself, cafeteria approach to religion that is non-institutional, individualist, subjective, and syncretistic. The cover of July-August 1998 *UTNE Reader* reads, "Designer God: In a mix-and-match world, why not create your own religion?" Pop spirituality is infused with an eclectic array of Eastern and neopagan spiritualities. "Contemporary American spirituality is largely a cut-and-paste affair," writes *Spin*'s Erik Davis, "perfectly in tune with today's musical mixology."

The central characteristic of contemporary spirituality is an "inner pluralism." All of the world religions are found in a single psyche. Traditional boundaries between religion dissolve and individuals hold multiple citizenship in a number of separate faiths with no complete allegiance to any. Princeton sociologist Robert Wuthnow recently interviewed a 26-year-old disabilities counselor for a study on American spirituality. She described her religious preference as "Methodist-Taoist-Native American-Quaker-

Russian Orthodox-Buddhist-Jew." Spirituality today is a divine deli where consumers of meaning pick and choose among increasingly exotic pagan alternatives. Art historian Camille Paglia argues that "Popular culture is an eruption of paganism... Judeo-Christianity never defeated paganism but rather drove it underground, from which it constantly erupts in all kinds of ways."

The rebirth of paganism is a return to varieties of pantheism, the worship of nature. Pantheism, C.S. Lewis observed, is "humanity's natural religion." Here one doesn't get "saved," one gets "connected." Pagan wisdom consists in the attempt to understand how our lives are to be properly placed and perceived within the forces of Nature. The aim is to open one's heart to these unseen realities. "Consumed with how much you get," Madonna chides, "you're frozen when your heart is not open." Pop spirituality combines personal autonomy with cosmic meaning. "You hold the key," Madonna explains.

G. K. Chesterton was right to warn, "That Jones shall worship the god within him turns out ultimately to mean that Jones shall worship Jones." Again *Spin*'s Erik Davis observes of the current music scene, "Mystical options such as yoga and pop cabala offer direct access to deeper essence, without the pesky moral codes of conventional religion. Unfortunately, this search can easily degenerate into another American cult of the self, a cult that already enshrines celebrities as the closest thing mortals come to being realized beings." Likewise, Princeton theologian Thomas Molnar concludes, "A good case can be made for the proposition that what attracts members of a weakened Christian civilization to Oriental creeds and occult doctrines is not Buddhism, the Tantra, the Tao, the Zen, Brahmanism, or shamanism. Much more important, is the presence in each of these new religions...of the hope of self-divination."

This is consumer spirituality well suited for the celebrity limelight and lifestyle. Paganism is spirituality attuned to the postmodern zeitgeist; for in the end, it celebrates self and sex. Whenever meaning is sought in Nature its practice takes a predictable course—and it has been this way from the beginning of time: a personal deity offers a personal morality reinforced by a personal power, which ends in the worship of the person and their passions. Paganism always ends in that which is violent and orgiastic. Chesterton again observes, "A man loves Nature in the morning for her innocence and amiability, and at nightfall, if he is loving her still, it is for her darkness and her cruelty." Paganism is a theology of hubris and hedonism.

Pop spirituality, then, quickly becomes the highest form of self-worship—the divination of ego, the spiritualizing of desire. This is religion adapted to therapeutic consumerism: cosmic meaning without personal morality, self-affirmation without self-constraint. Jewel, whose debut 1995 album *Pieces of You* sold over 10 million copies, asks, "Who will save your soul, if you won't save your own?" Who's my savior in pop spirituality? In the final analysis, I am. God is me and what I want is god.

Miseducation of Spirituality Lite

Enter Lauryn Hill, in her truly remarkable debut solo hip-hop album, *The Miseducation of Lauryn Hill,* she raises the stakes on pop spirituality lite. Here is a 23-year-old with spiritual unction. "There is always a spiritual war, but there's a battle for the souls of black folk, and just folk in general, and the music has a lot to do with it," she says. In interviews, Hill unequivocally describes herself as Christian (tinged with Rastafarian influences). Locating her prophetic message within the Christian narrative gives her words an unusual gravity and grace. Life is lived not for personal freedom, but personal responsibility. One's choices are made before the face of God. In her song, "Final Hour," she challenges the avarice of hip-hop: "You could get the money / You could get the power / But keep your eyes on the final hour." In "Superstar," Hill warns that no one—not even hip-hop superstars—can live above spiritual laws: "Now tell me your philosophy / On exactly what an artist should be / Should they be someone with prosperity / And no concept of reality? / Now who you know without any flaws / That lives above the spiritual laws / And does anything they feel just because / There's always someone there who'll applaud."

The significance of Lauryn Hill's accomplishments—10 Grammy Award nominations, 5 Grammy Awards (more than any other artist in history), a triple-platinum album—cannot be appreciated without understanding hip-hop. Mall America has become hip-hop. Hip-hop is pop style. No other musical genre has as much influence today in youth culture than rap. "Hip-hop is the rock of today," boasts MC Jean Wyclef. "It is the folk music of this generation," says Beck. Music critic Nelson George writes, "Now we know that rap music, and hip-hop style as a whole, has utterly broken through from its ghetto roots to assert a lasting influence on American clothing, magazine publication, television, language, sexuality, and social policy as well as its obvious presence in records and movies." In 1998, for the first time ever, rap out-sold what previously had been America's top-selling format, country music. White kids purchase more than 70% of hip-hop albums.

Nor is hip-hop known for its positive message. "Hip-hop is the rebellious voice of youth. It's what people want to hear," explains MC Jay-Z in *Time*'s cover story, "Hip-Hop Nation." "Kids don't want to be like Mike anymore. Their heroes are rappers," claims MC Sean (Puffy) Combs. The central tenets of hip-hop are rebellion, aggression, and materialism. It is pop culture's answer to commodified rebellion. "Hip-hop is perhaps the only art form that celebrates capitalism openly.... Rappers make money without remorse," writes *Time*'s Christopher Farley. Hip-hop is hoppin', writes Nelson George, because "materialism replaced spirituality as the definer of life's worth.... A voracious appetite for 'goods,' not good."

Hip-hop is the most image-driven part of pop music and has spawned a revolution in fashion. By 1996, Tommy Hilfiger had become the leading apparel company traded on the New York Stock Exchange largely due to its embrace of hip-hop. Finally, hip-hop promotes an in-your-face aggressive attitude toward others. Hip-hop rules the world of youth culture for a reason. It reflects what kids are thinking, an uncaring attitude about rules or responsibility. Lauryn Hill portrays a traditional spiritual search in the most unlikely of musical forms. A point not lost on Hill herself. Accepting the Grammy she beamed, "Wow, ya know what, this is amazing.

Pop Spirituality Assessed

The popularity of pop spirituality says that many are stopping the distractions long enough to ask the deeper questions of life. In this way, this trend in pop music is a significant spiritual accomplishment. Here is an honest look at the deeper longings of the heart. Here is a critique of the unreflective life. Here is an admission of the vanity of fame, fashion, and fortune. We all live cluttered lives.

Paganism may offer spirituality without morality, a religion that celebrates self and sex. But even paganism—with all its talk of fairies and spirits—puts to the lie the arrogant materialism that rules out the inner realities of the soul. C. S. Lewis observed, "Christians and pagans had much more in common with each other than either has with a post-Christian. The gap between those who worship different gods is not so wide as that between those who worship and those who do not." The discerning question is not "whether spirits," but "which spirits." In pop spirituality there is the recognition that we are not human beings having a spiritual experience, but spiritual beings having a human experience.

The spiritual is our highest and natural environment: life lived at its fullest. As Augustine concluded after years of hard partying and intellectual seeking, "You have formed us for yourself, and our hearts are restless until they find their rest in you." Pop spirituality is the outer voice of this inner search. Celtic scholar John O'Donohue has written a new book entitled, *Eternal Echoes: Exploring Our Yearning to Belong*. Our heart's longings to belong are, in fact, eternal echoes. O'Donohue said recently, "Maybe divinity is actually that secret tissue which links everything that is—matter, spirit, future, past, possibility, fact, question, quest. Maybe the divine is the great belonging." The Apostle John says, "Perfect love drives out fear." It is for this love that we long.

Qawwali : Islamic Devotional Music

Qawwali is the traditional form of Islamic song found in India and Pakistan. The word *qawwali* is derived from the Arabic word *Qaol* which means "axiom" or "dictum". A *Qawwal* is one who sings *qawwali*, or the dictums of the prophets and praises of God. The *Qawwali* is closely linked to the spiritual and artistic life of northern India and Pakistan.

The *qawwali* is inextricably linked to the *Sufi* tradition; Sufism is a mystical school of Islamic thought which strives to attain truth and divine love by direct personal experience. In Arabic, this mysticism is known as *tasawwuf*. The difference between Sufism and mainstream Islam is simple. All Muslims believe that man is on a path to God *(tariqah)*. However, where the mainstream Muslim believes that it is only possible to reach God after death at the final judgement, the *Sufi* believes that it is possible to reach God during ones life. To this end there are a number of different techniques and methods.

The Koran instructs man to remember God. This remembrance, known as *dhikr*, may be either silent of vocal. The *qawwali* may be viewed as an extension of the vocal form of this remembrance. The use of music as a spiritual force was discussed in great length by al-Gazali (1085-1111).

By the end of the 11th century, there arose the tradition of the *sama*. The *sama* was often a spiritual concert, which included a vocalist, and instrumentalists. These *samas* took place under the direction of a spiritually respected man *(shaikh)*.

There is a very specific psychological process which a *qawwali* follows. One starts with the singing of the song. In this psychological state the song is received in a manner that is not unlike standard forms of musical expression. The words are sung, quite repeatedly with variations intended to bring out deeper means of the lyrics. After awhile there is a repetition to the extent that the words cease to have a meaning. It is the goal here to lead the listener and performer alike into a trance *(hal)*. In the ideal situation the participant is moved to a state of spiritual enlightenment *(fana)*.

The origins of *qawwali* probably predate the birth of Muhammad. The earliest Islamic scholars discussed the spiritual effects of music, but it was only in the time of al-Gazali (1085-1111) that these principles were refined and codified. These principles were then expanded by the *Chisti* school of Sufism. It is this order that has been responsible for the propagation of the *qawwali* in India and Pakistan for then last few centuries.

The origin of the *Chisti* school is unclear. Most believe that it was established by Khwaj Moinuddin Hasan Chisti (1143-1234). However there are a some who hold that the originator was Abu Ishaq Shami Chisti who died in Damascus in 940 C.E. Khwaj Moinuddin Hasan Chisti was undoubtedly responsible for the widespread propagation of this school of Sufism. It is said that he was born in Sijistan. At a young age, he was influenced by several saintly men, including Ibrahim Qahandazi, and Shaikh Abdul Qadir Jilli. He immigrated to Delhi and became a very respected saint. He later grew tired of the life in Delhi and withdrew to the peace and quite of Ajmer (Rajasthan) where he lived the remainder of his days.

One of the followers of the *Chisti* school was a man by the name of Shaikh Nizamuddin Auliya (1236-1325). He was born in Budaun, but at the age of 20 he moved to Ajodhan and became a disciple of Fariduddin Ganj-i-Shakkar. It is said that it was here that he received the key to inner illumination. He was then sent to Delhi to instruct the populous. Here he acquired a reputation for using music in his devotional gatherings. This created a great amount of friction with the more orthodox Islamic elements in Delhi.

Nizamuddin Auliya was, and still is, a source of inspiration for countless people. Even today there is an annual gathering at his tomb. One man who was inspired by the Hazrat Nizamuddin was Amir Khusru. He was born in Mominpur (Patiala). His father was originally from Turkey, this gave the young boy a broader exposure to the rest of the Islamic world. His father died when he was eight years old, whereupon the job of raising him fell to his maternal grandfather. Amir Khusru was a legendary musician, statesman and philosopher. It is said that he was the advisor to 11 rulers of Delhi, particularly the rulers of the Khilji Dynasty.

Amir Khusru is so important to the development of *qawwali* that he is often (erroneously) said to be the inventor of it. It is said that he mixed the various musical elements from Turkey, greater Persia and India together. Even today, we find the curious mixture of Persian *moqquams* with Indian *rags*. The development of the *qawwali* up to the latter part of the Mogul empire closely parallels the development of the Hindu religious song known as *bhajan*. The degree of cross influence is so great that some musician / saints such as Kabir (circa 1440-1518) are to this day revered by Hindus and Muslims alike.

The tradition of *qawwali* has had numerous ups and downs. One particularly hard time was during the reign of Aurangzeb. Aurangzeb is known for his Islamic fundamentalism. The liberal traditions of the *Sufis* were not well received by this emperor. He took the fundamentalist injunction against music very seriously. Aurangzeb's dislike of music is well illustrated in a common story. It appears that during his administration a group of musicians, disheartened with their lack of patronage, took some musical instruments and wrapped them in the manner of a corpse and held a funeral procession in protest.

Aurangzeb enquires about the procession and is told it is a burial to signify the death of music. Whereupon it is said that the emperor declares, "Good! bury it so deep that never a sound should be heard again." The collapse of the Mogul empire and political fragmentation under the British was both good and bad for the *qawwals*. On one hand the political disarray meant that a major suppression of their artform was impossible, yet it also meant that their patronage was also uneven.

The rising film industry in the middle of the 20th century was a major vehicle for the rise in popularity of the *qawwali*. There was a period when a *qawwali* was a mandatory part of the formula Hindi films.

The film industry influenced the development of the *qawwali* in several ways. It is interesting to note that since the environment of the cinema house precluded the artist /audience interaction, it set the precedent for the more detached quality that characterises modern performances. The *filmi qawwali* also set the precedent for the "showy" quality that one finds in modern performances. Another effect of the *filmi qawwali* was the downgrading of the religious / devotional aspect. A typical example of a *filmi qawwali* is *"Sharam ke Kyun Sab"* from the film *"Chaudvin ka Chand"*.

The secularisation of the *qawwali* is an interesting phenomenon. One can see that the seeds of its secularisation are inherent in the *qawwali* itself. Themes of *qawwali* have traditionally revolved around very mundane or even coarse occurrences. However, the coarseness of the situations have always been interpreted as the coarse spiritual existence of our daily lives. The modern secular *qawwali* tends to strip the themes of their metaphorical and allegorical character thus producing a shallow, yet commercially marketable entity.

Recent years have seen the *qawwali* thrust into the international arena by such musicians as Nusrat Fateh Ali Khan. His fusion of traditional Indo-Pakistani influences with Western music has created quite a stir in the music world.

Characteristics

The performance of a *qawwali* is typically a group situation. This is different from a classical performance which revolves around one person. Within this group situation, there is one main vocalist or *qawwal*, and a group of supporting vocalist. The audience too is considered a participant in this event The musical accompaniment is varied; harmonium, tabla, dholak, sarangi, saringda, and rabab, are common instruments. Furthermore, a simple clapping of the hands is a ubiquitous rhythmic support.

There are several *tals* in common use in the *qawwali*. The most common is the fast *dadra* tal of 6 beats or the fast *kaherava* of four or eight beats. Unlike the more cerebral, classical forms these *tals* are played in such a way that they produce a driving hypnotic beat. Although the *qawwali* is not a classical form of singing, it does have some common elements. One finds fast *taans, meend gamaks* and the other forms of *ornamentation* which are typical of *Hindustani* performances.

The structure of the *qawwali* is also similar to the classical forms. It typically starts with the *alap*. This portion has no rhythm and is intended to create the right environment. One then moves into the main portion of the performance; this is usually in a medium tempo. The pace slowly increases until a state of extreme excitement is produced.

It is very common for audience members, moved by their state of ecstasy to give money to the performers. This is known as *vel.* The performance continues without stopping.

The most common *rags* used in *qawwalis* today are *bilawal, khammaj, kafi,* and *kalyan*. However one often finds *rags* which are more in common with the modal forms of Persia or Afghanistan.

Musical Instruments in Qawwali

— Bulbul Tarang
— Dholak
— Harmonium
— Kartal
— Rabab
— Santur
— Sarangi
— Saringda
— Tabla

3

Indian Classical Music

In Indian Classical Music, a Guru is a must; without his guidance and blessings one cannot go far. This is because of the spiritual content in our Classical Music. Our Classical Music is more than 5000 years old and has come from our temples. Our Gods were great musicians. Devi Saraswati played veena, Lord Krishna played flute, Lord Shankar played damaroo. 5000 years back Hinduism was the most established religion; respect to nature is very prominent in our religion. (eg: panch-mahabhootas, tulsi, cow, coconut, rivers, hills etc.) Indian Classical Music, as a part of Hindu religion, respected nature and followed laws of nature.

MELODY

Sound, which is useful for music, is melody. Sound of bomb-explosion or a harsh horn of a lorry cannot be a melody; whereas chirping of birds, whisper of breeze, sound of flowing river etc. can be melody. Melody has three characteristics: i) Volume/ Magnitude, which is loudness ii) Timber/quality, which enables us to know who is singing/speaking or which instrument is being played iii) Pitch, which is a result of frequency of vibration per second and it decides The octave.

Twelve Swaras

The octave can only be divided into 22 parts where our ear can distinctly hear the parts separately. Any additional part above 22, gets overlapped and our ear cannot distinguish. These are our 22 shrutis. Swara Sa occupies 4 shrutis, Re occupies 3 shrutis, Ga occupies 2 shrutis, Ma occupies 4 shrutis, Pa occupies 4 shrutis, Dha occupies 3 shrutis and Ni occupies 2 shrutis. Re, Ga, Dha and Ni have space to move backwards and hence can become komal, whereas Ma cannot move backwards but can only move forwards and hence can become teevra. Sa and Pa swaras are fixed at one place and are like Dhruv nakshyatra.

Thaats

The 7 swaras in different combinations give 10 thaats (groups)

Bilawal	Sa Re Ga Ma Pa Dha Ni	
Kalyan suddha	Sa Re Ga M'a Pa Dha Ni	Re, Ga, Dha
Khamaj	Sa Re Ga Ma Pa Dha Ni	
Bhairav	Sa Re Ga Ma Pa Dha Ni	
Poorvi komal	Sa Re Ga M'a Pa Dha Ni	Re. Dha
Marwa	Sa Re Ga M'a Pa Dha Ni	
Kafi	Sa Re Ga Ma Pa Dha Ni	
Asawari komal	Sa Re Ga Ma Pa Dha Ni	Ga / Ni
Todi	Sa Re Ga M'a Pa Dha Ni	
Bhairavi	Sa Re Ga Ma Pa Dha Ni	

Raga

Thaats give birth to all the ragas. The combinations of swaras for a raga must be aesthetically appealing. They must be artistically pleasing and entertaining. Aroha & Avaroha are must in a raga. They must have minimum of five swaras. Two variations of same swaras are not allowed consecutively in a raga. The raga will have Vadi (King), Samvadi (Queen / Minister), Anuvadi (Praja / subjects) & Vivadi (Enemy) swaras. Some ragas will have Vakra swaras. The raga will have a Pakad, which is the smallest combination of swaras depicting the raga.

— In a raga the aaroha or avaroha taking all seven swaras is known as sampoorna;

— the aaroha or avaroha taking only six swaras is known as shadav;

— the aaroha or avaroha taking only five swaras is known as auduv.

Thus we have nine combinations of ragas & a total of possible 484 ragas in one thaat ie. a total of 4,840 ragas in ten thaats as given below.

Samporna-Sampoorna	1
Sampoorna-Shadav	6
Sampoorna-Auduv	15
Shadav-Sampoorna	6
Shadav-Shadav	36
Shadav-Auduv.	90
Auduv-Sampoorna	15
Auduv-Shadav	90
Auduv-Auduv	225

Total ragas in one thaat : 484 Hence total ragas possible in ten thaats are 4,840

However all these possible ragas are not aesthetically appealing. Hence at a given period of time only about 350-400 ragas are in circulation and of these may be only about 100-150 are popular. With time some ragas go to the back-benches and some emerge to the front. You will now appreciate that it is futile to claim that somebody invented a new rags; at the most you may say that somebody re-invented the raga or somebody brought a raga from back-benches to the front row!

Development is slow unfolding of a raga. It should be done as if you are having a dialog with the audience (or with God/Guru when you are doing practice/riyaz). The raga starts with aalaps which is introducing the raga from all angles with progressive swaras. There is no rhythm involved at this juncture. Correctness of swaras and grammar of raga are important in aalaps. The rhythm without a cycle is then introduced in jod-aalaps. At the end of jod-aalaps we have jod-jhala where the rhythm becomes very fast and takes a pseudo-cycle without accompaniment of percussionist.

Then we have pre-set compositions in vilambit and drut tempo with the accompaniment of percussionist. The compositions are set to various time-cycles known as taals. Extempore development is then done within the framework of the compositions. We then have a fast jhala set to the time-cycle/taal, and finally a climax is achieved.

The basic raga and the compositions are to be given a beauty-parlour treatment so that the presentation becomes aesthetically pleasing and appealing to the mind. This is very very important exercise and this distinguishes a maestro from a mediocre artiste.

Kan, Meend, Murki, Gamak, Khatka, Behalava, Ghaseet, Krintan, Jamjama and a wide variety of Taans are the commonly used ornaments and cosmetics.

Fundamentals of Rag

The *rag* is the most important concept that any student of Indian music should understand. The Hindi/Urdu word "*rag*" is derived from the Sanskrit "*raga*" which means "colour, or passion". It is linked to the Sanskrit word "*ranj*" which means "to colour". Therefore *rag* may be thought of as an acoustic method of colouring the mind of the listener with an emotion. This is fine as a general concept but what is it musically? It is not a tune, melody, scale, mode, or any concept for which an English word exists. It is instead a combination of different characteristics. It is these characteristics which define the *rag*. Here are the characteristics.

- — There must be the notes of the *rag*. They are called the *swar*. This concept is similar to the Western solfege.
- — There must also be a modal structure. This is called *that* in North Indian music and *mela* in carnatic music.
- — There is also the *jati*. *Jati* is the number of notes used in the *rag*.
- — There must also be the ascending and descending structure. This is called *arohana /avarohana*.

Another characteristic is that the various notes do not have the same level of significance. Some are important and others less so. The important notes are called *vadi* and *samavadi*.

There are often characteristic movements to the *rag*. This is called either *pakad* or *swarup*.

In addition to the main characteristics of *rag,* there are some other less important ones. For instance *rags* have traditionally been attributed to particular times of the day. They have also been anthropomorphize into families of male and female rags (*raga, ragini, putra raga,* etc.). There is a tendency to downgrade the importance of these aspects due to their irrational and unscientific nature

Instruments used to play Rags:

— Bansuri
— Dilruba
— Esraj
— Gottuvadyam
— Harmonium
— Jal Tarang
— Mayuri Vina
— Nadaswaram
— Rabab
— Rudra Vina
— Santur
— Sarangi
— Sarod
— Sitar
— Surbahar
— Tabla Tarang
— Vichitra Vina
— Violin

TAAL

The time-cycles are known as taals. The taal has a tempo, has Matras (beats, ie. unit used to measure time), has Sam (Most important beat giving the impact), has Khali (which usually shows the mid-way). The taals have their distinct Bols. Our music is rich with several taals ranging from cycle of 6 beats to as high as 28 beats.

The Importance of Correct Riyaz

It is not necessary to practise for 12 hours a day as claimed by artistes of yester-years.For them it was necessary because they did not have modern gadgets like tape-recorder, electronic tabla etc. and they did not think of application of science to their musical effort. Even with a regular four hours a day riyaz many of today's younger artistes have reached the highest levels of success.

The student of music has to get the correct technique from through proper Guru, then and then only he can make extra-ordinary progress.

VARIETIES OF MUSIC

The music of India includes multiples varieties of folk and pop music, along with Karnatic and Hindustani classical music.

Pop music

The biggest form of Indian pop music is filmi, or music originated in films. Other forms of pop musicians include Alisha Chinai and rock bands like Bally Sagoo.

Filmi

The capital of the Indian film music industry is Mumbai (Bombay); consequently, the film industry there is referred to as Bollywood. Films in other regional languages are produced in the respective regions. Popular composers include Ilayaraja (Tamil, Telugu), Rajesh Roshan (Hindi), A.R. Rahman (Tamil, Hindi) and Raamlaxman (Hindi). Many of the films tend to be idealized visions of Indian life, and much of the music is similarly jolly and romantic. Prominent vocal stars include Lata Mangeshkar and S.P. Balasubrahmaniam.

Cinema began taking shape in India in the late 19th century, and silent films soon became very popular. In 1931, Ardeshir M. Irani's Alam Ara was adapted from a piece of Parsi theater and launched Indian talkies. The music became extremely popular, and was soon heavily advertised. One reason for the push was that India's linguistic diversity meant dialogue would be incomprehensible for a large portion of the audience, no matter what language it was made in. Music provided a neutral option.

A form of filmi based on ghazal is called filmi-ghazal and was introduced by Talat Mahmood; it was eventually modernized into ghazal-song.

Western fusions

In the late 1960s and early 1970s, rock and roll fusions with Indian music were well-known throughout Europe and North America. Ali Akbar Khan's 1955 performance in the United States was perhaps the beginning of this trend, which was soon centered around Ravi Shankar.

In 1962, Shankar and Bud Shank, a jazz musician, released Improvisations and Theme From Pather Pachali and began fusing jazz with Indian traditions. Future pioneers like John Coltrane continued this fusion, called indo jazz. George Harrison (of The Beatles) played the sitar, which he had learned from Shankar, on the song "Norwegian Wood" in 1965. Other Western artists like the Grateful Dead, Incredible String Band, Rolling Stones, The Move and Traffic soon incorporated Indian influences and instruments, and added Indian performers.

Though the Indian music craze soon died down among mainstream audiences, diehard fans and immigrants continued the fusion. In the late 1980s, Indian-British artists fused Indian and Western traditions to make the Asian Underground.

Folk music

The arrival of movies and pop music weakened folk music's popularity, but cheaply recordable music has made it easier to find and helped revive the traditions. Folk music (*desi*) has been influential on classical music, which is viewed as a higher art form. Instruments and styles have impacted classical ragas.

Brass bands

Brass bands, descended from English traditions, are now very popular especially at weddings and other special occasions.

Bhangra

Bhangra is a form of dance-oriented folk music that has become a pop sensation in the United Kingdom. The present musical style is derived from the traditional musical accompaniment to the folk dance of Punjab called by the same name, Bhangra.

Dandiya

A form of folk music adapted for clubs is called dandiya. It is based on *Gujarati* folk music, and includes best-selling artists like Falguni Pathak.

Rajasthan

Rajasthani has a diverse collection of musician castes, including langas, sapera, bhopa, jogi and manganiyar.

Baul

The Bauls of India and Bangladesh are a mystical order of musicians and played a form of music using a khamak, ektara and dotara.

Vocal music

Hindustani vocal music can be divided into several sorts, including *bhajan* and *ghazal*, while Karnatic vocal music is typically a hymn called *kriti*.

Dhrupad

Dhrupad is a sacred style of singing traditionally performed by men with a tampura and pakhawaj accompanying. The lyrics are in a midieval form of Hindi and typically heroic in theme, or else praising a particular deity. A more ornamented form is called dhamar.

Bhajan

Religious vocal music, bhajan is the most popular form in northern India. Famous performers include Kabir, Tulsidas and Mirabi. It arose out of the Alvar bhakti movement of the 9th and 10th century.

Ghazal

Ghazals are an originally Persian form of vocal music that is popular with multiple variations across Iran, Central Asia, Turkey and India. Ghazal exists in multiple variations, including folk and pop forms.

Khyal

An informal form of vocal music, khyal is partially improvised and very emotional in nature. Though its origins are shrouded in mystery, the 15th century rule of Hussain Shah Sharqi and was popular by the 18th century rule of Mohammed Shah. The best-known composer of the period was Sadarang, a pen name for Niamat Khan. Later performers include Faiyaz Khan, Abdul Karim Khan, Bhimsen Joshi, Shweta Jhaveri, Bade Ghulam Ali Khan and Amir Khan.

Kriti

Kritis are a form of Hindu hymn especially popular in southern India. It is commonly composed in Telugu, Tamil or Sanskrit.

Tarana

Tarana, and its southern equivalent Tillana, are rhymic songs with nonsense lyrics.

Thumri

Thumri is an accessible and informal vocal form said to have begun with the court of Nawab Wajid Ali Shah, 1847-1856. There are two types of thumri: Punjabi and Lucknavi. The lyrics are typically in a language called braj bhasha, and are usually romantic. Performers include Shobha Gurtu, Bade Ghulam Ali Khan and Girija Devi.

Bhajan: Hindu Devotional Music

Music to human ears is heavenly. And if it's purely devotional, it's truly divine. Such a genre of music is the Bhajan. Nothing can be more deeply rooted in the Indian tradition than bhajans. Bhajans are simple songs in soulful language expressing the many-splendored emotions of love for God, a complete submission or self-surrender to him through singing.

The groundwork for bhajans was laid in the hymns found in Sama Veda, the fourth Veda in the Hindu scriptures. They are distinguished from the Sanskrit shlokas (hymns that accompany religious rituals) by virtue of their easy lilting flow, the colloquial renderings and the profound appeal to the mass. These are sung in a group comprising devotees, with a lead singer. The fixed tunes, repetition of words and phrases lend a kind of tonal mesmerism. Anecdotes, episodes from the lives of Gods, preaching of saints, description of God's glories have been the subject of bhajans. Another form of the bhajanis the keertan or songs in the Haridas tradition.

Types of Bhajans

A plunge into the past reveals, that bhajans, as a genre, have come a long way weaving a home for itself into the core of human hearts. Traditions of bhajan — singing have been formed over the ages — Nirguni, Gorakhanathi, Vallabhapanthi, Ashtachhap, Madhura-bhakti are some of them. Each sect has their own sets of bhajans and ways of singing them.

The medieval age saw devotees like Tulsidas, Surdas, Meera Bai, Kabir and others composing Bhajans. In the modern times, composers like Pt. V. D. Paluskar and Pt. V. N. Bhatkhande have tried to mingle Raga Sangeet or Indian classical music - which had been an exclusive domain of the elite - with bhajans, thereby democratizing the Raga tradition.

The common mass indulges in bhajan-singing without realizing that such traditional methods of invoking the divine can have a tremendous stress-removing impact. Bhajan mandalis (a gathering to sing bhajans) that have been in existence in the Indian villages since the beginning of the Bhakti era, have proved to be great social leveller where individuals unhesitatingly participate in the singing, relegating their petty differences to the background. This participatory action elicits recreation and consequently a kind of mental relaxation. They close their eyes to ensure that they concentrate and thereby meditate on this near ecstasy. The words, tunes, rhythms and the typical repetitive style of the bhajans give a certain sense of permanency that is known as shashwat (freedom from the state of flux), something each one of us is secretly pining for.

Is Devotional Music Fundamentalist?

Can we not keep such a thing as music out of such criticisms? It is lamentable that the ruckus created around the issue of fundamentalism has not left even the devotional compositions out of its purview. The fundamentalist hullabaloo in the Indian scenario never misses an opportunity to constrict a gathering, which has come together for simple religious expressions such as singing of bhajans or popular devotional songs of the mass. To suspect that this trend of devotional singing may be in any way related to the spread of fundamentalism is nothing but naïve thinking.

To deem it propagandist in approach is anything but intelligible. Fundamentalism is a vested political interest whereas religion is something personal. It is only when religion breeds the desire to dictate mass feelings and direct it to a preconceived end, that it becomes fundamentalist, bringing communalism and destruction in its wake. Singing a bhajanor a quwwali is a cultural expression, and to equate them with fundamentalist outcries is nothing but erroneous. We must save the divine melody, and allow the benign force of music with its tremendous sustaining and benevolent power to drive out any number of 'isms'. This is only possible if we keep our musical sensibilities intact and expanding.

Saraswati—Goddess of Learning

The original concept of Saraswati was that of a feminine water deity. Over a period of time, this riverine goddess came to be associated with all coursing and flowing energies and forces. Today, Saraswati is hailed as the patron goddess for the thought process and all creative arts.

The Hindu religion or *Sanatana Dharama,* as it is called, recognizes a Supreme Godhead (*Paramatma*) who is omniscient, omnipresent and omnipotent. This supreme being performs three essential functions of creation (*shrishti*), sustenance (*samrakshana*) and annihilation (*samhara*) in relation to this universe and beyond. In his personalized manifestation, this Godhead assumes the triple forms of Brahma, the Lord of Creation, Vishnu or Narayana, the Lord of sustenance and Rudra or Shiva, the Lord of Annihilation. These three entities comprise the *Trimurtis* or the Holy Hindu Trinity. Each of these three gods has been associated with a consort or female aspect who provides the requisite support and energy to the respective Godhead in the discharge of his ordained functions. The *Vedas* which are the most ancient of the Hindu religious scriptures, postulate that Goddess Saraswati is the consort of Creator God Brahma.

The word Saraswati is of Sanskritic origin and etymologically, it denotes a person or being of the feminine gender. This name has different connotations which, in the final analysis, are all related with water bodies such as stream and river (*sarit*) and lake and pool (*saras*). In a figurative manner, all things that are fluid or free-flowing in nature have had their associations with Saraswati.

References to a river bearing the name Saraswati could be found in the *Vedas* and other Hindu scriptures of yore. The *Rig Veda* says that the River Saraswati originated in the Himalayas, flowed westwards and joined the Arabian Sea. At Prayag—modern day Allahabad—in Uttar Pradesh, the rivers Ganga and Yamuna are believed to be joined by a third river called Saraswati, which is invisible. Hindu faithfuls take the name of Saraswati, in addition to the Ganga and Yamuna, while they take a dip in any river held sacred by them. Thus, it can be inferred that the name Saraswati in itself has a purificatory significance.

As per Vedic lore, Goddess Saraswati manifested herself from the mouth-or tongue to be precise—of Lord Brahma. Having been bewitched by her beauty and grace, and impressed by her divine attributes, the Creator God decreed that Saraswati should become his consort and provide him assistance in his task of creation. Since Brahma was responsible for the creation of Saraswati, he was by logic her father. His act of marrying Goddess Saraswati was, therefore, regarded as a transgression of accepted norms of behavior and so Vishnu and Shiva uttered a curse that henceforth Brahma would cease to be worshipped as a God by faithfuls. Even to this day, this curse seems to be holding true since there are only a few temples dedicated exclusively to Brahma, whereas there are hundreds of thousands of temples and shrines dedicated to Vishnu and Shiva.

In this background, Goddess Saraswati traditionally has come to be worshipped in her individual capacity as the patron goddess for all knowledge and wisdom without her being associated with Brahma. Idols of Goddess Saraswati are installed in temples and shrines dedicated to her exclusively or sometimes find a place with other gods and goddesses of the Hindu pantheon in Vishnu, Devi and Shiva temples. Such temples are more in number in the southern and eastern parts of the country.

In the states of Tamil Nadu, Karnataka, Andhra Pradesh, Kerala, Rajasthan, West Bengal, Madhya Pradesh, Uttar Pradesh and the union territory of Pondicherry skilled craftsmen have been making beautiful icons of Saraswati since generations. Around the festival of Durga Puja in October, innumerable craftsmen move out from West Bengal to different parts of the country and display their artistry in making clay images of Saraswati and other deities that are ceremonially installed in the pavilions erected for the celebrations.

Saraswati worship spread during the medieval period from the Indian sub-continent to many south and east Asian countries. Several references to the Goddess can be evidenced in the local traditions and literature of those countries. Even sculptures and graphic representations of Saraswati have been identified in some of those countries, notably in Sri Lanka, Thailand, Cambodia and Indonesia.

Hinduism apart, Buddhism and Jainism have also accorded an honoured place to Saraswati. In modern times, wherever Indians have gone, they have carried the Saraswati lore and erected shrines for her worship.

The term Saraswati, besides referring to the goddess also stands as an appellation to the names of *sanyasis* (religious pontiffs or recluses) of the *Advaitic* (non-dual) religio-philosophic order. A sect of Hindu Brahmans in the western and northern parts of India go by the name of Saraswat Brahmans. Eminent poets and litterateurs are addressed as *Bharatis* by virtue of their scholarship, literary accomplishments or poetical ability which are all deemed to be the gifts of the goddess. A state level award instituted for the recognition of excellence in literature, fine arts and writing goes by the name Saraswati Samman. Trophies given to scholars, eminent artistes and craftsmen sometimes have the Saraswati motif or connotation. All in all, Saraswati dominates the entire scholastic, literary, cultural and aesthetic domains.

In the field of Indian classical music, the Carnatic system has accorded due importance to Goddess Saraswati who is the patron deity for music and dance. Innumerable musical compositions dedicated to the goddess can be identified in both Hindustani and Carnatic systems of music. *Saraswati Vandana* or invocation of the goddess forms an essential part of dance recitals. Saraswati is generally depicted in sculptures, icons and graphic representations either as seated on an ornate pedestal or standing on a fully blossomed white lotus. She is shown wearing a jeweled crown over her head and bedecked with resplendent pearl ornaments. Her face is said to resemble the full moon with a smile on it. She is fair complexioned and possesses four arms signifying her divine attributes. Her raiment is of white silk. She holds a stringed instrument, the veena, diagonally across her chest. In another arm she holds a palm leaf manuscript—the book of knowledge. Her fourth arm displays a rosary. The goddess radiates feminine beauty, grace and beatitude. Seen near her feet it the white swan which is her mount. In some depictions, instead of the swan, the colourful Indian peacock is shown standing at her feet. Likewise, in some pictorial representations, Saraswati is shown holding a pitcher containing holy water instead of a rosary. These symbols have been explained in esoteric texts as possessing philosophical connotations. The lotus, white swan, pearls and pitcher symbolize association of Saraswati with water. The colour white which predominates her personage alludes to purity, tranquility and equanimity. The manuscript held in her arm is symbolic of knowledge and intellectual excellence.

For the traditional worship of Saraswati elaborate rituals, supported by Vedic incantations, have been prescribed. While these are observed even today, the average householder installs an image, icon or pictorial reproduction of the goddess in a corner of his home and performs the rituals. Generally he recites verses in Sanskrit or in his own mother tongue, makes votive offerings and circumambulating it before the icon. He prays for the atonement of sins and then shares the votive offerings with members of his family. On festive occasions more elaborate worship is done and numerous delicacies are prepared by the housewife. The fare offered and blessed by the deity is partaken of as *prasadam* (benedictory meal).

Saraswati worship is done round the year. But certain specified periods of the Hindu calendar are regarded as especially propitious for her worship. *Basant Panchami* which is the fifth day of the fortnight following the new moon occurring during spring (*basant*), generally in the month of March or late February, is observed as the day dedicated to the goddess. On this day young men and women dressed in yellow attire and adorned with flower garlands congregate and sing verses in praise of the goddess' consecrated idol. The best part of the day is spent in music and dance and exchange of greetings. In West Bengal, the Nobel laureate, Rabindranath Tagore had organized such celebrations at Shantiniketan near Calcutta. The tradition started by him continues to this day. Wherever there are large concentrations of people of Bengali origin, there is bound to be a *Basant Panchami* celebration. Various cultural and entertainment programmes and competitions of skill are organized on this occasion, which sustain the interest of the young and old alike.

The other occasion on which ritualistic worship of Goddess Saraswati is done is during October every year coinciding with the first 10 days of the fortnight following the new moon (*Sharad Ritu*) in the autumnal month of *Aswina* of the Hindu lunar calendar. These 10 days are called Dussehra. In the southern part of India this period is denoted by term *Navratri* (nine nights) and the tenth day is called *Vijaya Dashami* (victorious tenth day). From the sixth day (*Shashti*) to the ninth day (*Maha Navami*) Saraswati is worshipped. In fact, the ninth day is termed as Saraswati Puja day in south India. On this day students are enjoined to worship the Goddess of Learning and seek her blessings for success in their educational pursuits. Factories and workshops are spruced up and the tools of production are worshipped since Saraswati Puja day is also the *ayudha* (implements) *puja day*. *Prasadam* made to the deity and tools are partaken by the management and staff.

In West Bengal, Saraswati Puja forms part of the Durga Puja celebration. Saraswati in the Bengali tradition is regarded as the daughter of the Mother Goddess Durga or Parvati, the consort of Lord Shiva. In Durga Puja, images of Durga and her children—Lakshmi, Saraswati, Ganesha and Kartik—are installed in the specially built pavilions and celebrations go on for four days, ending with the immersion of the images in the sea of river. Durga Puja is the most important festival for the Bengalis world over and it is not only a religious festival but also an occasion for promotion of fine arts, culture and universal brotherhood.

Instruments in Indian Classical Music

Musical instruments include the Sarangi, Sitar, Tabla, Tambora, and Tanpura.

Sitar

Sitar is the most popular stringed instrument of India and has been in use for about 700 years. It is fashioned from a seasoned gourd and teakwood and has twenty mental frets with six or seven playing strings and nineteen sympathetic strings below. It is played with a plectrum worn on the finger. Sitar has a long and complex heritage; its origin goes back to the ancient Veena. In the 13th century, Amir Khusru, in order to make the instrument more flexible, reversed the order of the strings and made the frets moveable. Ravi Shankar, the great musician-artist brought changes and a new perspective.

Sarod

Sarod is another popular stringed instrument. The body is carved from a single piece of well-seasoned teakwood and the belly covered with goat skin. There are four main strings, six rhythm and drone strings and fifteen sympathetic strings, all made of metal. These are played by striking with a plectrum made of a coconut shell. The Sarod has no frets. Sarod as been found in carvings of the 1st century in Champa temple and also in paintings in the Ajanta caves. It also has a similarity with the Rabab of Afghanistan and Kashmir. The instrument was modified by Amir Khusru in the 13th century. A definite change was made by Ustad Ali Akbar Khan in shape of the instrument for improving the tonal quality.

Sarangi

The name derives from Sau Rangi meaning 100 colours. Sarangi is played with a bow and has four main strings and as many as forty resonant strings. It is generally used to accompany singers but can also be a solo instrument.

Tanpura

Tanpura is a four or five stringed instrument which gives the essential drone background to all Indian music.

Esraj

Esraj is played with a bow and has many strings. It is one of the major instruments of North India.

Santoor

Santoor is a North Indian instrument originating from Kashmir. It has more than a hundred strings which run across a hollow rectangular box and the strings are struck by a pair of slim carved walnut mallets.

Vichitra Veena

Vichitra Veena is a comparatively recent addition to the Veena family. It is a fretless stringed instrument with four main strings, three drone and rhythm strings and eleven to thirteen resonating strings. The strings are plucked by a plectrum on the index or middle finger of the right hand.

Violin

Violin was introduced to India about 300 years ago and is a very important string instrument in the South of India. It is played in a sitting position and is held between the right foot and the left shoulder.

Tabla

Tabla is the overall term for two drums, which are played as accompaniment to North Indian music and dance. The musician uses the base of the palm as well as the fingers to produce great variations in sounds. The right hand drum is tuned to the tonic dominant or sub-dominant and the left-hand drum acts as the base.

Pakhawaj

Pakhawaj is a long bodied wooden drum with both ends covered in skin and is the most traditional drum of North India. Played horizontally with the fingers and palms of both hands, the right hand surface is tuned to the pitch required and the left hand surface provides the base.

Mridangam

Mridangam is similar in appearance to the Pakhawaj but the ends have a different texture. It is the most used drum in South Indian music.

Dholak

Dholak is a side drum, cylindrical in shape, bored out of solid wood. Its pitch is variable and is an essential accompaniment for folk music of North India.

Jal Tarang

Jal Tarang is essentially a water-xylophone. It is made up of a series of china bowls of varying sizes and they are filled with varying levels of water. These are then played with two light sticks.

Pung

Pung is a long bodied drum with both ends covered in skin and plays an important role in Manipuri dancing when it is played by men and women, either in a sitting position or standing position.

Flute

Flute is found in every part of India, carved from bamboo it is made in every possible size. It is usually played in a vertical position.

Shehnai

Shehnai is a double reeded wind instrument with a widening tube towards the lower end. There are eight or nine holes, the upper seven for playing, the lower ones for tuning. The Shehnai is considered auspicious and is played on all festive occasions in India.

The Tambora

Since Vedic times, Indians had been required to correctly recite, the Vedas. The correctness in recitation was very important as the Vedas were, in those days, transmitted through memory (Smriti) and were learnt through hearing (Shruti). This v so, as writing was absent in early Vedic times. Even today the Vedas are traditionally learnt through oral studies.

This kind of an emphasis on recitation the correct pronunciation lead to studies in phonetics and sound manipulation. This was the birthplace of Indian Musical Raga (metre) and Swaras (rhymes). That Music in ancient India was given considerable recognition is illustrated by the fact that Saraswati, the Indian goddess of learning is shown to be holding a musical instrument (Veena) in her hand.

Traditionally, vocal music in India has tended to be devotional music (Bhakti-geet), and temples have been places (as they still are) where musicians used to practice music to please the deity and the devotees. Indian vocal music is broadly divided into two schools viz. the Hindustani or north Indian school and the Carnatic or South Indian school. As far as instrumental music goes there is a general identity of instruments that have been used.

However, as far as, devotional vocal music goes, Indian musical traditions did travel to the countries of South east Asia. The instrumental and vocal music of Korea has many elements of Indian music; which it received along with the Buddhist invocative and devotional songs and slokas (religious couplets). Along with Buddhism, some Indian musical instruments like the flute (bansi), temples bell (Ghanta), etc., went to the countries of south-east Asia. Even

Europe owes certain instruments to India. Two popular European musical instruments namely the flute and violin are believed to be of Indian origin. Though we do not know about the process of transmission of these instruments, however in India the flute (bansi) and the violin (a variant of the Veena) are definitely indigenously Indian.

4

Music Performance

Music performance provides a rich domain for study of both cognitive and motor skills. Performers dominate many aspects of our musical culture today. Concert attendance and recording sales, for example, often reflect listeners' preferences for performers and abilities to distinguish among performances. Although public consumption of music tends to highlight performance differences, there are also strong commonalities across performances that reflect cognitive functions of grouping, unit identification, thematic abstraction, elaboration, and hierarchical nesting.

Music performance is based on both individualistic aspects that differentiate performers and normative aspects shared by performers. Both the commonalities and differences among music performances can be modeled theoretically in terms of general cognitive abilities. The majority of studies focus on the performance of musical compositions for which notation is available, thus providing unambiguous performance goals. The focus has also been on piano performance, in which pitch and timing measurements are simplified. Common forms of music performance in the Western tonal tradition include sight-reading (performing unfamiliar music from notation), performing well-learned (prepared) music from memory or from notation, improvising, and playing by ear (performing music from aural presentation).

Correlations among these abilities tend to be high and to increase with training, although some studies show differences in abilities across performers. For instance, accompanists perform better than soloists on some sight-reading tasks. Although there are few studies of long-term changes in performance ability, diary and interview studies suggest that differences in performance levels across individuals are largely a function of experience and practice.

Psychological studies of music performance aim to develop theories of performance mechanisms (what cognitive or motor constraints influence performance). A second aim is to explain the treatment of structural ambiguities (in what contexts do ambiguities arise, what kinds of choices do performers make). A third aim is to understand relationships between performance and perception (how are listeners influenced by performance aspects). During a performance, musical structures and units are retrieved from memory according to the performer's conceptual interpretation, and are then prepared for production and transformed into appropriate movements.

Serial Order and Timing Issues

Speaking, typing, and performing music are among the most complex forms of skilled serial action produced by human beings. Seminal theories of motor control often use music performance as the ultimate example of human motor skill. Based on capacities such as the trilling speed of concert pianists (on the order of 16 notes/s), Lashley suggested that successive elements of this kind of activity must be centrally linked; a centrally controlled mechanism determines movements in a predetermined order. This open-loop (motor program) theory is based on two types of evidence: There is little time for feedback to affect the planning of the next movement, and some skills can be performed in the absence of kinesthetic feedback.

The control of complex, temporally structured behaviours such as speech production or music performance embodies two problems: the serial order of sequence elements, and their relative timing. The serial order problem arises from the fact that chain-like organization of behaviour is inadequate to explain certain serial order effects in sequence perception and production. For instance, strong constraints on the order of words within phrases and of phonemes within words must be met for speech to be acceptable. Musical and linguistic sequences that are well-formed in their serial order, however, are often not understandable unless additional constraints hold on the relative timing of the individual sequence elements.

Music performed without accurate temporal control is considered deficient because it lacks the property of rhythm, in which the timing of elements is influenced by the timing of other (adjacent and nonadjacent) elements. The domain of music performance is ideal for developing models of timing mechanisms because it offers theoretical consensus on the nature of the temporal relationships that must be present for a sequence to be considered accurate. Questions of serial order, relative timing, and how rhythm (temporal patterning) constrains the planning and production of musical sequences are addressed below.

Methodological Issues

Several methodological issues influence the interpretation

of research in music performance. First, the wealth of data from a single performance (roughly 3000 pieces of information in one second of digital audio sound recorded at a low sampling rate) results in problems of separating signal from noise. Carl Seashore, one of the first to conduct psychological studies of music performance, developed a piano camera system to record only gestural (movement-based) data from hammer and foot-pedal movements, greatly reducing the amount of data necessary to capture essential performance aspects.

Current computer music technology relies heavily on movement-based information and records only event onsets, offsets, and their relative intensities from electronic- or computer-monitored musical instruments. Despite the reduction of information, problems with separating the signal-performance expression-from random noise fluctuations remain. Performance expression refers to the large and small variations in timing, intensity or dynamics, timbre, and pitch that form the microstructure of a performance and differentiate it from another performance of the same music.

Musicians can replicate their expressive patterns of timing and dynamics for a given musical piece with high precision, and attempts to play without expression significantly dampen these patterns but do not remove them altogether , which suggests that some variations are intentional. Expression is often analysed according to the deviation of performed events from their fixed or regular values as notated in a musical score. However, performance can be expressive without reference to a score (as in musical improvisation). Expression can also be analysed relative to the performance itself; for instance, expression within a unit such as a phrase is the pattern of deviations of its parts with respect to the unit itself. Consequently, measurements of performance expression sometimes differ across studies, which makes comparisons difficult.

A second methodological problem is determining which performances should be considered representative, given the large variations that can occur among competent performances of the same music. There are few objective criteria for performance success; most experimenters opt for a recognized level of performer expertise. Large samples of famous performers are hard to find, however, and exploratory (nonexperimental) methods or case study methods are often used. A similar representativeness problem arises in choice of musical stimuli. Because of complexity issues, experimenters often use simplified or reduced musical compositions. For these reasons, the domain of music performance relies heavily on converging evidence from both small and large sample studies conducted with different musical stimuli.

INTERPRETATION

Music performance is often viewed as part of a system of communication in which composers code musical ideas in notation, performers recode from the notation to acoustical signal, and listeners recode from the acoustical signal to ideas. Each performer has intentions to convey; the communicative content in music performance includes the performers' conceptual interpretation of the musical composition. Western tonal music has developed a notation that represents pitch and duration information fairly explicitly but intensity and tone quality only approximately.

Other relationships, such as group boundaries, metrical levels higher than the measure, and patterns of motion, tension, and relaxation are unspecified or only implicitly specified in notation. Thus, ambiguities in musical notation allow a performer considerable freedom in deciding how to interpret the music's content. Interpretation refers to performers' individualistic modeling of a piece according to their own ideas or musical intentions. Differences in interpretation can account for why the same musical score is performed differently by different performers or why the same performer may perform a piece differently on separate occasions.

As in other art forms, there is no single ideal interpretation for a given musical piece; every performance involves some kind of interpretation or analysis. The field of music analysis offers various explanations for the content of a given composition. For instances, a piece can be viewed as a hierarchy of part/whole relationships, as a linear course that follows the harmonic tension, or as a series of moods that result in a unity of character. However, music analysis does not indicate how a performer actually produces a desired interpretation..One goal of interpretation is to convey the meaning of the music. Definitions of musical meaning abound, but several theorists define it as having major components that relate to structure, emotion, and physical movement, which contribute to performers' interpretations.

One function of interpretation is to highlight particular structural content. Some experimental work evaluates the effects of individual performers' structural interpretations on performance expression. Nakamura compared musicians' performances of a baroque sonata with their notated interpretations of musical dynamics (patterns of intensity changes). Performers' notated intentions generally corresponded to changes in sound level. Listeners' perceived dynamics matched performers' intended dynamics fairly well, even when underlying acoustic changes were not identifiable.

Palmer compared pianists' notated interpretations of phrase structure and melody with expressive timing patterns. Onsets of the melodic voice preceded other voice onsets in notated simultaneities (termed melody leads), and slowing in tempo was greatest at phrase boundaries. Expressive timing patterns decreased when pianists attempted to play without interpretation, and these patterns increased in exaggerated interpretations, similar to other findings of modulations in expressive level. Further studies indicated that the expressive timing patterns increased from novices to experts, increased during practice of an unfamiliar piece, and changed across different interpretations of the same piece performed by the same pianist.

Interpretations of structural content affect both the expressive marking of individual events and the likelihood that events will be correctly retrieved and produced. Error analyses (based on comparison with the notated score) of piano performances with different phrase structure interpretations indicated that pitch deletions tended to occur within phrases and perseverations at phrase boundaries, which suggests that interpretations strengthen phrase boundaries relative to other locations. These findings were replicated in later experiments, which also indicated that melodic interpretations increased the likelihood that melodic events were correctly retrieved and produced relative to nonmelodic events.

Another function of interpretation is to highlight particular emotional content of the music. An extreme view holds that the structure of music is isomorphic to the structure of moods or feelings; music should sound the way moods feel . Gabrielsson compared performers' interpretations of emotional content with their use of expression. Flute and violin performances of the same music interpreted with different emotional characters indicated general patterns of change in expression. Performances of happy and angry emotions were played with faster tempo and larger dynamic range, whereas soft and sad emotions were performed with slower tempo and smaller dynamic range.

Tone onsets were abrupt in the angry version and more gradual in the sad version. Related patterns of performance expression were found in violin performances of a Beethoven theme with tender or aggressive interpretations. Later experiments replicated these patterns, and most of the emotion categories were accurately conveyed to listeners. The emotional content of music has also been examined recently in terms of narrative, with emphasis on dramatic characterization, thematic content, and conceptions of large-scale structures.

Musical experience enhances both performers' use of expression to emphasize interpretations and listeners' ability to identify interpretations and expressive aspects of performance. Listeners without musical experience do pick up some interpretive aspects. Nonmusician listeners were able to discern general differences among mechanical (inexpressive), expressive, and exaggerated levels of performance as accurately as musician listeners. Some evidence suggests that type of musical experience matters: All musician listeners were influenced by expressive timing cues when asked to choose the intended phrase structure in piano performances, but only listeners with piano training were influenced by expressive timing cues (melody leads) when choosing among melody interpretations.

Planning

Planning and memory retrieval processes in music

performance reflect multidimensional relationships among melodic, harmonic, and diatonic elements. In Western tonal music, individual pitches, chords, and keys are posited as conceptually distinct units of knowledge, that reflect levels of melodic, harmonic, and diatonic structure, respectively. Some compositional structures, such as homophonic music, emphasize across-voice (chordal) associations between melody and accompaniment, whereas others, such as polyphonic structure, emphasize within-voice (single-note) associations among multiple important voices.

Analyses of piano performances indicated that chord errors occurred more often in homophonic styles and that single-note errors occurred more often in polyphonic styles, which suggests that the relevant musical units change across different musical contexts. Knowledge of diatonic and harmonic structure influences performance as well. Mistakes were more likely to originate from the key of the piece than from another key and to be of the same chord type as what was intended. Child singers' pitch errors were also likely to be harmonically related to intended events, and pianists' errors during sight-reading of pieces in which deliberate pitch alterations had been placed indicated tacit knowledge of likely melodic and harmonic relationships.

Theories of skilled performance often assume that people prepare complex sequences for production by partitioning them into shorter subsequence. Phrase structure is one feature that influences the partitioning of musical sequences; evidence from performance timing and errors suggests that musical sequences are partitioned during planning into phrase segments. Errors that replaced intended pitches in piano performances were more likely to originate from the same phrase as the intended event than from different phrases. Interacting elements rarely crossed phrase boundaries, similar to findings in speech errors. Segmentation during performance planning is also influenced by relationships among musical accent structures.

Adult pianists' and children's abilities to reproduce melodies were increasingly disrupted the more that melodic, metrical, and rhythmic grouping accents were shifted out of alignment in the performed tunes. Both structural relations and the serial distance between sequence events influence the range over which performers can plan, presumably because of limitations on memory capacity. Supporting evidence is seen in eye-hand span tasks, in which pianists reproduced briefly presented musical sequences. The mean eye-hand span was 7-8 events beyond the location at which the notation disappeared, and it tended to extend only to phrase boundaries. However, eye-hand span measures may reflect effects of both memory capacity and anticipatory eye movements. Range of planning in memorized piano performances (with no notation) was affected by both serial distance and structural relations among sequence elements.

Errors and timing measures indicated that the planning of current elements was affected by elements that spanned larger serial distances in the absence rather than in the presence of intervening phrase boundaries, similar to interactions of distance and structural constraints in language production. These findings suggest two possible invariants in the planning of complex serial behaviours in many domains: the co-occurrence during planning of elements that share structural features, and constraints of structural boundaries on serial distances over which elements are concurrently planned.

Syntax of Musical Structure

The performance of music is also constrained by style-specific syntactic properties that transcend individual interpretations. Many theories of Western tonal music have meter and grouping as their primary syntactic elements. Meter refers to periodic features: the regular alternation of strong and weak beats. Positions of metrical accents form hierarchical levels, with different periodicities represented at each level. Meter provides a temporal framework in performance for when to do what, as supported by evidence that only those rhythmic patterns that can be accommodated to a metrical framework are correctly reproduced, and the same duration pattern is performed with different expressive timing when placed in different metrical contexts.

Grouping refers to the segmentation of a sequence into smaller subsequence that also form hierarchical levels, based largely on pitch relationships. Some metrical and grouping levels are more salient than others. Tactus refers to the most salient periodicity or metrical level, which corresponds to the rate at which one might tap a foot to the music, and phrases are thought to be the most salient level of grouping structure. Events at the most salient levels are commonly emphasized in performance and may be most precisely or consistently produced and perceived. Probably the most widespread structural characteristic of Western music is its hierarchical nature; both pitch and rhythm structures are represented in a series of levels, between which relationships of reduction or elaboration operate.

For instance, Schenker's music theory views the melodic and harmonic organization of a musical piece as a series of progressively more complex elaborations of a simple foundation, the background, from which the surface level or foreground (the note-to-note aspects of the musical score) is generated. These hierarchical levels not only embody music-theoretic principles but also have implications for perceptual and cognitive processes, such as the prediction that more important events are processed at deeper levels and thus memory should be facilitated for those events.

Improvisation tasks have been used to address hierarchical implications for music performance. Pianists' improvisations on a musical theme tended to retain from the theme only structurally important events from abstract hierarchical levels of reduction. A neural network model trained to produce reduced memory representations represented structurally important events more efficiently than others, by accounting for the musical reduction in terms of a recursive auto-associative mechanism. The network's weightings of relative importance corresponded with both the musical events retained across improvisations and the predictions of structural importance from a reductionist music theory, which suggests that reduction may be a natural consequence of hierarchical encodings of musical structure.

Schmuckler used an improvisation task to test performers' expectancies for which events would follow in open-ended musical fragments. Performers' improvised continuations reflected influences of both the contents of the musical fragments and the abstract tonal and metrical hierarchies typical of Western music. Other studies indicated a correspondence between the events most often produced in improvisations and listeners' ratings of how highly expected those events were. These findings suggest that music perception and performance are both influenced by the hierarchical properties of musical styles.

Structure-Expression Relationships

Many findings have established a causal relationship between musical structure and patterns of performance expression. One of the most well-documented relationships is the marking of group boundaries, especially phrases, with decreases in tempo and dynamics. Patterns of rubato (tempo modulations) often indicate a hierarchy of phrases, with amount of slowing at a boundary reflecting the depth of embedding. The more important the musical segment, based on a hierarchical analysis of meter and grouping principles, the greater the phrase-final lengthening.

The greatest correspondence between expressive timing and intensity in performance is found at an intermediate phrase level, and performers' notated and sounded interpretations tend to differ most at levels lower than the phrase. Metrical structure also influences performance expression. Metrical accents (events aligned with strong beats as implied by notated metrical information) are often emphasized by lengthened durations and delayed onsets in piano performance and in vocal performance. Pianists presented with the same melodies in different notated metrical contexts played events aligned with metrical accents louder, with longer durations, and with more legato (smooth) articulation.

Listeners' subsequent judgments of meter for the different performances aligned with performers' metrical intentions most often for the most experienced pianists' performances (whose expressive markings of meter were clearer). When the different expressive cues were independently manipulated in computer-generated simulations, listeners most often chose the intended meter primarily on the basis of articulation cues. Loudness cues alone communicated meter also, but they were not present in all performances. In all, these findings suggest that there is no one set of necessary and sufficient expressive cues to denote meter.

One of the first types of musical structure for which systematic patterns of performance expression were documented is the duration patterns that form characteristic rhythms. An example is the Viennese waltz (based on a repeating pattern of three equal-duration beats with a metrical accent on the first beat), typically performed with a short first beat and a long second beat. Gabrielsson documented systematic deviations in the note durations and amplitudes of pianists' and percussionists' performances of repeating rhythmic patterns to a metronomic tempo; the first note of each measure was louder, and notated duration ratio relationships were increased.

Listeners' ratings of similarity among these performed rhythms and performances of polyphonic (multivoiced) rhythms suggested that the expressive timing patterns can be grouped according to three factors: structure, motion, and emotion. Structure included meter, accent pattern, and simplicity (of duration ratios). Motion included rapidity (sound event density), tempo, and forward movement. Emotion included vitality, excitedness, and playfulness. Factor analyses of the timing profiles from piano performances of a Mozart sonata replicated some of the same structure-expression relationships found with the simpler rhythm patterns, in which other types of musical structure were not present.

The mapping between structure and expression is modulated by several factors, however, including the musical context. Drake & Palmer examined whether accents associated with different musical structures affect performance expression independently or interactively.

Three types of structure were systematically combined in melodies presented to pianists: meter, rhythmic grouping, and melodic accents (pitch jumps and contour changes). Performance expression corresponding to rhythmic grouping and meter remained the same when those two structures were presented separately or combined, and they remained the same when the two structures coincided or conflicted. Expression associated with melodic accents and sometimes metrical accents, however, was altered by the presence or absence of other accents. These findings suggest again that the mapping between particular musical structures and performance expression is not consistent across contexts.

Performance expression also serves to differentiate among simultaneously occurring voices in multivoiced music. Voices can be distinguished by their intensity or timing. Early analyses of Duo-art (player piano) rolls indicated that pianists played tones comprising the melodic voice sooner than other tones notated as simultaneous. Recordings of wind, string, and recorder ensembles also indicated asynchronies among the voices for notated simultaneities, with a spread of 30-50 ms and a small relative lead (7 ms) of the instrument leading the ensemble. The amount of spread was larger for instruments whose rise (attack) time was longer, which suggests that musicians may adjust the asynchronies to establish appropriate timing of perceptual onsets.

Measurements of both acoustic and electronic piano performances indicated a 20-50 ms lead of the melody over other voices, longer than the 20 ms needed for listeners to determine the order of two isolated tone onsets. As interpretations of the melodic voice changed across performances, the voice that preceded other notated simultaneities changed accordingly. Melody leads may serve to separate voices perceptually. Experiments with simple tone sequences indicate that tones that are temporally offset tend to be perceived as belonging to separate streams.

Do performers use a syntax or formal set of rules to generate expression? According to the view that musical structure is related to performance expression in terms of explicit generative principles, systematic patterns of expression result from transformations of the performer's internal representation of musical structure. Three types of evidence support the view that structure systematically generates expression: the ability to replicate the same expressive timing profile with very small variability across performances, the ability to change an interpretation of a piece and produce different expression with little practice, and the ability to perform unfamiliar music from notation (sight-read) with appropriate expression. Structure-expression relationships have been formalized in computational models that apply rules to input structural descriptions of musical scores. In one model, three types of rules affect event durations, intensities, pitch tunings, and vibrato. Differentiation rules enhance differences among categories, grouping rules segment the music, and ensemble rules coordinate multiple voices or parts.

Another computational model of performance expression formalizes the inner pulses (reflecting individuality and viewpoint) of individual nineteenth-century composers; pulses defined at different levels of musical structure are applied similarly to all pieces by a given composer to generate performance expression. Perceptual judgments of model-generated simulations and comparisons with live performance expression provide some support for these models, but they indicate in general that piece-specific factors contribute to performance expression as much as the piece-transcendent factors captured by the models' rules.

The view that musical structure generates expression also predicts that performers should find it more difficult to imitate a performance that contains an arbitrary relationship between expression and structure than a conventional one. In fact, pianists most accurately imitated a performance that contained a conventional relationship between phrase structure and phrase-final lengthening, but they could also reproduce synthesized versions that contained distorted structure-expression relationships. Reproduction accuracy worsened with increasingly disrupted structure-expression relationships, although accuracy improved over repeated attempts even for the most distorted timing patterns. Listeners' ratings of the quality of the performances decreased as the structure-expression relationship became more disrupted. Evidence that performers can imitate expressive timing patterns that have an arbitrary relationship to the musical structure suggests that performance expression is not generated solely from structural relationships.

Perception of Performance Expression

Performance expression can communicate particular interpretations and resolve structural ambiguities, as suggested by the studies reviewed above. Performance expression may also function to compensate for perceptual constraints of the auditory system. According to a bottom-up argument based on psychoacoustic mechanisms, musicians play some events louder or longer because they are heard as softer or shorter otherwise. Listeners showed decreased detection accuracy for experimentally lengthened events placed right before a long duration in simple rhythmic patterns, the same locations at which performers tended to lengthen events in richer musical contexts.

Similar findings have been noted for intensity changes. Under instructions to play melodic tones with equal intensity, pianists systematically intensified the second tone of each group of four tones, contrary to predictions of metrical accentuation on the first tone of each group. Perceptual ratings of the same sequences indicated that the tones in original performances as well as simulated equal-intensity versions were judged to have equal intensities, compared with simulated versions of randomized or altered intensities. These initial findings suggest that perceptual sensitivity to temporal and intensity changes is modulated by structural aspects of musical sequences, and performance expression may compensate for those modulations.

The compensatory psychoacoustic explanation of performance expression can be contrasted with a top-down explanation that musical structure elicits expectations via listeners' internal representation of structure-expression rules. Listeners' detection of a single lengthened event in an otherwise temporally uniform (computer-generated) performance indicated that lengthening was more difficult to detect in places where it was expected to occur (at ends of structural units, strong metrical positions, and points of harmonic tension). Furthermore, listeners' detection accuracy (percent correct per event location) for lengthened events was inversely correlated with a performer's natural use of expressive lengthening in the same musical piece.

Detection accuracy also correlated with bottom-up acoustic properties of musical stimuli, including intensity and tone density characteristics inherent in the musical score. These findings were taken to reflect both top-down and bottom-up influences on the perception of performance expression. Further experiments replicated the detection findings for lengthenings and extended the detection paradigm to intensity changes. Although bottom-up and top-down explanations cannot be completely separated, the findings suggest that the structure given in a musical composition has inherent relational properties that constrain both perception and performance, rather than perception simply constraining performance or vice versa.

Psychological tests of music-theoretic models of musical expectancy and tension-relaxation point to a similar explanation of the influence of compositional structure in perception and performance. Narmour's model of melodic expectancy predicts which events are most likely to occur in a given musical context. The more expected events are those that match their preceding contextual implications. Lerdahl's model predicts patterns of tonal tension and relaxation that arise from harmonic relationships across large musical sections. Both music theories are based on a combination of bottom-up (hard-wired) and top-down (acquired) processes that account for listeners' expectations.

Perceptual experiments suggest that listeners can apprehend the music-theoretic predictions of melodic expectancies and tension-relaxation from just the categorical score information presented in computer-generated (expressionless) performances. Comparisons of the music-theoretic predictions with piano performance indicate that expressive cues emphasize melodic expectancies and tension-relaxation. Unexpected events were played louder than expected events, and events with higher tension were performed with longer durations. These findings suggest that performers' and listeners' interpretations of certain structural relationships are constrained in similar ways by the musical composition.

Movement

After musical structures and units are retrieved from memory according to a performer's conceptual interpretation, they must be transformed into appropriate movements. Movement plays many roles in theories of music and its performance; for example, musical rhythm is often defined relative to body movement. Different views exist on the causal relationships between musical rhythm and movement in performance. For instance, movement can generate rhythm and timing, or rhythm and timing can generate movement. These two views are considered below.

Timekeeper Models

Movement generating timing is the motor control view: Structural information (such as a sequence's rhythm) may be the input to a motor system, which then produces some kind of temporally structured behaviour, perhaps with the use of internal clocks or timekeepers. Internal clocks were proposed to account for behaviours such as the anticipation and coordination of gestures or acts, e.g. accompanying musical sounds with tapping. Accompaniment reflects a synchronization between perception and production that requires the anticipation of upcoming events. In music performance, motor systems are thought to construct the information for upcoming movements on the basis of internal clocks, which act as timekeepers by controlling the time scale of movement trajectories.

A clock constructs beats at an abstract level that provide temporal reference points for future movements. The primary role of an internal clock is to regulate and coordinate complex time series such as those produced between hands or between performers. Evidence to support clock models comes mainly from reproduction tasks, in which subjects hear and then reproduce musical rhythms by tapping. People are more accurate at reproducing musical rhythms whose interonset intervals are based on 1:1 or 2:1 ratios than on other ratios . Both musicians and nonmusicians reproduce duration patterns most accurately when the durations are related in integer ratio relationships. Early models of the temporal control of rhythmic sequences posited a single clock, whereas others contrasted multiple timekeepers. Because reproduction tasks combine perceptual and motor processes, some models of reproduction timing attribute internal timekeeping to perceptual encoding, whereas others attribute it to production mechanisms.

At what hierarchical level of musical time does an internal clock operate? Most clock models exert their influence at the level of the tactus, or most salient metrical level in a musical sequence. Evidence from some tasks suggests that 600 ms may be the preferred pace of the tactus: People most often generate beat patterns around 600 ms in spontaneous rhythmic tapping tasks, the typical interstep interval found in neutral walking is 540 ms, and listeners most often use motion terms to describe rhythmic patterns whose interbeat intervals center around 650 ms. Most internal clock models applied to music performance produce time periods greater than or less than the primary timing level by concatenating or dividing beat periods, rather than by positing additional clocks.

A further implication of a motor system paced by an internal timekeeper or clock is that temporal variance in performed event durations may be attributable to the timekeeper or to the executing motor system. Early models of the timing mechanisms underlying tapping behaviours partitioned the temporal variance into lack of precision due to an internal timekeeper and due to motor response delays, based on covariance analyses of the interresponse intervals. Extensions of this model were developed to test hierarchical organizations of timekeepers operating at multiple metrical levels or beat periods in single rhythms and in polyrhythms. Covariance analyses also allow comparison of whether the timing of event durations is constructed directly or indirectly; performed durations at the metrical level directly controlled by a timekeeper should be less variable than the durations of residual nested events within that level.

Tests of hierarchical clock models operating at various metrical levels, based on covariance analyses, were applied to music performance. Comparisons of temporal variance in skilled piano performances indicated that timekeeping was most directly controlled (least variable) at intermediate metrical levels of the subbeat (below the tactus), the beat, or the bar. Further tests of solo piano performances indicated that timing was directly controlled at the beat level (above the level of individual notes), which allowed the two hands some temporal independence in co-ordinating note events below the beat level that differed in duration. In extensions of covariance analyses, Shaffer concluded that separate timekeepers controlled the timing of individual hands in piano performance.

Duet performances indicated that each pianist's timing had highest precision (least variance) at the bar level, which suggests how performers might co-ordinate in the absence of an external conductor. Although covariance analyses rely on an assumption of constant global tempo that is rarely seen in music performance, these findings suggest that temporal precision in performance is influenced by the structure of the sequence-in particular, the salience of the beat level or tactus.

Performance timing can also exhibit stability at more abstract hierarchical levels, such as entire musical pieces. The durations of string quartets over repeated performances by the same performers were highly consistent. The standard deviation of the total piece duration (30-45 min) was about 1%, smaller than that of individual movements within the piece. If one movement was shortened, another compensated in duration, which suggests temporal control at a level higher than the individual movements.

A related theory predicts that the performance tempos of successive sections of music form simple integer ratios, called proportional tempos. The various periodicities that comprise a performance display phase synchrony, particularly at structural boundaries. Like Clynes & Walker, Epstein proposed oscillator mechanisms that track periodicities of tempo in performance and perception and specify relationships among successive movement durations and tempo changes in quantized steps.

Similar mechanisms have been proposed in a model of rhythmic attending, based on internal referent periods (preferred attentional periodicities) that may be shared by performers and perceivers. However, large-scale tempo measurements may reflect performers' memory for tempo as well as timekeeper stability, and findings based on live performances are limited by practical constraints such as concert hall rental periods. Nevertheless, these theories do suggest that a large range of periodicities influences the timing of music performance.

Motor Programs

Another theory of temporal control of performance stems from motor programming views. A motor program contains representations of an intended action and processes that translate these into a movement sequence. The basic idea is that a sequence of movements can be coordinated in advance of its execution. The goal of motor programming is to account for motor equivalence across contexts; the fact that the same sequence can be performed with different actions and retain its fluency, expressivity, and adaptivity. One view accounts for performers' ability to produce the same sequence in different ways with a single generalized schema that takes parameters.

Changes in global tempo across performances of the same musical piece have been conceptualized in terms of a parameter change. If timing of music performance is relationally invariant across tempo changes, then a change in tempo amounts to multiplying all event durations by a constant value. Relational invariance would support the existence of a generalized motor program, in which a variable rate parameter accounts for performers' ability to produce the same sequence at different rates.

Tests of relational invariance for speech, typing, and walking have produced mixed results. Tests of relational invariance in music performance generally indicate that the relative durations of note events tend to vary across performances of the same music played at different tempi by the same performer, although in some cases the relative timing patterns remain highly similar.

One hypothesis for the relative timing changes across tempi is that structural interpretation does not remain constant across performance tempo; for instance, the number of group boundaries increased with slower tempo in piano performances of the same musical piece. Lack of relational invariance suggests a failure of transfer of learning; practicing a pattern at a different rate than the intended performance rate might be counterproductive. These findings also warn against drawing structural conclusions based on performance data averaged or normalized across tempi.

Is the perception of musical structure invariant across tempo changes? Perceptual experiments with performed monorhythms and polyrhythms suggest that tempo changes do affect the perception of duration patterns. If performers use expressive timing to bring about a desired structural organization for a particular tempo, different perceptions might result for the same relative expressive timing pattern played at a different tempo. Repp independently manipulated the amount of expressive timing (incremented in terms of a power function) and the global tempo (incremented in terms of total piece duration) of performances.

Listeners gave higher ratings of aesthetic quality to the reduced expression at fast tempo and to the augmented expression at slow tempo for the same musical pieces, which suggests that listeners preferred the amount of expressive timing to change with tempo. Although these perceptual findings do not indicate the mechanisms controlling performance timing, they suggest that a perceptual analogue exists for the tempo effects on expressive timing documented in performance.

Kinematic Models

The view that rhythm generates movement is reflected in

the notion that music performance and perception have their origins in the kinematic and dynamic characteristics of typical motor actions. A rhythmic framework may be transmitted from performers to listeners through sound, as suggested by computational models of music performance in which the auditory system interacts directly with the motor system. The kinematics of movement allow a common origin for performance and perceptual phenomena, based on similar kinematic properties applying across individuals. Consequently, aesthetically satisfying performances should be those that satisfy kinematic constraints of biological motion.

Kinematic models were first applied to the large decelerations in performance tempo that commonly occur at the ends of pieces, called the final ritard. Pianists' final ritards were modeled in two parts-a variable timing curve followed by a systematic, constant decrease in tempo (called linear tempo). The "motor music" used in the studies, which contains a regular sequence of events with short durations, may create associations for listeners with experiences of physical motion. Feldman et al modeled both ritards and positive accelerations that occurred throughout performances. Based on modeling fits to the timing of a few ensemble performances, cubic polynomial models were chosen to minimize the jerk or jumpiness in connecting points of tempo changes (ritards) to the constant tempo that preceded them. Repp modeled the expressive timing of a short melodic gesture in piano performances of a Schumann piece, finding a best-fitting quadratic polynomial.

The three parameters represented a positive constant that corresponded to overall tempo, a negative linear coefficient that corresponded to vertical and horizontal displacement of the parabola, and a positive quadratic coefficient that corresponded to degree of curvature. Synthesized performances for the same melodic segment based on altered parameter values were played for listeners, who preferred timing profiles that fit the original parabolic functions. Although most models of motion in performance address timing, some apply to dynamic (intensity) changes as well.

Some measurements of performance suggest a coupling between expressive timing and dynamics in singing and piano performance, in which tempo and intensity increase and decrease together over a musical section such as a phrase. Todd proposed an underlying kinetic energy model for performance expression, in which intensity is proportional to the square of musical velocity (number of events per unit time). Contrasting the fit of different parabolic models to intensity and timing patterns in piano performances, Todd settled on a model with constant acceleration (linear tempo). Like Sundberg & Verrillo, Todd proposed that musical expression induces a percept of self-motion in listeners.

The notion that performance expression has its origins in the kinematic and dynamic properties of motor actions was extended in a general framework of perception and performance . A linear tempo model equivalent to Kronman & Sundberg's was fit to the expressive timing of piano performance segments, which were identified by changes in the sign of acceleration. Todd proposed an auditory model of rhythm performance and perception, based on a time-domain process that computes temporal segmentation of onsets (low-pass filters) and a frequency-domain process that computes a periodicity analysis (bandpass filters).

In addition, a sensory-motor feedback filter has two periodic components: the tactus (a filter centered at 600 ms), modeling beats, and body sway (a filter centered at 5 sec), modeling large-scale body movements. Performers' body and limb movements can specify some aspects of music performance, as evidenced in observers' ratings of performances based on visual information only from point-light displays. Todd's model requires further testing to eliminate potential overfitting of data, and its identification of line segments can be problematic. The model's advantage is that it is a purely bottom-up segmentation method that requires no input structural markers, as are required by several of the kinematic models discussed above.

Arguments against kinematic models suggest that physical notions of energy cannot be equated with psychological concepts of musical energy. An alternative explanation suggests that tempo changes in performance are guided by perceptual rather than kinematic properties. For instance, large tempo changes cannot occur too quickly, because the rhythmic categories that occur within the region of tempo change will not be perceived intact.

Rhythm identification and discrimination tests suggest that categorical distinctions underlie the perception of rhythmic structure, and performers use expressive timing to separate durational categories of note events even more when the events' absolute durations are converging at fast tempi.

Thus, tempo changes in performance may operate in a noncontinuous, stepwise fashion across absolute durations to retain the perception of intended rhythmic categories, which is another explanation for why relational invariance may not hold across tempo changes. Although this explication is not yet fully developed, it incorporates perceptual constraints and sensitivity to musical structure in explaining the control of movement in music performance.

Composing Affective Music with Generate and Sense Approach

There is a high application potential for affective music players. Consider, for example, physical training. Various studies have shown that music has a significant impact on the performance of athletes. However, the selection of appropriate music constitutes a problem for many people since the music does not necessarily match their individual motion rhythm. A personalized coach could sense and collect physiological data in order to monitor the user's physical exercise and to keep him or her in a good mood by playing appropriate music. In-car entertainment is another promising sector for adaptive music players.

Nobody questions that a driver's affective state has an important impact on his or her driving style. For instance, anger often results into an impulsive and reckless behaviour. The private disk jockey in the car might realize the driver's emotional state and play soothing music to make him or her feel more relaxed. On the other hand, driving on a monotonous road may lead to reduced arousal and sleepiness. In such situation, soft music may even enhance this effect. Here, the personalized disc jockey might help the driver stay alert by playing energizing music.

Last but not least, an adaptive music player could be employed for the presentation of background music in computer games. Unfortunately, music in games usually relies on pre-stored audio samples that are played again and again without considering the dramaturgy of the game and the player's affective state. A personalized music player might increase a player's engagement in the game by playing music which intensifies his or her emotions.

Measuring the Emotional Impact of Music

The most direct way to measure the emotional impact of music is to present users with various music pieces and asking them for their impression. This method requires, however, intense user interaction which increases the user's cognitive load and may seriously affect his or her perception of the music. In addition, asking users about their emotional state means an interruption of the experience. In the worst case, the user might no longer remember what he or she originally felt when listening to the music.

Furthermore, inaccuracies might occur due to the user's inability or missing willingness to report on his or her true sensations. Another approach is to exploit expressive cue profiles to identify the emotion a certain piece of music is supposed to convey. For instance, to express fear, many musicians employ an irregular tempo and a low sound level. While this approach offers an objective measurement, it does not account for the fact that different users might respond completely differently to music. Also, expressive cue profiles rather characterize the expressive properties of music and are less suitable to describe what a user actually feels.

The recognition of emotions from physiological signals bears a number of advantages. First of all, they help us to circumvent the artifact of social masking. While external channels of communication, such as facial expressions and voice intonation, can be controlled to a certain extent, physiological signals are usually constantly and unconsciously transmitted. A great advantage over self-reports is the fact that they may be recorded and analysed while the experience is being made and the user's actual task does not have to be interrupted to input an evaluation. Nevertheless, there are also a number of limitations. First of all, it is hard to find a unique correlation between emotion state and bio signals. By their very nature, sensor data are heavily affected by noise and very sensitive to motion artefacts.

In addition, physiological patterns may widely vary from person to person and from situation to situation. Self-reports are employed for new users with the aim to derive typical physiological patterns for certain emotional states by simultaneously recording their physiological data. If the system gets to know users, they are no longer required to explicitly indicate what they feel. Instead the system tries to infer the emotional state based on their physiological feedback.

A Music Composition Approach Based on Emotion Dimensions

The question arises of how the user should specify his or her emotional state. Essentially, this depends on the underlying emotion model. Two approaches to the representation of emotions may be distinguished: a categorical approach which models emotions as distinct categories, such as joy, anger, surprise, fear or sadness, and a dimensional approach which characterizes emotions in terms of several continuous dimensions, such as arousal or valence.

Arousal refers to the intensity of an emotional response. Valence determines whether an emotion is positive or negative and to what degree. Emotion dimensions can be seen as a simplified representation of the essential properties of emotions. For instance, stimulating music could be described by high valence and high arousal while boring music is rather characterized by low valence and low arousal (Fig. 1).

We can follow a dimensional approach and examine how music attributes that correspond to characteristic positions in the emotion space are reflected by physiological data which seems to be easier than mapping physiological patterns onto distinct emotion categories, such as surprise.

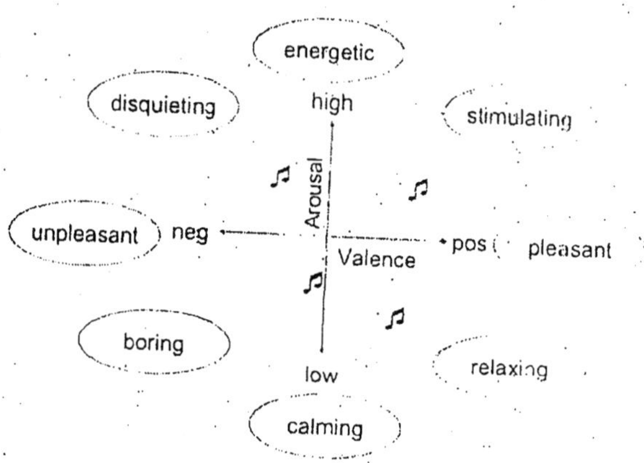

Figure 1. Emotion Dimensions for Music

While the users are listening to the music and inputting their evaluation, their physiological response is recorded. Based on these data, the system tries to derive typical physiological patterns for the emotion attributes. For instance, the system might learn that energetic music tends to increase skin conductance.

The next step is to produce music that influences the user's arousal and valence in a way that corresponds to the positions of the attributes in Fig. 1. To accomplish this task, the candidates that represent a position best are combined by a genetic optimization process starting from randomly created solution candidates. The objective of this process is to obtain better solutions for each attribute after a number of reproduction cycles.

The affective state of the user is influenced by means of music samples that are selected with respect to their presumed effect on the valence and arousal dimensions. For instance, if the users' arousal is high and should be lowered, a relaxing, boring or calming music sample might be presented to them depending on whether we intend to activate them in a pleasant, unpleasant or neutral manner.

Experimental Setting

For training purposes, there are 10 experimental sessions of 1-2 hours duration with subjects recruited from Augsburg University. In the sessions, the subjects had to evaluate 1422 automatically generated rhythms according to pairs of opposite attributes in the emotion space. In case, none of the attributes applied, the music should be evaluated as neutral. In each session, the subjects had to concentrate just on one attribute pair. If subjects have to fill in longer questionnaires, there is the danger that they don't remember the experience any more after some time. While the subjects listened to the rhythms and inputted their evaluation, four types of physiological signals were taken using the Procomp+ sensor equipment:

— Electrocardiogram (ECG) to measure the subject's heart rate.

— Electromyogram (EMG) to capture the activity of the subjects' shoulder musculature.

— Galvanic Skin Response (GSR) to measure sweat secretion at the index and ring finger of the non-dominant hand.

— Respiration (RESP) to determine expansion and contraction of the subjects' abdominal breathing.

The ECG signal was taken with a sampling rate of 250 samples per second, the EMG, the GSR and the RESP signal with a sampling rate of 32 samples per seconds. Following , 17 features were extracted from the ECG, 2 features from the EMG, 4 features from the RESP and 10 features from the GSR signal.

The subjects had to listen to a rhythm for at least 20 seconds before they were allowed to evaluate it. This time period corresponds to the duration determined by in which the skin conduction values may develop their full reaction. After the user has evaluated the music, the tonic measures of the signal values are observed without any music stimuli for a period of 10 seconds. After that, a new generated music sample is played for at least 20 seconds. The recorded data are then used to identify characteristic physiological patterns with a strong correlation to user impressions.

Music Generation with Genetic Algorithms

There have been a number of attempts to compose music automatically based on techniques, such as context-free grammars, finite state automata or constraints. For this kind of problem, genetic algorithms have been proven useful.

The basic idea of genetic algorithms is to start with an initial population of solution candidates and to produce increasingly better solutions following evolutionary principles. A genetic algorithm consists of the following components:

1. a representation of the solution candidates called chromosomes
2. mutation and crossing operators to produce new individuals
3. a fitness function that assesses solution candidates
4. a selection method that ensures that fitter solutions get a better chance for reproduction and survival

Genetic Algorithms are applied iteratively on populations of candidate problem solutions. The basic steps are:

1. Randomly generate an initial population of solution candidates
2. Evaluate all chromosomes using the fitness function
3. Select parent solutions according to their fitness and apply mutation and crossing operators to produce new chromosomes
4. Determine which chromosomes should substitute old members of the population using the fitness functions
5. Go to step 2 until a stopping criterion is reached.

As a first step, we can concentrate on the automated generation of rhythms. In particular, to determine an appropriate combination of percussion instruments and beat patterns. Rhythms are represented by four 16-bit strings. A beat event is represented by 1 while 0 refers to a rest event.

To create new rhythms, implemented a number of mutation and crossing operators. For example, use of a One Point Crossover Operator that randomly chooses a position out of 16 bits of two rhythms and swaps the components to right of these bit positions to create new rhythms.

Table 1: Illustration of the Evolution Process for Relaxing and Disquieting Rhythms

Experiment 1: Production of Different Populations for Relaxing and Disquieting Rhythms	Random Phase	Evolution of Relaxing Rhythms		Evolution of Disquieting Rhythms	
	Session 1:	Session 2: Relaxing Rhythms	Session 3: Relaxing Rhythms	Session 4: Disquieting Rhythms	Session 5: Disquieting Rhythms
Duration	1:05':49"	1:50':59"	1:51':06"	1:59':18"	1:49':18"
# Evaluated as Relaxing	5	120	172	0	1
# Evaluated as Disquieting	40	40	20	159	199
# Evaluated as Neutral	71	40	8	41	0
Overall Produced Number Rhythms/ Generations	116	200/1-10	200/11-20	200/1-10	200/11-20

Table 2: Illustration of the Evolution Process for Pleasant and Unpleasant Rhythms

Experiment 2: Production of Different Populations for Pleasant and Unpleasant Rhythms	Random Phase	Evolution of Pleasant Rhythms		Evolution of Unpleasant Rhythms	
	Session 1:	Session 2: Pleasant Rhythms	Session 3: Pleasant Rhythms	Session 4: Unpleasant Rhythms	Session 5: Unpleasant Rhythms
Duration	59':04'	55':52"	56':20"	56':17"	55':01"
# Evaluated as Pleasant	18	45	31	0	0
# Evaluated as Unpleasant	18	21	3	63	80
#Evaluated as Neutral	70	34	66	37	20
Overall Produced NumberRhythms/Generations	106	100/1-5	100/6-10	100/1-5	100/6-10

Table 3: GSR Table with Emotions Disquieting (D) vs. Relaxing (R) and Neutral (N)
HPAmp = maximal amplitude within the time window corresponding to a stimulus

GSR-Signal			High Peak Amplitude		
Statistical Analysis		Pattern of HPAmp	Mean (HPAmp)	Two Group t-Test: Groups	Two Group t-Test: Correlated significantly?/result
Emotion	Disquieting	High/Very High	3.0480131	Group 1: D, Group 2: N and R	Yes/t(914)=25.399; p<0.001
	Relaxing	Very Low	0.0402349	Group 1: R, Group 2: D and N	Yes/t(914)=-21.505; p<0.001

Table 4: EMG Table with Emotions Pleasant (P) Versus Unpleasant (U) and Neural (N)
NumPeaks = number of peaks within the time window corresponding to a stimulus

EMG-Signal			Number of Peaks		
Statistical Analysis		Pattern of NumPeaks	Mean (NumPeaks)	Two Group t-Test: Groups	Two Group t-Test: Correlated significantly?/result
Emotion	Pleasant	Medium	1.5078111	Group 1: P, Group 2: N and U	Yes/t(504)=-23.422; p<0.001
	Unpleasant	High	2.0283725	Group 1: U, Group 2: N and P	Yes/t(504)=8.151; p<0.001

There are two methods for assessing the fitness of rhythms. The first method relies on explicit user judgments and is used for new users to train the system. For users the system knows already, the fitness is computed on the basis of their physiological response. For example, if our goal is to employ music for relaxation and the system predicts a relaxing effect on the basis of the determined physiological data, the chromosome is assigned a high fitness value.

Tables 1 and 2 illustrate the genetic evolution process. The experimental sessions 1-5 in Table 1 served to create populations with individuals that are supposed to disquiet or relax the user. In Session 1, the user was presented with 116 randomly generated rhythms. Five of the rhythms were classified by the user as relaxing, forty as disquieting and seventy-one as neutral, i.e. neither relaxing nor disquieting. The four most relaxing and four most disquieting individuals were chosen for reproduction and survival. As a result, obtained two new populations each of them consisting of 20 individuals with either relaxing or disquieting ancestors. The same procedure was iteratively applied to each population separately until 20 generations were produced.

Table 1 shows that relaxing rhythms may be found rather quickly. For instance, already after 20 reproduction cycles most of the individuals were perceived as relaxing. For disquieting rhythms, the evolution process was even faster. Already 10 reproduction cycles led to generations with rhythms that were, for the most part, classified as disquieting. It was easier to generate rhythms with a negative valence than rhythms with a positive valence.

A similar experiment was conducted to create populations with individuals that correspond to pleasant and unpleasant rhythms (see Table 2). Nevertheless, Table

2 shows that the algorithm is also able to find pleasant and unpleasant rhythms after a few generations.

Correlating Subjective Measurements with Objective Measurements

The genetic evolution process results into rhythms that match a certain attribute quite well after some reproduction cycles. The question arises of whether the subjective impression of users is also reflected by their physiological data. After a first statistical evaluation of the experiment, the GSR-signal was identified as a useful indicator for the attributes "disquieting" and "relaxing".

Table 3 provides a comparison of the GSR for "disquieting" and "relaxing" rhythms. In particular, a very low GSR indicates a relaxing effect while a higher GSR may be regarded as a sign that the music disquiets the user. Our results are consistent with earlier studies which revealed that arousing music is usually accompanied by a fast increase of GSR.

To discriminate between positive and negative emotional reactions to music, EMG measurements have been proven promising. A study by detected increased zygomatic EMG (activated during smiling) for subjects that were listening to happy music as opposed to sad music. Earlier studies by revealed that facial corrugator EMG activity (eyebrow contraction) were significantly higher for unpleasant sounds as compared to pleasant sounds. As shown in Table 4, higher activity of this muscle is linked to unpleasant rhythms while lower activity is linked to pleasant rhythms.

Aesthetic Perception in Music

Music is a Kunstart, in German as in Danish, literally: a 'species of art'. This biological analogy - a 'species' of art is imaged as a living being - may have inspired the general History of Art. The underlying intuition about these beaux arts, the 'beautiful arts', may be the conceptual metaphor that *Beauty is life;* the kinds or types of aesthetic expression, thus conceptualized as animal species, "Arten", are maybe also seen as inscribed in a sort of genetic evolution, but basically, there is a conceptual zero-to-positive grading scale, spanning from 'not beautiful' = 'not alive', to 'very beautiful' = 'very much alive'.

Beauty is not only an ideological term or an outdated norm, but is a real cross-cultural and transhistorical phenomenon, an experiential fact about the human mind, the one that motivates the genre of objective phenomenology we call art criticism. Art really conveys beauty. Art is in fact 'good' when beautiful, and bad when not. As mentioned, good art is praised for being metaphorically 'alive', and bad art is scorned for being 'dead'. Furthermore, it is a characteristic of the experience of art that this bio-critical evaluation of its objective source, the work of art, is a part of its perception, rather than an estimation by external normative parameters. There is an aesthetic perception, an Einstellung which in this and other respects differs from a non-aesthetic perception, where there is no such inherent critical evaluation.

The evaluation of art therefore does not mainly depend on external, circumstantial criteria, as some modernist schools inspired by Marcel Duchamp have claimed, but is primarily determined by the specific internal content of an aesthetic perception of art. How the specific determination works is not clear to critics, though; and critics do not need to know it in order to judge perfectly well. But one of the tasks of neuro-aesthetic research will be to elucidate this issue. The determination might of course work differently in different sense modalities; so, musical beauty does not have to depend on exactly the same neural processes as, say, pictorial beauty. There are some important inter-aesthetic correlations.

In history of art, it is non uncommon to distinguish the spatial arts (architecture, sculpture, painting...), which create material objects, and the temporal arts (music, dance, poetry and the narrative genres: drama, fiction, film, video...), which create immaterial objects. Their respective histories do not always unfold in parallel; but their anthropology seems to be much the same. So, whether material or immaterial, these objects, the artefacts call works of art (Kunstwerke), tend to attract and affect us in comparable ways, namely either as means of celebration of culturally important events or as 'self-celebrating' things, as activities important in themselves. So, music can hail a king, animate a military parade, accompany a declaration of love, or be played at concerts and, as chamber music, in intimacy, for its own sake.

All of the 'species' of art use expressive signs that already serve evident cultural purposes as well as that of creating celebrative energy or pure beauty ; the arts are indeed often functional conveyors of pragmatic information, or give performative force to events of communal interest, at the same time as they are sources of aesthetic pleasure. But works of art always call attention to their own making, as to a manifestation of what artists will call pure form, the structural organization of the expression as such, as important in itself, and these objects display an 'auto-referential' insistence that makes them paradoxically be signs of themselves; this 'formalism' of art as such is another feature that makes aesthetic perception different from pragmatic perception, and perhaps the most important feature. One of the tasks of neuro-aesthetics will be to find the mechanisms underlying this variation in perception from pragmatic to aesthetic and formal.

As Susanne K. Langer suggested, the aesthetic experience of form and the paradoxical feeling of the object being 'alive' in good works of art may be interrelated and cognitively constitutive. Artfulness may 'animate' the object and let us experience it as if it were a sort of autonomous animal, equipped with an autonomous consciousness, with mind and intentionality. As if it were an auto-referential biological structure, in fact. This strange aesthetic feeling is extremely strong in experiences of music. Music is said to 'breathe'.

If architecture presides the spatial arts, music probably presides the temporal arts in human evolution, all the way from the Neolithic to the historical cultures of Cro-Magnon civilization. Architecture and music are both primary. Furthermore, the optical and the acoustic aspects of the creations are intimately related; they apparently integrate whenever and wherever we perform a socially significant act: our habitats must resound, and our musical displays must fill our spaces and 'take place'.

Our embodied minds connect to each other in optico-acoustic spaces, where the gestures of our bodies seek to attune to each other. For our minds to obtain intersubjective attunement, establish communicative contact in time and space, and to produce or perceive art and formal structures, are perhaps one and the same. In that case, Beauty may by evolutionary and cognitive definition be the special quality ascribed to those phenomena, in particular cultural objects or performances that make human minds attune. For e. g.:

"This music is beautiful...". The aesthetic judgment is grammatically impersonal, and in this Kantian sense, Beauty is represented as objectively given, probably because this 'feeling' when present is perceived as being shared by an indefinite number of minds as something that attunes them.

Accordingly, music (along with architecture) appears necessarily in the behaviour of our species in relation to prominent elementary fields of shared activity in all societies, such as Work, Love, and Worship : work songs, love songs, and hymns. Music and architecture are no doubt the two most important integrative semiotic factors of social life, besides language. But language would probably never work without them.

Brains specialize cognitively for space and for language, but also for music. Both are bodily grounded. If we accept to approach music through the classical triad: rhythm, melody, harmony, we might consider these three acoustic substructures as naturally grounded in three corresponding ways.

Firstly, musical rhythms involving beats performed in recursive numerical series (called bars) facilitate muscular motor coordination in collective (multi-body) doings, e. g. of the sorts mentioned (Work, Love, Worship), and typically those involving locomotion (legs and posture); people count and move together.

Secondly, tonal sounds arranged in sequences of pitch variations, also called melodic lines, help us coordinate gestures, as in rituals and communicative interaction, typically those involving movement of hands and arms; people sing or chant and gesticulate together.

Thirdly, maintained tonal clusters containing pitch intervals whose interfering formants produce consonance and dissonance, also called harmonic clusters, or chords, are directly related to our vocal and facial expressions of mood and empathic disposition, hence the double meaning of German 'Stimmung' (mood, tuning). People purr, hum, sigh, moan, groan, grunt or screech, scream, yell, bawl, shout, squall, squeal etc. at each other and their faces configurate accordingly, when they mean to let each other know what their mood and the shared situation are. This variation is even most often automatic and hardly needs the subject's intervention, unless it is repeated, simulated, theatricalized, or quoted.

Music addresses our body in these remarkably concrete and direct ways, when heard. It might also be reported that when played, music appears to emanate from the body of the orchestra or the musician, and thus that it constitutes a significant metonymy for an embodied person, the one that the musicians take on as a role while playing, or the very person that the musician is. We know from cognitive semantics, and as well from classical rhetoric, that metonymic representations of things, and in particular of individuals, are perceived as far more pithy than their referents, and that if perceived as representative of a person, they are more personalizing and even more 'alive' than the person herself: they are the person's signature. This particular authenticity-making phenomenon of metonymy and metonymic compression of personhood may explain the Langer-effect of vitalism in form.

A style is a signature of (numerical) identity. As to the corresponding activation in the brains of listeners and musicians, the processing of tonal hearing and thinking appears to happen in specialized neurons in the superior temporal and some frontal regions of the cortex, particularly in the right side, but recent scanning studies (PET and fMRI) by R. Zatorre and his group show additional bilateral activity in occipital areas normally involved in visual processing, despite the absence of visual input. Also parts of motor cortex are activated. And paralimbic areas that are active in emotional processing are shown to be involved in the evaluative aspects of musical experience.

This suggests that the auditory processing in music is integrated with spatio-visual imagery as well as with something like imaginary motion or gesture, and imaginary emotion. There is (in the referred experimental situations) only an acoustic input, but it triggers in the listener's mind a multimodal imaginary activity implying scenarios in time and space, landscapes and architectural sites, possibly with persons that move, gesticulate, and behave emotionally - virtual scenes of embodied intersubjectivity. Music thus appears, as suggested by C. Trevarthen, to guide our minds into communitary attitudes, to prepare us for cooperation and expressive exchange based on empathy, shared attention and volition - attitudes and 'share' with the imaginary musical gestalts themselves and then with each other.

This imaginary aspect of musical hearing prepares our minds for a semantics of human interaction: our imaginary gestures and imaginary emotional states are 'meanings'. They possess imaginary reality, in the sense that what we experience when music is played, whether by others or by ourselves, is given immaterially but really, as a thought without a head, one that someone could have, including ourselves but independently of ourselves. "Sad" music heard by us when we are already sad makes us more impersonally and communally sad: it makes us feel like sharing that mood with others, and thus brings us comfort, even pleasure.

The neural 'imaginarization' of visual space-time, motion, gesture, and facial expressions, as associated with musical thinking and hearing, makes these meanings of tonal experiences appear to us as distinct from any individuals that might be factually having them here and now. As mentioned, they form autonomous gestalts or fantoms of possible people of whose presence they would be metonymies. Abstract (ownerless, just possible) ideas or forms are results of metonymic disembodiment; and they are then readily re-embodied in architecture and imagery in general, when music is performed and experienced collectively in socio-cultural locations, settings, and sites - as the 'meaning of' that site.

We then get the genius loci effect: the place is felt as having a 'spirit' attached to it... Here, meaning migrates musically from our bodies into architectural receptors in space. Individual re-embodiment of meaning subsequently occurs, mainly in the shape of experiences of participation in the resounding collective activities that the architectural spaces hence determine and contain. This happens when we 'interpret' music. We then become fillers of the role of the 'genius' reembodied in the space of performance. By metonymy, our minds thus disembody and reembody, but the reembodiment has a generalized, communal gestalt, a principled activity or active principle in the place of the original source body; so, the resounding expression is now a sign of this principled thing, a filling of a role. It has become an abstract symbol. Symbolization takes place.

Disembodiment: BODY -> musical expression

Reembodiment: ROLE performed as symbolic activity <-

Let me present a technical three-step version of this view of music and meaning in terms of conceptual integration and blending analysis, as developed by Mark Turner and Gilles Fauconnier, and then cast into a semiotic mould by the Danish school of cognitive semiotics. A conceptual blend has two mental spaces as inputs, one Presentational, the other Referential; the blend is stabilized by a binding process that ties and maps it to the schematic contents of a Relevance space.

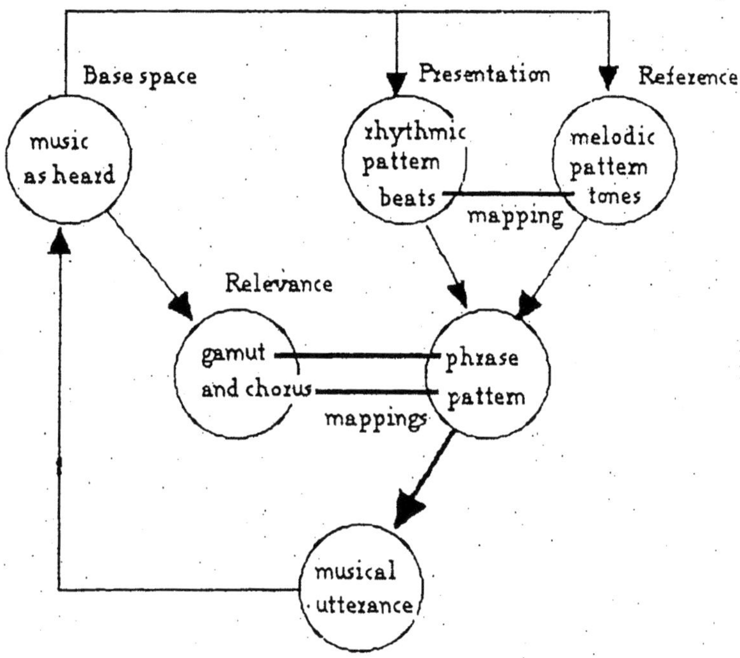

Figure 2. Rhythmic Pattern

In a first, perhaps excessively simplified analysis, there is in the auditive perception of music—not of other, functional or pragmatic sounds—a first integration cycle, in which rhythmic forms and tonal forms blend into the melo-rhythmic phrase. Then this phrase blends with some harmonic pattern to form a complete 'utterance', which is projected to the 'Base space' of ongoing experience.

Beats in a rhythmic pattern are mentally mapped onto notes in a melodic pattern, and the 'note' beats' of the resulting phrase is mentally interpreted by a harmonic and temporal format that make a series of phrases meaningful, so that they can form a musical utterance.

Then, in a second step, the integrated musical utterance, now as a Presentational Input, further integrates with the gestural and the emotional, semiotic components of imagination during the experience of hearing:

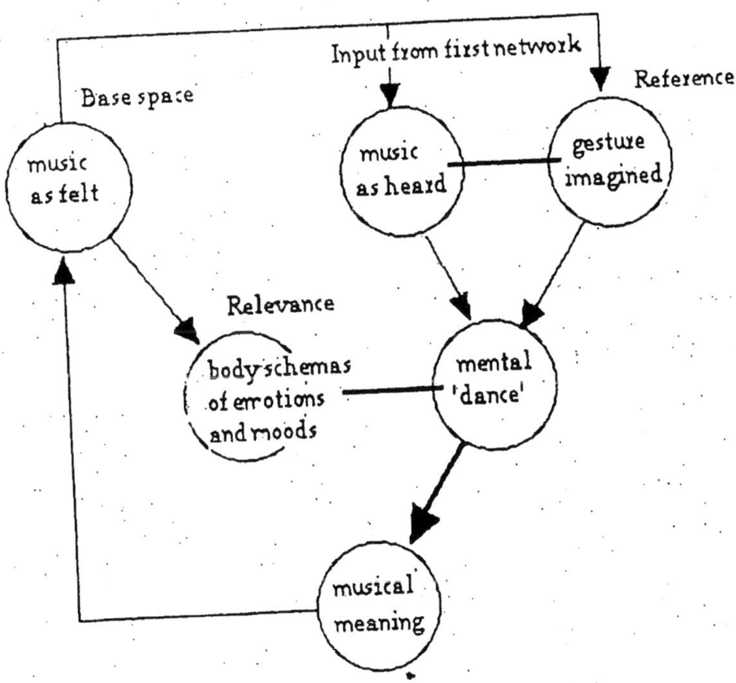

Figure 3. Imaginary Process of Possible Gestures

What we hear is mapped onto an imaginary process of possible gestures that our body could perform, if conditioned by affective states and its inherent schemas of motion and sound expressing such states.

Finally, in a third step, this result again integrates with the contextual social setting and its possibly celebrative circumstances, where the affective charge carried by 'music as felt' can be important for the actual attunement of the participants, their shared attention and subsequent memorization. The social setting is the workshop of abstraction:

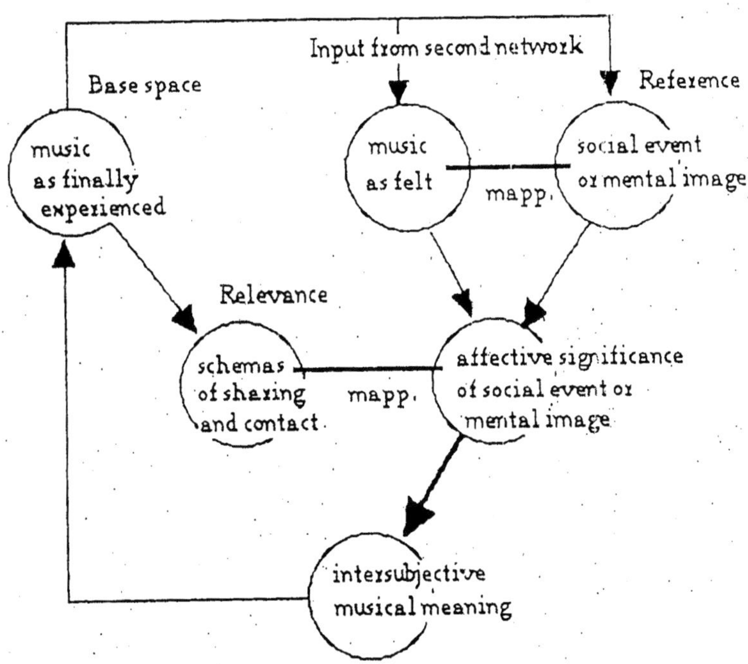

Figure 4. Integration of Musical Phenomenon

At this stage of integration, the musical phenomenon, affectively invested, is mapped onto the occurring events in the experiencer's present situation - either social or mental (and instead of real events there could be a text or a fiction, as in film, whose meaning would then be accompanied by the music).

This third step has the same network design as the two first. Through the three steps, the series of integrations form a blending cascade. At the third level of this cascade, the perception of music has a referential content filled by the context of its performance. But as initially mentioned, sometimes there is no such definite situation of performance! Music is then just perceived as music in its own right. Systematically provided in modern cultures, music is performed and enjoyed without an already significant 'resorbing' situation, the inherent reference space is simply left open.

For most or all music practicians it is characterized by abstract figurations, often synaesthetic sensations, especially of colours linked to tonal entities, and existential thoughts. In critics and other specialized listener minds, it may be filled by poetic, philosophical or narrative discourse, or rather such discursive intuitions, sketches, and ideas. The best description of the cognitive but non-conceptual state of mind created by forceful musical experiences of this auto-referential kind might be the tautological account: "It means what it means". This tautology probably just states that such an impression-of-abstractness is being experienced.

In the classical theoretical literature of aesthetics it was called the Sublime (das Erhabene). In this sense, beauty can be said to lead us to the Sublime, which is the Abstract as such If you will allow me another Kantian expression, it is also the realm of Freedom, in the sense that abstraction is the one operation which frees thought from the local necessities of life. Good art 'lives' in the sense of an unimpeded embodiment: a feeling of 'possibility'. This is perhaps the ultimate sense and value of art. In music it is immediately accessible to us, and sometimes lets us take on the imaginary shape of baroque angels moving around in the universe on forceful wings of shining sound.

5

Music in Christianity

According Christian belief music is far more than a human art form. It is an inseparable part of creation. More than even this, however, it seems an integral part of God's own nature. We could define music as man exploring the wonders of two of God's creations - time and sound. This definition is in line with much Christian music: God gets a mention, but thereafter it's all in the hands of men and women. God is in the soul saving business, not in musically assisting the church organist.

Christians believe that God is the origin of every good and perfect gift is the source of all knowledge. He deserves - but seldom receives - full credit for all human ingenuity. Christian Scripture acknowledges God as the source of even humanity's most rudimentary understanding of agriculture. The Bible asserts that without insight that is ultimately traceable to God Himself, none of us could even recognise the foolishness of forever ploughing a field and never stopping to plant. This dependence upon God for knowledge is a staggering concept. It means that not even a militant atheist or a devil-worshipper could produce music were it not for God. It is He 'who gives songs in the night; who teaches us more than the beasts of the earth, and makes us wiser than the birds of the air'. In the words of

Paul, 'What have you that you did not receive?' So credit for the development of music ultimately belongs not to man but God.

However, divinely given ability can be put to trivial use. Is music some freakish human fad, on the level of Rubik's cubes and hopscotch, or is it something far nobler? The answer to this question has the potential to revolutionise the Christian attitude to music. It could be like discovering that the rock in your back-yard is not just pleasant to look at - it's solid opal!

The Power of Song

The history of the songs of the Bible is full of suggestion as to the uses and benefits of music and song. Music is often perverted to serve purposes of evil, and it thus becomes one of the most alluring agencies of temptation. But, rightly employed, it is a precious gift of God, designed to uplift the thoughts to high and noble themes, to inspire and elevate the soul. As the children of Israel, journeying through the wilderness, cheered their way by the music of sacred song, so God bids His children today gladden their pilgrim life. There are few means more effective for fixing His words in the memory than repeating them in song. And such song has wonderful power. It has power to subdue rude and uncultivated natures; power to quicken thought and awaken sympathy, to promote harmony of action, and to banish the gloom and foreboding that destroy courage and weaken effort.

It is one of the most effective means of impressing the heart with spiritual truth. How often to the soul hard-pressed and ready to despair, memory recalls some word of God's, —the long-forgotten burden of a childhood song, — and temptations lose their power, life takes on new meaning and new purpose, and courage and gladness are imparted to other souls! The value of song as a means of education should never be lost sight of. Let there be singing in the home, of songs that are sweet and pure, and there will be fewer words of censure and more of cheerfulness and hope and joy. Let there be singing in the school, and the pupils will be drawn closer to God, to their teachers, and to one another.

A Weapon Against Discouragement: If there was much more praising the Lord, and far less doleful recitation of discouragements, many more victories would be achieved.Song is a weapon that we can always use against discouragement.

To Impress Spiritual Truth: Song is one of the most effective means of impressing spiritual truth upon the heart. Often by the words of sacred song, the springs of penitence and faith have been unsealed.

A Means to Conserve Christian Experience: Evening and morning join with your children in God's worship, reading His Word and singing His praise. Teach them to repeat God's law. Concerning the commandments, the Israelites were instructed: "Thou shalt teach them diligently unto thy children, and shalt talk of them when thou sittest in thine house, and when thou walkest by the way, and when thou liest down, and when thou risest up." Accordingly, Moses directed the Israelites to set the words of the law to music.

If it was essential for Moses to embody the commandments in sacred song, so that as they marched in the wilderness, the children could learn to sing the law verse by verse, how essential it is at this time teach our children God's Word! Let us come up to the help of the Lord, instructing our children to keep the commandments to the letter. Let us do everything in our power to make music in our homes, that God may come in.

Song Helped Jesus Resist the Enemy: When Christ was a child like these children here, He was tempted to sin, but He did not yield to temptation. As He grew older He was tempted, but the songs His mother had taught Him to sing came into His mind, and He would lift His voice in praise. And before His companions were aware of it, they would be singing with Him. God wants us to use every facility which Heaven has provided for resisting the enemy.

Bringing Heaven's Gladness: —The early morning often found Him in some secluded place, meditating, searching the Scriptures, or in prayer. With the voice of singing He welcomed the morning light. With songs of thanksgiving He cheered His hours of labor, and brought heaven's gladness to the toil-worn and disheartened.

He Sang Songs of Praise: —Often He expressed the gladness of His heart by singing psalms and heavenly songs. Often the dwellers in Nazareth heard His voice raised in praise and thanksgiving to God. He held communion with heaven in song; and as His companions complained of weariness from labor, they were cheered by the sweet melody from His lips. His praise seemed to banish the evil angels, and, like incense, fill the place with fragrance. The minds of His hearers were carried away from their earthly exile, to the heavenly home.

Effective Use Of Music In Israel's Experience

Music was made to serve a holy purpose, to lift the thoughts to that which is pure, noble, and elevating, and to awaken in the soul devotion and gratitude to God. What a contrast between the ancient custom and the uses to which music is now too often devoted! How many employ this gift to exalt self, instead of using it to glorify God! A love for music leads the unwary to unite with world lovers in pleasure gatherings where God has forbidden His children to go. Thus that which is a great blessing when rightly used, becomes one of the most successful agencies by which Satan allures the mind from duty and from the contemplation of eternal things.

Music forms a part of God's worship in the courts above, and we should endeavor, in our songs of praise, to approach as nearly as possible to the harmony of the heavenly choirs. The proper training of the voice is an important feature in education and should not be neglected. Singing, as a part of religious service, is as much an act of worship as is prayer. The heart must feel the spirit of the song to give it right expression.

Music can be a great power for good; yet we do not make the most of this branch of worship. The singing is generally done from impulse or to meet special cases, and at other times those who sing are left to blunder along, and the music loses its proper effect upon the minds of those present. Music should have beauty, pathos, and power. Let the voices be lifted in songs of praise and devotion. Call to your aid, if practicable, instrumental music, and let the glorious harmony ascend to God, an acceptable offering.

But it is sometimes more difficult to discipline the singers and keep them in working order, than to improve the habits of praying and exhorting. Many want to do things after their own style; they object to consultation, and are impatient under leadership. Well-matured plans are needed in, the service of God. Common sense is an excellent thing in the worship of the Lord.

Effective Pathos: —There is a great pathos and music in the human voice, and if the learner will make determined efforts, he will acquire habits of talking and singing that will be to him a power to win souls to Christ. The melody of song, poured forth from many hearts in clear, distinct utterance, is one of God's instrumentalities in the work of saving souls. All the service should be conducted with solemnity and awe, as if in the visible presence of the Master of assemblies. In every school, instruction in singing is greatly needed. There should be much more interest in voice culture than is now generally manifested. Students who have learned to sing sweet gospel songs with melody and distinctness, can do much good as singing evangelists. They will find many opportunities to use the talent that God has given them, carrying melody and sunshine into many lonely places darkened by sin and sorrow and affliction, singing to those who seldom have church privileges.

One of God's Entrusted Talents: —The human voice in singing is one of God's entrusted talents to be employed to His glory. The enemy of righteousness makes a great account of this talent in his service. And that which is the gift of God, to be a blessing to souls, is perverted, misapplied, and serves the purpose of Satan. This talent of voice is a blessing if consecrated to the Lord to serve His cause.

Choir and Congregational Singing: —In the meetings held, let a number be chosen to take part in the song service. And let the singing be accompanied with musical instruments skillfully handled. We are not to oppose the use of instrumental music in our work. This part of the service is to be carefully conducted; for it is the praise of God in song. The singing is not always to be done by a few.

Undesirable Qualities

Shrieking Sacred Words of Hymns of Praise: —Music forms a part of God's worship in the courts above. We should endeavor in our songs of praise to approach as nearly as possible to the harmony of the heavenly choirs. Those who make singing a part of divine worship should select hymns with music appropriate to the occasion, not funeral notes, but cheerful, yet solemn melodies.

No Jargon or Discord: God is not pleased with jargon and discord. Right is always more pleasing to Him than wrong. And the nearer the people of God can approach to correct, harmonious singing, the more is He glorified, the church benefited, and unbelievers favorably affected.

Sing With the Spirit and Understanding: Do not hire worldly musicians if this can possibly be avoided. Gather together singers who will sing with the spirit and with the understanding also. The extra display which you sometimes make entails unnecessary expense, which the brethren should not be asked to meet; and you will find that after a time unbelievers will not be willing to give money to meet these expenses.

Secular Music

Qualities of Acceptable Secular Music: —For about an hour the fog did not lift and the sun did not penetrate it. Then the musicians [on the ship] who were to leave the boat at this place entertained the impatient passengers with music, well selected and well rendered. It did not jar upon the senses as the previous evening, but was soft and really grateful to the senses because it was musical.

Beautiful Instrumental Music at the Swiss Beer Garden: — The same night there was beautiful music and fireworks close by across the road. There is an extensive beer garden owned by the city and carried on by the city. This garden is made attractive with flowers and shrubs and noble trees, giving a nice shade.

The Musical Performers

Ambition for Display: —Musical entertainments which, if conducted properly, will do no harm, are often a source of evil. In the present state of society, with the low morals of not only youth but those of age and experience, there is great danger of becoming careless, and giving especial attention to favorites, and thus creating envy, jealousies, and evil surmisings. Musical talent too often fosters pride and ambition for display, and singers have but little thought of the worship of God.

Music That Offends God: —Display is not religion nor sanctification. There is nothing more offensive in God's sight than a display of instrumental music when those taking part are not consecrated, are not making melody in their hearts to the Lord. The offering most sweet and acceptable in God's sight is a heart made humble by self-denial, by lifting the cross and following Jesus. We have no time now to spend in seeking these things that only please the senses. Close heart searching is needed.

Music Acceptable to God. Music is acceptable to God only when the heart is sanctified and made soft and holy by its facilities. But many who delight in music know nothing of making melody in their hearts to the Lord.

Facets of Music and the Musician

Music is of heavenly origin. There is great power in music. It was music from the angelic throng that thrilled the hearts of the shepherds on Bethlehem's plains and swept round the world. It is in music that our praises rise to Him who is the embodiment of purity and harmony. It is with music and songs of victory that the redeemed shall finally enter upon the immortal reward.

There is something peculiarly sacred in the human voice. Its harmony and its subdued and heaven-inspired pathos exceeds every musical instrument. Vocal music is one of God's gifts to men, an instrument that cannot be surpassed or equaled when God's love abounds in the soul. Singing with the spirit and the understanding also is a great addition to devotional services in the house of God.

SCRIPTUARL EVIDENCE

Solomon's Birds

The King James Version of Psalm 104:12 speaks of birds which 'sing'. However, 'give voice' is a more literal translation. In this instance, the original text carries no musical connotations. However, a Hebrew word, which Scripture elsewhere applies exclusively to human music, is used in Song of Solomon 2:12, apparently to describe the singing of birds.

Furthermore, in Zephaniah 2:14, we read of birds which 'sing in the windows'. Here, the underlying Hebrew word is different to the one used in Solomon's Song and yet it again is a term usually reserved for human singing.

The expression 'daughters of song' may also be relevant. According to the scholarly Hebrew Lexicon by Brown, Driver and Briggs, it is probably a reference to birds.

It might be going too far to conclude that the above Scriptures put certain bird calls in exactly the same category as human music. It seems, however, the divinely inspired writers wished us at least to see the similarity.

Nature Worship

All of nature seems more involved in praising God than most of us would have guessed. The stars declare God's glory. Sun and moon, wind and hail, hills and trees, beasts, birds, fish and insects are all urged to praise Him. Wild animals honour Him. Moreover, Scripture speaks of pastures, trees, hills and skies singing. In the original language, the clearest example is Psalm 65:13:

> 'The pastures are clothed with flocks;
> The valleys also are covered with corn;
> They shout for joy and SING.'

Other references abound, though their musical implications are not as obvious as some English translations imply.

> 'Sing O heavens;
> For the Lord has done it:
> Shout, you lower parts of the earth:
> Break forth into singing, you mountains,
> O forest and every tree therein.'

Perhaps we would miss something significant if we dismissed all of this as poetic expressions that tell us nothing about sub-human creation. The link between human music and the sounds of even inanimate creation might be stronger than we think. Behind the design of wind, trees and animals is the same Person who created man with the ability to produce music.

If flowers were planted to spell out an Arabic word, we could easily miss the significance. We would not recognise the language and, since flowers are mindless, we might assume the arrangement was simply random. We would see things in an entirely different light, however, if the gardener - the intelligence behind the design - explained.

Similarly, creation would take on a whole new meaning if God revealed that what we have mistaken for mindless sounds are a symphony of praise orchestrated by the One who sustains them. In the words of Edith M. Thomas, 'The God of music dwelleth out of doors'.

Confirmation that this view of creation is a product of special revelation, rather than human imagination, is found in the spiritual experiences of a host of Christians, for whom a divine encounter has edged them closer to seeing sub-human creation musically exalting its Creator. Perhaps the suffer from a narrow musical appreciation, snobbishly rejecting forms of musical expression other than their own, and so failing to recognise the musical qualities of nature's sounds. Meditating upon the relevant Scriptures and prayerfully seeking the One who inspired them might open their ears to nature's melodies.

> 'Let the sea roar, and all that is in it:
> Let the fields rejoice, and all that is therein.
> Then shall the trees sing before the presence of the Lord,
> For He comes to judge the earth!'

Verses similar to the above appear in a total of three of the Bible's songs. Let's examine the context of one of them, Psalm 98. The psalmist urges 'all the earth' to audibly praise God. He then expounds what he means by addressing human instrumentalists and singers *and nature*. The psalm begins with a call to sing a new song to the Lord. It builds up to a plea to human musicians and climaxes by appealing to nature to complete this orchestra of praise. The first half of the psalm explains *why* a new song should be sung and the second half answers the questions *how* (with harp, trumpet, clapping rivers etc) and *who* ('all the earth' - an expression the psalmist subdivides into man and nature). At the very least, this psalm suggests a strong link between the worship of God's musicians and the sounds of God's sub-human creation.

Singing Star

Job 38:7 speaks of the time 'when the morning stars sang together'. This probably refers to heavenly intelligences, rather than stars, because it appears in a poetic couplet paralleling 'sons of God'. However, the possibility of a strictly literal interpretation alerts us to something significant: God's music in nature need not be confined to what is audible to us.

'See deep enough, and you see musically: the heart of nature being everywhere music, if you can only reach it,' mused Carlyle.

Clestial Musicians

The sounds of lower forms of creation may seem so primitive that we hesitate to regard it as music. But who can deny the possibility that angelic music may be equally superior to humanity's highest attempts? We know with certainty that angels worship. We also know that at least some heavenly beings are superior to us in many ways, including 'might and power', mobility, and ability to disappear. They have a greater capacity to afflict, protect and deliver. Their power over nature astounds us, and they are superior in wisdom, intellect, knowledge, physical appearance, dazzling brilliance, size, name, and proximity to God.

With a list as impressive as that, it is difficult to believe heavenly creatures would lack our musical ability. Indeed, it would be surprising if their musical powers were merely equal to ours. Imagine what skills could be developed by sinless beings unaffected by aging who have been living since the creation of the universe.

Moreover, there is much Biblical evidence that angelic beings have greater than human vocal abilities.

According to Thomas Fuller, music is simply '... wild sounds civilised into time and tune'. Certainly, from a heavenly perspective, our music might be more like the unsophisticated sounds of nature than we wish to admit.

If logic suggests superior heavenly beings would be musical, is it confirmed by direct Scriptural reference? Most of us would immediately think of the angelic choir announcing to awe-struck shepherds the most significant birth in human history.Heaven seems so excited, it sent the world's first inter-galactic singing telegram.

There are also recorded instances of angels blowing trumpets; Job 38:7 is strong evidence:

> 'When the morning stars sang together
> and all the sons of God shouted for joy.'

But for the hard to convince, Revelation 5:8 f is the clincher:

> 'The four beasts and the twenty-four elders ... every one of them having harps ... sang a new song ...'

Even our brief examination of creation - from the chirping of insects to the harp playing of heavenly beings - reveals that music is far more than a merely human activity. Music in all its various forms throughout creation, has as its common factor, not human idiosyncrasy, but the Creator Himself.

Some Bible scholars find the Scriptural evidence for angelic music less than compelling. We are indeed exploring the very frontiers of revealed knowledge. Down through history there have been innumerable reports from reliable Christian witnesses of angelic visitations. A number of these are particularly relevant to musicians. Though this subject seems bizarre, reports are too numerous and the implications too profound to be ignored in a serious work on the Christian view of music.

Our final authority is Scripture alone. Yet few would deny that testimonies of conversions can help our dull minds see with greater clarity what Scripture means by being born again. Similarly, Christian testimony may help sharpen the image of music drawn from our Biblical research.

Even if the phenomena described were a mere trick of the human mind, they could still be indirect evidence for the existence of music in the next world. The possibility of such music seems so strongly stamped upon the human psyche as to invite the conclusion that it was placed there by the One who made us. If so, we cannot imagine God placing within us expectations that will never be satisfied.

John Cage's belief that the entire world is the product of nothing but chance caused his music to degenerate into literally random sounds. As another example, consider a musician whose general attitude to life is that what's new is best. Such a person will almost inevitably produce quite different music to someone who believes in 'the good old days'. Likewise, a Christian's belief in heavenly music is likely to affect his or her musical composition. In fact, heavenly strains have apparently directly influenced some Christian music.

Facets of Music in the Light of Christian Scriptures

Christians tend to use music as bait, to allure; a novelty, to entertain; a sedative to soothe, a stimulant to whip-up emotions: or a glimmering orb to mesmerise the wavering wayward into a decision.

According to Christian belief, the most crucial thing in the entire universe is involved - God's will. So we need something much more concrete than an educated guess. Emotions, traditions, worldly trends, love of music and commendable intentions must all bow to God's will. The will of God, however, always agrees with the Word of God. An exploratory Bible probe is therefore imperative; Scripture's evaluation of music must be determined with precision.

Time-wise, we may be closer to the sparkling new heaven and earth, than to the era when the Bible was penned. In character, however, our shabby world is far closer to that of the Bible than to the new age. So we can take the Biblical findings and apply them to our era with little or no modification.

Ancient musical instruments may have been rudimentary, but the Bible's approach to music is so sophisticated that it makes some of our modern attempts seem simplistic. This is to be expected from a book that claims to be not just God's history book, but His guide book for all generations.Facts gleaned from thhe Bible discovery tour will provide significant guidance and confirmation in our effort to set precise, divinely directed goals for music.

When seeking Biblical guidelines for the music, Old Testament references tend to predominate. But should Christians be led by pre-Christian Scriptures? Music receives significantly less emphasis in the New Testament.

Does this indicate that the Lord meant music to play a lesser role in the Christian era?

The amount of space Scripture allocates to a subject does not necessarily reflect God's view of its importance. The New Testament's attitude to musical instruments is typical: little mention is made of them, and yet it gives them the highest possible status, speaking of 'harps of God' and revealing that musical instruments are played in heaven itself.

The casual way the New Testament mentions the singing of hymns shows that it regards music as a normal part of a Christian's life.

> 'And, having sung a hymn, they went out ...'
> 'And at midnight Paul and Silas were praying and singing praises to God ... And suddenly ...'
> 'When you come together, every one of you has a hymn ...'
> '... speaking to yourselves in psalms and hymns and spiritual songs'
> 'Is any among you afflicted? Let him pray. Is any cheerful? Let him sing hymns.'

These New Testament Scriptures give the impression that for the Christian, hymn singing is as natural as breathing. The centrality of such music to Christian living is taken for granted.

Little wonder that when reporting to the Roman emperor the activities of Christians in about AD 110, Pliny the Younger zeroed in on hymn singing.

> 'They are accustomed to meet on a fixed day before daylight to sing a hymn of praise to Christ as God. They read from their own sacred writings and partake of a very simple meal consisting of bread and wine ...'

In about 125 AD a Greek described to his fellow pagans a typical Christian funeral. The Christians would escort the 'body with songs and thanksgiving as if he were setting out from one place to another nearby'.

The New Testament speaks of singing under the Spirit's influence and implies that singing is a natural consequence of being filled with the Spirit. Clearly, music is linked with one of the most fundamental aspects of the New Testament era - the outpouring of God's Spirit.

Jesus sang. Indeed, He still sings. And it is the New Testament, rather than the Old, that gives the greater insight into music beyond this world. Furthermore, there are possibly more hymns and remnants of early Christian hymns locked in the New Testament text than most of us realise.

It is hardly surprising that something that will out-last our planet, had no difficulty surviving the passing of the old covenant!

If the entire Old Testament had been made obsolete by the New, we would have to gloss over the Bible's earlier musical insights. But the earlier Scriptures were not a crumbling ruin that had to be demolished to make way for the new. On the contrary, they are the very foundation upon which the New Testament stands.

When Jesus confidently declared, 'It is written', He quoted from the pre-Christian Scriptures that, He said, 'cannot be broken'. And it was these that Paul was referring to when he wrote:

> 'ALL Scripture is given by inspiration of God, and is profitable for doctrine, for reproof, for correction, for instruction in righteousness: That the man of God may be perfect, thoroughly equipped for every good work'.

The Old Testament was written for people belonging to the New Testament era.

> 'Whatever things were written previously, were written for OUR instruction ...'

The Lord didn't go to the lengths He did in giving musical instructions in the Old Testament, only to ignore it and laboriously repeat it all in the New. The Old Testament's hymn book is the most frequently quoted book in the New Testament. According to one calculation, of the approximately 287 Old Testament quotes in the New Testament, more than forty-four percent are from the Psalms.

Since singing in tongues occurred in the New Testament period, it is likely the other verbal gifts of the Spirit were also commonly set to music. Singing in tongues is mentioned unambiguously in only part of one New Testament verse - just three Greek words. The use of music in delivering utterances of the Spirit is already established in the Old Testament. Further confirmation in the latter part of Scripture is not necessary. Some pre-Christian practices have been superseded, but music is obviously not one of them. Christian musicians can learn from the Old Testament as readily as from the New.

Instrumental Interlude

One final thing before commencing: when reading Bible references to singing, there is no reason for instrumentalists to feel left out.

Paul and Silas were probably not permitted to bring their grand piano and drum set into the cramped Philippian jail to accompany their singing. Nevertheless, singing to the accompaniment of instruments is the norm in Scripture.

Harps, alone, are mentioned some fifty times. References to trumpets are twice as frequent. David appointed 4,000 instrumentalists for sacred music. David himself was renowned not only as a song writer, but as a highly skilled harpist and a maker of fine musical instruments.

Scriptural Ways of Using Music

Worship directed solely to God

If music began in the heart of God, it is only fitting that it be offered back to Him. And so we find such Scriptures as:

> 'I will sing unto the Lord as long as I live:
> I will sing praise to my God while I have any being.'

Scripture abounds with such exhortations to sing God's praises. They occur up to four times in one verse as the Bible seeks to drive home the importance of musically worshipping the Creator.

Worshipping the majestic Lord of heaven and earth is the highest use anything can ever be put to. The fact that the Almighty has ordained that music be used for this exalted purpose indicates how highly esteemed earthly music is.

It is customary to place musical worship at the beginning of church services. This is consistent with Psalm 100:

> 'Come before His presence with singing.'
> 'Enter into His gates with thanksgiving, and into His courts with praise.'

The Levitical musicians lived in the temple chambers 'free from other duties' because they were in service 'day and night'. However, the temple was - at least usually - closed at night. Our information is scanty, but perhaps these musicians worshipped the Lord not just when other worshippers were present, but at times when only the Lord was listening.

That the Lord appointed these Levites, confirms what by now must be obvious: music is no gimmick. It is a holy ministry of the highest order. In fact, it is about the only temple ministry to survive the revolutionary consequences of Christ offering the ultimate sacrifice. So much has been superseded; Levites, priests, ceremonial cleansing, unclean food, burnt offerings, sacrifices and the veil to the holy of holies have all gone. But music remains.

To Express a Prayer

Music has done much to encourage prayer. The book of Psalms is not only Scripture's hymn book; it is its prayer book. Of all the prayers recorded in God's Word, a large proportion, perhaps nearly half, were originally set to music. Many of these prayers were associated with worship.

Two-thirds of the Bible's songs are either entirely prayers or contain prayers. Each of these songs has such expressions as 'unto THEE, O Lord,' clearly indicating that God is being personally addressed.

Frequently the Psalms' prayers contain a commendable declaration of faith and praise in the midst of adversity. Psalm 13, for instance, commences:

> 'How long, O Lord?
> Will you forget me forever?
> How long will you hide your face from me?
> How long shall I take counsel in my soul,
> Having sorrow in my heart daily?
> How long shall my enemy be exalted over me?'

A few lines later, however, this once-dreary psalm triumphantly concludes,

> 'I will sing unto the Lord, because He has dealt bountifully with me.'

To Diclare God's Greatness to Fellow Humans

Most frequent of all, is music directed to God but deliberately played in the presence of other people. That way, two of music's two most important functions - ministering to God and to people - are achieved at the same time. Furthermore, it effectively focuses both the musicians' and the audience's attention upon the Lord, who alone is the Source of effective ministry. The audience is drawn into worshipping the Creator, rather than idolising the dust the music is coming from.

.As an Aid to the Worship of Others

We have seen that exhorting others to praise God is a very common theme in the Bible's songs. Sermons on praise can be helpful, but the psalmists usually went far beyond this. By singing their song they provided a living example. Moreover, they created an atmosphere conducive to praise and even provided words for their hearers to use.

> 'O magnify the Lord WITH ME and let us exalt His name together.'

> 'And all the congregation worshipped, and the singers sang and the trumpeters sounded: and all this continued until the burnt offering was finished.'

> 'All the people of the land rejoiced and blew trumpets, the singers with their musical instruments LEADING the praise.'

Some psalms were probably intended to be sung by a choir, with responses by the congregation. In fact, the nature of Hebrew poetry means that most psalms can be readily adopted to this form of singing. At least by the first century

AD, there were three different types of responsive singing, alternating between a leader and the congregation.

An Impcrtant Aspect of Spiritual Warfare

Christians believes that music that woos the Spirit of God must, of necessity, make demons quake. When God's chosen people comprised one nation, wars involving that nation had spiritual overtones. For instance, when the Israelites slaughtered the former inhabitants of the promised land, they were executing God's judgment, not expressing personal hostilities. This is highlighted by the Lord repeatedly rebuking Israel for being too lenient. As the Lord told Jehoshaphat centuries later, 'The battle is not yours, but God's.'

The Lord of hosts was deeply involved in Israel's wars; whether it was giving victory to Joshua's army whenever Moses raised his rod, pounding the Amorites with hailstones, teaching David's 'hands to war,' revealing Syrian war secrets to Elisha, or slaying Sennacherib's army, to mention just a few exploits of the One who is 'mighty in battle'. On the other hand, we would expect evil spiritual powers to have an active interest in attempts to annihilate or subjugate God's people.

Since these wars clearly had a spiritual dimension, they may encompass principles of relevance to the spiritual warfare each of us face today. This could be a major reason why God has preserved these accounts in Scripture.

Consider this divine instruction:

> 'If you go to war in your land against the enemy that oppresses you, then you shall blow an alarm with the trumpets; and you shall be remembered before the Lord your God, and you shall be saved from your enemies.'

Trumpet blowing played a significant role in the defeat of God's enemies under both Joshua's and Gideon's leadership. In each case, the decisive point of the battle was won before they even physically touched the enemy.

In Jehoshaphat's time, God's secret weapon was taken one step further: the enemies annihilated each other. The most strenuous thing God's people had to do was to collect the booty. Musicians played the key role in this glorious victory, right from the initial prophecy, through to the victory celebration.

Following in this tradition, a Jewish hero in the intertestament era is reported to have loudly sung psalms as he successfully attacked the enemy.

Isaiah connected the playing of godly music with the Lord executing His judgment upon Assyria. The blows of God's judgement would fall upon anti-God forces to the accompaniment of the drums and stringed instruments (and singing) of God's people.

Half of Psalm 149 may be roughly thought of as dealing with the subject of musical praise, and the other half, with the defeat of God's enemies. These two, seemingly diverse activities, might be closely related.

With David, certain leaders were involved in the appointment of the Levitical musicians. Though acknowledging that there are other views, Payne insists that the Hebrew of 1 Chronicles 25:1 unambiguously identifies these leaders as military commanders, an interpretation favoured by several Bible translations. If military commanders had a particular interest in the appointment of musicians, it suggests a strong link between music and warfare.

Another aspect of spiritual warfare is seen in David's skilful harp playing which relieved King Saul of his oppression from an evil spirit. In this context, note Psalm 138:1:

> 'I will praise you with my whole heart:
> Before the gods will I sing praise unto you.'

'Gods' often represent demonic powers. So this verse is yet another Scriptural suggestion that musically praising God directly affects evil spiritual powers.

This discussion is important because spiritual warfare is inevitable for the Christian. Even after Christ's victory, Peter declared Satan to be the enemy and Paul affirmed that we wrestle against principalities, powers and rulers of darkness. This, of course, is not merely defensive. We should be on the attack, as suggested by the NIV rendering of Psalm 141:5 b, 'My prayer is ever against the deeds of evildoers'.

A Tyndale publication, *Attack From the Spirit World* is a compilation of reports from 38 different Christian workers (mainly missionaries) in a total of 24 different countries. Though the sources are so diverse, account after account testifies to the power of Christian songs over the demonic realm. As Ruth Noack put it, years of experience in pre-Communist China had taught her that 'demons do not like hymn singing'.

An Act of Obedience to God

There are times when personal feelings must not be allowed to dictate to us.Music was a central feature of King Hezekiah's celebration of the purification of the temple. This emphasis, however, was not the result of a royal whim or ecclesiastical embellishment: it '... was the commandment of the Lord by His prophets."To obey is better than sacrifice' This applies to melodic sacrifices of praise, as much as animal sacrifices.

To Deliver a Prophetic Utterance

The Bible's hymn book is crammed with prophecies. This is no coincidence. In fact, we believe the relationship between music and prophecy is so strong that rather than present just a smattering of the evidence.

To Increase one's Receptivity to the Spirit

During the dedication of Solomon's temple, music played and the cloud of God's glory spectacularly filled the sanctuary. The biblical account hints at a link between this music and the awesome manifestation of the Lord's presence.

After privately anointing Saul as king, Samuel told him,

> '... you will meet a company of prophets coming down from the high place with a psaltery, and a tambourine, and a pipe, and a harp, before them; and they will be prophesying: And the Spirit of the Lord will come upon you, and you will prophesy with them, and will be turned into another man.'

Clearly, Saul's spiritual experience on that day was closely associated with music, though it is uncertain how critical the music was in initiating the experience.

In the above examples, the use of music to induce a manifestation of the Spirit may not necessarily have been deliberate. Any element of doubt, however, is removed in the case of Elisha. On one occasion, when he wished to prophesy, he specifically arranged for a harpist to play.

It was probably common knowledge amongst the bands of prophets such as those Saul met that, under God's direction, music can enhance one's receptivity to the Holy Spirit. Whilst the harpist played, the Spirit of God came upon Elisha and the Lord spoke through him. Since Elisha's message was apparently in prose, it is unlikely the music was used to accompany a prophecy in song. On this occasion, music was used to elicit a prophecy, rather than to deliver one.

To Edify yourself

In the chorus of Psalms 42 and 43, the psalmist sang to himself, in an attempt to break through depression, and exercise faith in God. As is typical of Biblical music, however, he did not force the entire ministry burden upon music alone. In addition to melody, he used prayer, praise and a positive Scriptural mentality to lift himself from his despondency.Furthermore, this godly songwriter did not use music as a means of escapism. He faced his problems head-on; neither pretending his trials were trivial, nor letting them stifle his faith.

To Edify Others

We cannot always be with people. But we can teach them encouraging songs that will remain with them wherever they go.

To Share a Testimony

'Come and hear, all you that fear God, And I will declare what He has done for my soul,' sang the Psalmist. A number of psalms fall into this category. The book of Psalms is filled with references to being saved from sin, sickness, death, etc. Often these testimonies are combined with praise or petition to God. These songs reveal a standard of frankness and honesty that we should emulate. They are not all glowing testimonies of victory. They neither hid, nor gloried in, past failings.

A personal testimony in song necessitates having an experience. Frequently, it involves an initially adverse situation. We cannot, for example, give a personal healing testimony without first being sick! Very few Scriptural miracles occurred without someone being in an unpleasant dilemma that necessitated divine intervention.

Scripture commands us to rejoice when we encounter trials because such trials produce a depth of character and a greatly enhanced ability to minister to others. If our experience is only second-hand, this is likely to be reflected in our music, especially its composition.

An Important aid to Memory

The Lord wanted to impress a message upon the minds of His people that would remain with them for generations. So He wrote a song. God declared that although in generations to come Israel would forget Him, they would never forget the song.

Andrae Crouch failed his high school algebra. He couldn't remember the formulas. His father suggested he set them to music. It worked! He later used the same method to learn Scripture.

The more Scripture is put to music, the easier it becomes to fulfil God's command to Joshua, and Paul's command to the Colossians.

> 'This book of the law shall not depart out of your mouth; but you shall meditate therein day and night

...

> 'Let the word of Christ dwell in you richly ... in psalms and hymns and spiritual songs ...'

To Teach

Music's value of as a memory aid, coupled with its ability to entertain and arrest attention, makes it a powerful medium for instilling truth. But the Scriptural standard of music is not achieved by using song merely to drill people with biblical facts. The goal should be to instruct and enlighten. And beyond even that, the goal of all ministry gifts - of which teaching is one - is to lovingly release people into their own ministry and to help them reach 'the measure of the stature of the fullness of Christ'.

For hundreds of people to quote a preacher is almost unheard of. In contrast, it is common-place for thousands to sing words composed by a song-writer.

Consider the Wesley brothers: Hundreds of thousands, no, millions more people have sang Charles' songs than have read any of his famous brother's sermons.

> '... teaching and admonishing one another [by means of], psalms and hymns and spiritual songs ...'

In fact, teaching is the primary or secondary aim of a number of Biblical hymns.

Psalmists sang:

> 'Give ear, O my people, to my teaching.'
> 'I will teach you the fear of the Lord.'

In Psalm 49 the teacher expounded his wisdom to the accompaniment of a harp.

Everyone engaged in teaching should take the following words very seriously:

'Let not many become teachers, knowing that we shall receive the greater judgment. For in many things we all offend.'

To Challenge and Inspire others to Action or Commitment

The attitude-changing power of music is vividly portrayed in the words of Jeremy Collier: 'Music is almost as dangerous as gunpowder; it may be requires looking after no less than ... the mint.'

Many of us pray earnestly for our politicians and never give our nation's secular songwriters a thought. Yet 'a very wise man' felt music is so persuasive that if he could write a nation's songs, he would be unconcerned about who wrote its laws.

Shortly before he died, Dwight L. Moody was visited by hymn-writer, Will Thompson. 'Will', said the famous evangelist, 'I would rather have written [your hymn] *Softly and tenderly*, than anything I have been able to do in my whole life.'

Psalm 95 is one of many Biblical songs seeking to raise its hearers to new spiritual heights. It urges hearers to worship God and not harden their hearts. How it does this should be of particular interest to us. It is, after all, no ordinary hymn. It carries God's seal of approval in a way no extra-Biblical song can claim. This psalm ministers to the whole man - intellect, will and actions, as well as emotions. The writer used to the fullest, every means at his disposal to effect a God-glorifying response in his hearers. This is in marked contrast to some modern musicians, who seem content to rely almost solely upon a musical appeal to the emotions. One of the features of this psalm is its use of the words 'us' and 'we'. The psalmist did not have a 'holier-than-thou' or stand-offish attitude. He identified with his listeners. This can be a powerful way of influencing people. Furthermore, as many of the great intercessors have discovered, identification - which reaches its pinnacle in Christ crucified - is an attitude that touches not just human hearts but God's heart. And God's approval is obviously crucial in Christian ministry.

To the power of music and identification, the psalmist adds rational argument. Persuasive reasons, both positive and negative, are given for worshipping God:

— He is the Rock of our salvation.
— He is above all gods.
— He is the Creator.
— We are His people.
— If we harden our hearts we could miss God's rest, as did our fathers.

Not content with even this impressive list, the psalmist adds yet another powerful means of influencing others: the magnetism of personal example. 'Make a joyful noise unto Him with psalms,' he sings and immediately he does just that, singing a psalm of praise to God in the next three verses.

Psalms 96 and 98 employ the same principles. They commence with, 'O sing unto the Lord a new song' and that is exactly what the psalmist proceeds to do, at the same time giving rational reasons for following his example.

Evangelism

To look for evangelistic content in the Bible's Song Book is nearly like scanning the works of Shakespeare for references to rock 'n' roll You are looking in the wrong era. Evangelism is essentially a New Testament concept. Less than one eighth of the Bible belongs to the era initiated by the Great Commission. Nevertheless, if the Bible's Songs are as deep as we suggest, you never know what you might find. Before plunging into this, however, let's step back a little and ask ourselves if people who wish to use music for evangelism are not closer to the spirit of New Testament evangelists than their critics.

The New Testament portrays its model evangelist, the apostle Paul, as a man desperate to employ almost any and every means to propagate the gospel.

'I have become all things to all people that I might BY ALL MEANS save some,' he declared.

> 'Some indeed preach Christ because of envy and strife ... from selfish ambition, not sincerely, supposing to add affliction to my bonds ....' Can you imagine such debased motives attached to such a holy task? Yet in even this scandal Paul rejoiced because what mattered most was that in 'every way, whether in pretence or in truth, Christ is preached ...'

If we had Paul's passion for evangelism brewing within us we would need pretty strong evidence that something was unacceptable to God before refusing to press it into service for the King.

'Music and the Bible are the two most important agencies with which to reach the world' declared Dwight Moody in the latter part of his life, 'And I've made as much of singing as I have of preaching.' That's the evaluation of one of the greatest evangelists the world has seen - someone who himself was totally unmusical.

If we had just one percent of Moody's conviction of music's power to 'reach the world' we would beg God to let us use it to snatch souls from the flames of hell.

We don't know how regularly Paul used music but we know he burst into a duet at midnight in the midst of criminals in the Philippian jail, and that was about as far from a church setting as one can go. If he sang with his wounds throbbing in a stinking jail in the dead of night surrounded by such a potentially hostile audience, one wonders how often he sang to non-Christians in less trying circumstances

Geoff Bullock sees the initial outpouring of the Spirit upon the church as a blueprint for what should happen when the Holy Spirit comes upon Christian musicians. At the birth of the church, the 'sound of divinity and humanity being struck together in the power and the presence of God by the Holy Spirit' did not remain within the four walls where the church had gathered. It reached outside and touched people of diverse cultures, not in the normal language of the first Christians, nor even in Greek, the international language with which all must have had some familiarity, but in the mother tongue - the heart language - of every hearer.

'For too long we've been making our music more relevant to within the walls [of the church] than outside the walls. And yet God, from the day of Pentecost, burst out of those religious walls ... because He wanted this sound ... heard in the marketplace in the language of every culture represented.' The result, of course, was thousands of conversions.

Note the key facets:

1. The message went out from the church into the world
2. It penetrated cultural barriers and reached hearers in a form they could readily identify with
3. There was a strongly supernatural element.

It is often asserted that there is no Biblical precedent for using music for evangelism, but even in the Old Testament not only were God and the godly sung to, but also the ungodly. Some psalms were addressed not just to Israel, but to 'all inhabitants of the world'. This is rather staggering, written as they were, centuries before Jesus commissioned His church to preach to Gentiles. The significance was not lost to Paul, who twice quoted psalms to prove that Christ came 'that the Gentiles might glorify God'. His first quote is particularly strong:

'Therefore will I give thanks unto you, O Lord, among the heathen, and sing praises unto your name.' This verse appears three times in the Bible.

The Song of Moses focuses on people who have turned their back on God. Psalm 94 admonishes evil-doers to take heed. Psalm 52:1-7 is directed to sinners, warning them of God's judgment and Psalm 75:4-10 is similar.

Psalm 82 has lyrics apparently designed to coax the ungodly into a right relationship with God. The song says:

> 'How long will you judge unjustly,
> And be partial to the wicked? Selah.
> Defend the poor and fatherless:
> Do justice to the afflicted and needy.'

Note also Psalm 4:2-5:

> 'O you sons of men, how long will you turn my glory into shame?
> How long will you love vanity, and seek after lies? Selah.
> But know that the Lord has set apart him that is godly for Himself:
> The Lord will hear when I call unto Him.
> Stand in awe, and sin not:
> Continue with your own heart upon your bed, and be still. Selah.

> Offer the sacrifices of righteousness,
> And put your trust in the Lord.'

Several psalms come close to telling us to use music to evangelise the world:

> 'Sing to the Lord, bless His name;
> Tell of His salvation from day to day.
> Declare His glory among the [heathen] nations,
> His wonders among all people ...
> Say among the nations that the Lord reigns ...'

Since most of our Biblical understanding of music comes from the Old Testament, it is not surprising that references to evangelism are muted. Nevertheless, Carman has an interesting thought. This innovative and controversial artist believes the scriptural emphasis indicates that the primary function of music is to magnify the Lord. Emphasising Jesus declaration, 'If I be lifted up ... I will draw all people to myself', he concludes that if music causes Jesus to be exalted, conversions will result. Praise and worship directed solely to the Lord will woo the Spirit of God so effectively that unbelievers present will be saved. He warns that some Christian artists, rather than casting the burden of evangelism upon Jesus, seem to think *they* must be lifted up, so that *they* will draw people to Jesus.

To Express Pent-uo Feelings

Christians have used music as an emotional release. Is this a perversion of God's gift? Not according to Scripture. James wrote, 'Is anyone happy? Let him sing psalms.' Clearly, such a supposedly 'unspiritual' motivation has God's approval. Isaiah virtually commands the barren to sing for joy because of the exciting things that will happen to them.

Ideally, Christian music is like a rope made strong by the entwining of many strands. Emotional appeal is one of those strands. Some of us are tempted to rely almost exclusively upon it. But God intends music to accomplish far more than mere emotionalism can achieve. Others of us would like to weaken the emotional strand, but that would weaken the entire rope.

The psalmists confessed feelings of confusion and frustration. Jesus openly wept and displayed anger. Early Christians 'made great lamentation' over Stephen. The Ephesian elders 'all wept sore' at Paul's departure. Many of us, in contrast, seem reluctant to even admit that dedicated Christians can have feelings other than peace and moderate joy. We could hardly be surprised if, locked within many Christians from time to time, are strong feelings that they have no idea how to express in an authentically Christian manner.

Some Christian traditions fear 'excessive' enthusiasm, there are others equally wary of any expression of sorrow. Yet in the book of Ezra we see both, on the same occasion and associated with music.

A jubilant expression of joy seems to be gaining acceptance in Christian circles. The expression of sorrow, however, often seems less common in today's Christian music than in Scripture.

In his youth, William Muhlenberg wrote a melancholic hymn. He afterwards regretted its tone and for years tried to brighten it. To his repeated frustration, the hymn was widely accepted only in its original form.

Sad songs should not seem strange to us - consider the innumerable pop songs of our era expressing the pain of broken relationships. In P. B. Shelley's opinion, humanity's 'sweetest songs are those that tell of saddest thought'.

There is considerable scope for such Christian songs; especially dealing with Jesus' suffering and death, the sorrow of knowing a loved one is going to a Christ-less eternity, grieving over past sin, lamenting the future judgment of this world, and so on.

Christians in great distress have always been able to turn to biblical songs for comfort. Many of today's song-writers would have let them down. But what about those pressures unique to our era - unemployment, AIDS, the power of the mass media, the ecological time-bomb, fear of getting mugged, the fragmentation of Christ's body, the exploitation of sex, and so on? While we're busily burying such problems in the 'too hard' basket, real flesh and blood Christians are forced everyday to try to cope with them.

To Accompany Physical Movements

Processions: When Nehemiah dedicated the city wall, he divided the people into two processions, each with their instruments and singers. This religious use of processions had a long history in Israel.

Dancing: Though worldly excesses and 'religious' fears make us hesitate, Scripture forces us to confess that godly music was frequently associated with dancing. Being thoroughly convinced from childhood that all dancing is worldly has made it difficult for us to face these Scriptures.

Psalm 150 gives the impression that dancing was such an integral part of Biblical music that it was impossible to speak at length about music without referring to dancing. The psalmist mentioned it in the midst of a list dealing exclusively with musical instruments. Perhaps it was as much a part of their music as hand-clapping is in some Christian circles today.

Dancing may have been much more a part of the Biblical scene than we generally realise. For example, as Johnson points out, '... it is hard to imagine the music and ecstasy of prophetic bands [such as those which Saul met] without rhythmic movement ...' They even played the instrument most frequently associated with dancing - the tambourine.

Christ had no hesitation in including dancing in His Prodigal Son parable and when mentioning children's games to make a point. Physical movement is a natural and legitimate way to express joy and if the New Testament emphasises anything, it is that joy did not die with the making of the New Covenant. Even when persecuted, we should 'jump for joy,' said Jesus. The God who in the Old Testament era turned mourning into dancing has in no way diminished in power or lost His desire for us to exuberantly share in His joy.

As instrumentalists use their instruments and singers their voices, so dancers use their bodies to magnify the Lord. '... the body is ... for the Lord,' declared Paul, '... glorify God in your body ...' Later he expressed his desire 'that the life of ... Jesus might be made manifest in our body.' In a third epistle he wrote of his longing that 'as always, so now also Christ shall be magnified in my body.'

As instrumentalists often unite with singers to heighten the power of their individual ministries, so they can both unite with dancers for a further enhancement.

Nevertheless, the fact that dancers can use their bodies for sensual purposes should thwart us no more than the fact that singers can misuse their voices. The very real possibility of abuse only accentuates the glory when that path is spurned in favour of passionate purity. Though the servant in Jesus' parable resisted the urge to squander his talent on sensual pleasure, he still incurred the master's wrath because he failed to use that talent positively.

Special Occasions

Obviously music played an important role in Israel's holy festivals. There are numerous Biblical references to the use of music in weddings, funerals, coronations, victories, banquets, farewells, completion of public works projects and harvests.Generally, this reflects the secular use of music, acceptable to God, though not specifically ordained by Him. The prophets, when speaking of God's judgment, often said that the Lord would cause a people's music to cease. According to Werner, music in Biblical times contrasted with our society in that it 'was an organic part of daily life, linked with a thousand bonds to all human concerns, from birth to death'.

To Accompany Animal Sacrifice

The Jewish Talmud suggested that the absence of Levitical music invalidated a sacrifice. So strong was the link that when sacrifices ceased in AD 70, so did Levitical music. This use of music certainly shows that it is sometimes valid to play music while another important spiritual activity is in progress. Music while the sacraments are being administered is probably the closest modern parallel. One might also be tempted to use it to support the common practice of playing music while the offering is being received.

Music Manifedtation of Divie Extravagence

The long list established above shows how highly God prizes music. That divine approval rests on using music for such diverse and sacred purposes should forever silence anyone tempted to belittle music. The dine purpose of music is to show forth the beauty and mind-boggling extravagance of almighty God.

If the Lord wanted us to see, black and white vision should have sufficed. Instead, he lavished upon us the ability to revel in an estimated seven million discriminable hues. In the magnificent garden of Eden, just one tree was forbidden. A lesser god might have banned every tree but one. One bland, nutrient-rich food-type could keep us healthy. Instead we have been divinely showered with a vast array of tastes, aromas and textures. Wherever we look we see the creative genius and extravagant generosity of the One who invites and empowers us to imitate Him. Music is our opportunity to reflect this aspect of the divine nature.

Beautiful music is like gold in Solomon's temple. It theoretically was not necessary, but God is worthy of nothing less.

The Bible graphically shows that not all music pleases God. Like all of God's precious gifts, music can be corrupted. Scripture speaks of it being associated with slander, idleness, drunkenness, immorality, hypocrisy and false religion.

Nebuchadnezzar used an orchestra as part of a sinister attempt to bludgeon and bewilder Shadrach, Meshach and Abednego into idolatry. Scripture emphasises this corrupt use of music by laboriously listing all the different instruments four times in the space of eleven verses. Some of those instruments were almost certainly foreign to the Hebrews. No doubt, the exotic music would have raised some pious eyebrows back in Jerusalem. Nevertheless, the biblical account is devoid of the suggestion that there was anything *intrinsically* decadent about the pagan music or the 'weird' instruments.

Music and pomp and public pressure were all employed, but the furnace held centre stage. Possibly, the furnace was of a type never before mention in Scripture. However, new ways of doing things are not inherently evil. It was the godless use Nebuchadnezzar's furnace was put to that was evil, not the furnace itself. Perhaps the same could be said for Nebuchadnezzar's unorthodox music.

It is sometimes asserted that when Satan was the highest angelic being God appointed him as chief musician. If the theory is right, it focuses on pre-fall Lucifer and so it says nothing about fallen music. On the contrary, if the Lord entrusted music to the most important arch-angel it yet again confirms God's exalted view of music.

Spirit-led ministry is always Scriptural, yet gloriously unpredictable. Beware of the temptation to make it predictable by suppressing the Spirit's leading!

Soldiers on a mission, are handed maps of the terrain. Then they are briefed concerning intelligence reports and their objectives. Without the briefing there would be chaos. But without the map, they'd get lost.

Scripture is your map. The Spirit briefs you, nominating your daily destination and filling in any personal details you need. The Spirit's guidance is not a substitute for those too lazy to seriously study the Bible. Nor is the Bible an alternative for those too preoccupied to maintain a daily, intimate walk with God. Both are indispensable.

We've now left the biblical era and are speeding towards the time indicated on our twentieth-century watches. The centuries blur by. Lest we overshoot the mark we begin to decelerate. Peering down, we can make out certain peaks in God's use of music. Glimpsing a few of them as they whiz by will heighten our conviction that Spirit-empowered music is a tremendously versatile, God-given way of firing the infinite power of the cross into the lives of men and women.

Most of our peeps below the clouds will stop short of our era. This will help us see contemporary music in an historical perspective. Some of us seem to imagine that God has been on vacation from the closing of the New Testament until this century! And neither are our trials unique to our era. Consider, for example, Ira Sankey and his old-fashioned Gospel Songs.

Even a Christian heavy metal band has a greater kinship with D. L. Moody's soloist, Ira Sankey (1840-1908) than most of us would imagine - including bitter opposition from seemingly pious sections of the church. His music was so much like the popular secular music of the day that, wrote one journalist, ' ... it is sometimes difficult to realise that what we hear is sacred song ...'

Many lovers of classical music would regard Sankey's simple gospel songs as lightweight, yet, according to one estimate, in just one year more people heard Sankey sing than listened to actual performances of Bach's works during the entire nineteenth century. In the first fifty years, sales of his collection of hymns have been estimated at between fifty and eighty million copies.

Contemporary music would suspect that the secret of Sankey's popularity was that people were starved of modern alternatives. Pollock observes that Sankey is judged harshly today because his song book was published before the snail of time could kill off the inferior songs and because we have heard only poor imitators of this great soloist.

A Godly Addiction

Thomas Hornblower Gill was brought up a Unitarian. However, he loved the Isaac's Watts' hymns. This gradually lured him away from his sect until finally he fully embraced orthodox Christianity. Dr. Frederick Faber, a convert to Roman Catholicism lamented the fact that many Catholics delighted in Protestant hymns. He confessed that these very hymns had earlier held a spell-like influence over him, for years acting as 'a counter-influence to very grave convictions' and keeping him within the Protestant fold. 'Even now,' he wrote, these hymns 'come back from time to time unbidden into the mind.'

This correlation between new moves of God and new songs continues outside of the Bible, climaxing in the prophesied 'new song' in the age to come. Dr. Schaff notes that not only were the great revivals of the Reformation, Pietism, Moravianism and Methodism 'sung as well as preached,' the leaders of each of these revivals 'were themselves hymnists'. Again, the founding of the Salvation Army meant the development of new musical expressions of old truths, and the founder himself contributed to the movement's songs. Moody's enormous influence in Great Britain was inseparably linked with the introduction of Gospels songs. Until then, especially in Scotland, anything but metrical versions of the Psalms was banned in very many churches.

In a Northern Ireland revival in the mid-nineteen century, music played an unexpected role. The move of God so affected the crime rate that the police formed quartets and sang in churches in an attempt to find something to do! Far from being an insignificant consequence of new moves of God, however, music was often in the forefront, actually helping to carry the revival. Brown and Butterworth strongly support an oft-quoted observation of Coleridge that Luther's hymns accomplished as much for the Reformation as did his translation of the Bible into German.

A moment's reflection will confirm the enormity of this statement. A return to the Bible was at the very heart of the Reformation. Moreover, Luther's Bible translation has been called 'one of the greatest human achievements of all time'. Yet music is seen to have rivalled even this as a means of spreading the Reformation. Even without the wisdom of hindsight, the centrality of music to the reformation was widely recognised by contemporaries. 'We seek poets everywhere,' wrote Luther about the importance he placed upon obtaining suitable songs. On the other side, Roman Catholic monks said, 'Luther has done us more harm by his songs than his sermons'.

Likewise, the songs of the Wesleyan revival are claimed to have had a greater impact than even the sermons and Biblical expositions. New moves of God have generally had songs which were not only of recent origin, but were of a new type. Thus, Dr. A. E. Gregory believes he can see in many of Wesley's hymns a style designed to arouse the attention of casual passers-by. Open-air meetings played an important part in the Wesleyan revival.

Salvation Army songs, with their military symbolism and different tempo, fitted this movement's needs better than any other type. For the Charismatic Movement, Scripture choruses, markedly different from hymns, were an ideal vehicle for introducing a new form of worship and a renewed emphasis upon taking Scripture at face value. In the hands of God, music can not only transform individual lives, it can shape entire movements and fan the fires of mass revival.

Today, few people who sing his songs are aware that Isaac Watts had significant abilities in addition to hymn-writing. His songs have outlasted his other achievements. As illustrated by the following quotes, there is little in the whole of Christendom that can rival the durability and worth of good music. James Montgomery, a poet of uncommon ability, was asked which of his works would 'live'. 'None,' came the reply, 'except for a few of my hymns.' At the time, few would have believed him, yet his prediction proved remarkably accurate. On another occasion, Montgomery wrote that he would rather be the anonymous author of a few hymns that were permanently embraced by God's people than be ranked with the greatest poets the world has seen.

According to Lord Shaftesbury, if Ira Sankey had done nothing but teach the hymn 'Hold the fort,' he had bestowed upon the British Empire a blessing of incalculable worth. Henry Ward Beecher said he would rather have written the hymn *Jesus, Lover of my soul* 'than to have the fame of all the kings that ever sat on the earth. It is more glorious. It has more power in it. Moody's musical limitations were such that he was moved to tears by what he imagined to be his daughter's-in-law rendition of *Rock of Ages.* She had mischievously played a soulful rendition of *Yankee-Doodle*! Yet this gifted evangelist was not so easily fooled about the power of music to out-run the spoken word. When asked why he placed so much emphasis upon getting his audience to sing heartily, he indicated that whilst they would soon forget what he said, Gospel songs would have a more permanent impact.

Fanny Crosby's prayer was that her hymns would play a key role in the conversion of one million people. Many believe her target has already been passed, and the work of her songs is still far from over.

Luther was inspired to commence hymn-writing by two young martyrs singing praises to God while being burnt alive for their reformed faith. According to Beattie, the playing of *Nearer my God to Thee*' enabled passengers on the 'Titanic' to die with dignity. Some researchers dispute this particular instance, but the role of music in comforting countless dying Christians is beyond dispute.

Bio-chemical Changes

Music can reduce susceptibility to hypothermia and boost the body's immune system. It has also demonstrably improved both the quality and quantity of milk produced by lactating mothers in third-world countries. It has been reported to ease hunger pains in malnourished children and there is strong evidence that music can actually lower infant mortality rates. The mechanism by which these little-recognised powers of music operate is fully understood - money!

The dramatic changes referred to above were accomplished, not by some mysterious force, but by the use of music in fund-raising. Like everything else he does, Satan's use of music is much less powerful than God's. Nevertheless, if we let him, he will use this force for his own perverted ends. So one role of Christian music is to displace worldly music. This use of music is not some crack-pot idea dreamed up in the last decade. It was even one of Luther's motivations in writing hymns. He wished to provide youths with something to counter the corrupting influence of what he called 'amorous and carnal songs'.

As Jimmy Owens discovered, even mature Christian musicians can be mesmerised by its heady surge and be swept into ungodly ego trips. This nitroglycerine of the mind and emotions must be handled with fear and trembling. The forces of evil are unmoved by musicians 'playing church'. But when musicians are locked into the power of God, Satan shudders.

God's Music

We have seen that throughout history supernatural moves of God in music have occurred through divine sovereignty, but for music miracles to occur with greater frequency requires two things:

(1) to use music God's way

(2) to have the faith to receive divine intervention in our music.

It was the American Civil War. Rev. Rankin bent over a critically wounded soldier. Seeking to minister to him, the chaplain asked if there was anything he could do. The unexpected reply hit the reverend like a sickening blow. He was asked to sing *Jesus, Lover of my soul.* He knew the song, but never in his life had he sung it. His United Presbyterian Church taught that only psalm-singing was acceptable to God. A chill swept his spine. Suddenly, the folly of shallow Bible study was all too apparent. The soldier was but seconds from death. It was too late now to feverishly scour the Word for an authoritative answer.

New Christians, cigarettes drooping from their mouths, have witnessed to the saving power of Jesus Christ in the only way they know - in speech peppered with foul language. It would be hypocritical to be shocked by the Spirit empowering such witnessing. God even prophesied through the man who sent Jesus to the cross. If not even church tradition guarantees divine approval of our methods, neither will godly motives. We have noted the disastrous consequences of David's minor deviation from Scripture's ark-carrying instructions. The purity of David's and Uzzah's motives did not insulate them from God's judgment.

Scriptural reference to 'psalms, hymns and spiritual songs' is difficult to interpret with definite accuracy. Commentators have often regarded 'spiritual songs' as synonymous with singing unknown words 'with the Spirit'. But even without such precise identification, it is most unlikely that a writer would use in succession three separate terms if he simply meant the book of Psalms. Surely, at least one of the terms must refer to songs not found in Scripture.

Corinthians 14:26 may also hint at divinely approved extra-Biblical songs:

> 'When you come together, each one of you has a hymn, or a teaching, a tongue, a revelation, or an interpretation.'

Delling, in Kittel's Theological Dictionary, says this 'obviously' refers to a song composed and sung by the person in the gathering. In other words, an extra-Biblical song. Notice how 'a hymn' is placed side by side with gifts of the Spirit. Some commentators even wonder whether this implies the song is a gift of the Spirit.

So the Bible supports our hunch: at least in principle, God endorses the singing of lyrics not preserved in Scripture. This, however, has been hotly debated at various times and in various parts of the Christian Church. Rev. Rankin sang the hymn to that soldier. Before he had finished, the man was dead. But the light on the soldier's face amazed him. He arose, an eyewitness to God's ability to empower songs not found in the Psalter.

We can now complement that subjective evaluation with reassuring hints from the authoritative Word of God. We have a scriptural basis for affirming that a divine blessing upon such music is neither exceptional, nor a reluctant accommodation to the weakness of man. Perhaps we should be cautious, however, about a wholesale musical rejection of the Bible's songs, in favour of man-made ones.

Non Christian Material

A study of the biblical adaptation of pagan lyrics will give us greater confidence in the use of non-Christian melodies. Before proceeding to this, however, let me illustrate the power of this practice. Music which, just moments before, was moving dancing feet was now bending penitent knees. Such is the power of a musician sold out to God. That night a new hymn was added to the Christian Church. More significantly, new names were added to the Lamb's *Book of Life*. The tune wasn't new, but the reverence in that tavern certainly was. A man had converted dance-hall music. God had converted dancers. Casson changed their song. God changed their hearts.

A word of caution, however. Though we have established that musical ability is from God, it does not logically follow that, lyrics aside, every musical style must be of God. And although some worldly music can be reclaimed for the cause of Christ, this does not automatically imply that all secular music is capable of such use. The world can misuse God's gift of sex, turning it into sin and yet that exact behaviour could be placed in a godly, marital context and glorify our Maker. However, this gift can be not merely misused but so perverted (eg bestiality) that there is no acceptable context in which that perversion could be used for the glory of God. As another example, consider God's gift of speech, something that is so much of God that His Son is call the Word.

Then there are those who conclude that if Christians can play a certain type of music then they can fill their minds with the worldly equivalent. More than two entire New Testament chapters are devoted to the care we should exercise in ensuring we do not risk a bother's or sister's spiritual welfare by doing something which causes us no qualms of conscience. There are people who would not dare touch alcohol for fear of offending a 'weaker brother' and yet spare no thought for the casualties their music might produce. Musicians worthy of the name of Christ are ministers of the Gospel, servants of the body of Christ, not egotists intent of having a good time or establishing their own rights.

With our knowledge of ancient tunes being so slight, it is hardly surprising that a search for the Biblical use of pagan or secular songs is more productive when we examine the lyrics. Some divinely inspired psalms bear striking similarities to Canaanite and Akkadian psalms. Many scholars even believe Psalm 29 was originally a Canaanite hymn. Whilst this might be going too far, it does seem that songs used in Baal worship have strongly influenced the form of some of the Bible's psalms.

The full extent of Scripture's use of heathen works is not known. It certainly goes beyond the book of Psalms. Paul's famous sermon on Mars Hill contains pagan poetry, as does two of his letters. So if expressions in a pop song, or even from a non-Christian cult, happen to be particularly applicable to the true God, we apparently have Biblical support for adopting them.

So christians are vindicated in adapting, but not diligently researching, unchristian material. For example, perhaps a converted Muslim could cautiously draw upon his past experience. After becoming a Christian, however, no-one should engage in further pagan studies without definite guidance from heaven. Scripture is the songwriter's treasure house. Every spiritual truth on earth is deposited there. Delving into its depths is a life-long pursuit worthy of humanity's noblest minds supernaturally expanded by the Spirit of God. To mount in a worthy setting, just one of Scripture's priceless jewels is a challenge of superhuman proportions; a calling as high as the heavens.

Gaining Musical Insights

Like tongue-speaking, instrumental praise can be edifying to the participant and pleasing to God, without the message being verbally explicit. It is perfectly suited for private worship. For public performance, however, they should carefully consider the implications of Pauline teaching about interpretation of tongues. From this unlikely source, we can distil a principle of great significance to musicians. This principle, however, must not be confused with an infallible law of God.

Christians may have differing ideas as to whether the gift is still given, but all are united in declaring that God made no mistake in preserving these New Testament chapters for us. Whilst wordless music conveys *some* meaning, it does so no more than singing 'with the Spirit'. In both cases, there is a tune without intelligible vocalisation. Even without a tune, speaking in incomprehensible words can communicate something through the tone of voice. However, Scripture demands that these sounds be followed by intelligible words so that everyone present benefits from those sounds and hears from the Lord.

When playing the melody of a well-known song without vocal accompaniment, it may seem sufficient to rely on the hearer's memory. The obvious problem, however, is that the message is clearest only to those who have fully memorised the entire song. This conflicts with the apostle's concern that every part of a service should minister to the 'unlearned or unbelievers' as well as the thoroughly initiated.

Entirely instrumental music is much less likely to offend outsiders than uninterpreted singing in tongues. Moreover, it can be played while something else, clearly intelligible to outsiders, is simultaneously occurring. No-one need feel left out. When used wisely, so as not to detract from whatever else is happening, background music is unlikely to offend newcomers. So interpreting the gist of *background* music seems less essential than for tongues. When music is the focus of attention, however, Scripture's teaching about glossolalia is more directly applicable.

It may be objected that some music has no need of words or verbal explanation. Music can do things beyond conveying a message to the congregation. But so can tongues.

Paul's teaching about interpretation is obviously applicable to those uses of music which parallel the functions of tongues, especially prayer, personal edification and delivering a message. Nevertheless, even when music is put to other uses, it still usually fits Biblical teaching about making a spiritual activity intelligible to inexperienced listeners.

For example, wordless music can create an atmosphere in which the Spirit moves by speaking through someone, or by overcoming spiritual opposition. But in the former case, Paul would want the person receiving the Spirit's burden to share it with the whole congregation. In the latter case, sometimes spiritual warfare could perhaps be just as effective if restricted to background music. Furthermore, the enemy-defeating music of Gideon's and Jehoshaphat's armies was verbalised.

Lyrics

Not even the use of a known language guarantees that they have fulfilled their obligation to new-comers. The jargon-infested lyrics of some Christian songs would hardly be less intelligible to non-Christians if they were sung in tongues! Then there's the issue of how clearly the lyrics are heard. 'It took a miracle to put the stars in place,' sang George Beverly Shea. The song completed, he sat down, satisfied that he had exalted the Lord before this British audience. Imagine his shock when he learnt about the irate woman who slated Billy Graham for having the audacity to allow a soloist to come to England and sing, 'It took *America* to put the stars in place'.

Few people could make music with unclear or non-existent words seem so eloquent. Yet even he considers words so important that he takes enormous care in selecting music with unmistakably clear lyrics. The spiritual burden of music may be clarified by accompanying words, whether distinctly sung, spoken or written. Even pictures or mime may help. Modern technology opens up many possibilities.

It is not always essential that it be synchronised with the music. Sometimes the theme may be effectively expounded before or after your rendition.

Regardless of sequence, however, the verbal or visual 'interpretation' is an integral part of your performance. As much care should be taken with this as with the music itself.

Some musicians' spoken introduction to their works are like mounting exquisite jewels in settings of scrap iron.

Each note of your music is precisely planned and executed, representing countless hours of writing, arranging and practice. Stumbling through a spur-of-the-moment introduction is ridiculously incongruous.

Just as an utterance in tongues and its interpretation are equally Spirit inspired, so our rendition of the music's message is as important to God as the music itself.

A few, well chosen words can be powerful. You don't have to preach a sermon. As much as possible, let your music do the talking. If, however, your comments add clarity to the message, they could be the linchpin, validating your whole performance in God's sight. Like clothing one's naked body, making the theme explicit renders one's music publicly presentable. Otherwise, it might be too private for public exposure. You are a minister of God, not an exhibitionist!

Even if reading between the notes is easy for most of your audience, less discerning hearers still deserve your loving concern. For someone, your explanatory remarks could be the key to transforming a mere sound into a life-changing experience.

Lighting, movement, video clips, and so on have the power to enhance the message. Ideally, everything should be like a whirlpool drawing people to the central message. Too often, however, they detract from it. Not many experienced pastors preach while a James Bond movie is showing on the screen behind the pulpit, a spotlight is on an acrobat performing on one side and a fireworks display is in progress on the other. The greater the complexity, the smaller the chance of people grasping the message in one hearing. The more you are sure you will repeat your performance to the same audience, however, the more justified you are in adding to the complexity.

Too often we think if it works in the world it will work in the church. What we fail to see is that much worldly music seeks simply to entertain, not convey a life-changing message. In fact, even entertainment is too lofty a goal for some music. Making money is the ultimate for many. Their goals and our goals; their measure of success and Christ's measure of success, are worlds apart. Look at the ministries of the prophets, of Christ, of Paul. You will find no-one whose goal was popularity and no-one whose goal was to have a good time. Their passion was to serve and if that meant ostracism or pain or death, so be it.

There is an additional consideration, however. The Bible teaches are sacred. It is they, rather than a church building, which house God's Spirit. The Lord counts our bodies so important that He will resurrect them for eternity. That God treasures our bodies should hardly surprise us. Christians may be required to endanger their bodies in times of persecution, or be specifically led to minister in dangerous places.

Muscial Excellence

Not through training, practice and effort. Not through righteous living, Bible study and prayer. *Through Him* involves more than performing in Jesus' name.

A horrifyingly large number of sincere church people falsely imagine they are serving Christ. They mumbled a prayer asking God's forgiveness through Jesus' shed blood and since then they have been virtually indistinguishable from true Christians. However, their certainty that they are forgiven, heaven-bound, born again Christians is nothing but a tragic delusion. Being good, clean-living, hard-working musicians in the best church does not guarantee we have been forgiven. Neither does believing the right doctrines. Adam's sin, with its cataclysmic results, was not mass murder, hideous perversion or demon worship. In fact, by human standards, it was two saints who were forever banished from Eden. It is blissfully easy to define sin a manner that make us feel good.

Many people, though they would never admit it, want to keep their favourite sin more than they want forgiveness. Though it would grieve God greatly, we will rot in any sin we deliberately choose to remain in. This would result in not only our music, but our entire lives being cut off from God. Imagine a head of state with the legal power to pardon anyone he chooses.

The Bible calls it repentance - a change of heart regarding sin; a genuine desire to surrender to God's holiness. Another heart attitude essential to salvation is our willingness to forgive others. God treats us the way we treat other people. Unforgiveness is sin.

Musical Sacrifice

This encourages us to realise how highly God values our musical praise. Consider how costly animal sacrifices were. Moreover, in Bible days, these animals were more than four-legged hamburgers. They were also tractors, trucks and threshing machines. And you could bet your bottom shekel, that forced the price up. Though a blind animal may not fetch the highest market price, it would be of significant value for slaughter. But since it was not the best possible specimen, it was unacceptable to God.

New Zealand senior music lecturer, John Cousins made 'spectacular' music at Britain's 1984 Edinburgh Festival by publicly urinating on drums. Surely your music is of more significance to God and our dying world than that! How many times more important than that insult to dignity would you rate your music ministry? One hundred times? One thousand? More? Then are you willing to be that many times more dedicated to your ministry than Cousins was to his questionable act?

If we are 'walking in the realm of the Spirit' we can hear the redeemed in heaven sing their songs 'and join in with them,' says Roberts Liardon. He implies that by this means, songs composed in heaven can become part of earth's repertoire. However, he adds that some compositions in heaven 'have not yet come to earth, because no man has yet paid the price for them'. You can remain sceptical like me. You can add that Christ has already paid the price. But it is undeniable that in terms of dying to self, resisting opposition, slogging on despite the pressure to slacken off, effective ministry is costly.

God delights to use the weak to astound the powerful; the unlearned to put intellectuals to shame. It is then obvious to everyone that God has acted. In most cases, however, the critical factor is not abilities or lack of them. Nor is it merely a question of knowing God. The issue is whether we place our confidence partly in our own abilities or solely in God.

It's a disturbing paradox that the closer we get to the musical excellence God deserves, the greater the likelihood that pride will nullify our ministry. The more we improve musically, the more diligently we have to fight the delusion that our dependency upon God is becoming less chronic., We were once certain we couldn't complete a single performance without God's miraculous intervention. Now, we're not so sure.

Ideal Musician

In James Montgomery's expert opinion, George Sandys' psalms were 'incomparably the most poetical in the English language, and yet they are scarcely known'. Genius alone is insufficient for an effective music ministry. Every Christian should musically extol the Creator. However, as we have scanned the pages of God's Word a picture is beginning to emerge of the person who specialises in the music ministry.

In the Old Testament, the main people with a ministry in music were Levites. There were probably no others engaged in this ministry full-time. Like the high priest himself, Levites did not volunteer for ministry, but were chosen by God. They were chosen solely on the basis of their parentage. Talent was not the critical factor. They were literally born for this specific ministry.

Just as we could not choose the human family we were born into, no amount of effort on our part can cause us to have a God-ordained ministry in music. It is not for us to decide to have a music ministry and then seek God's blessing upon it. Musical ability and a love of music are suggestive, but are not infallible proof, of God's calling. It's obviously futile to spend the rest of our lives wringing our hands, wondering whether God has called us. But neither should we be presumptuous. By all means, continue with music if you feel at peace about it, but keep your ear attuned to the Lord, being aware that in time He could lead you into another ministry.

The ideal musician:

1. delights in GOD's will

Consider spending every second of the rest of your

existence doing nothing but God's will. If that prospect seems a little cold, drab, claustrophobic, you have missed so much.

Do you believe God is all-powerful? Then you believe He could ask nothing of you that would be too hard for you. An omnipotent God could turn a mouse into a superman. It's exciting when God asks the impossible of you. A miracle is around the corner!

Do you believe God is all-knowing? Then you believe that in every situation you face, God knows all the facts - past, present and future - so much more than you could possibly comprehend. When God asks you to do something, He is granting you the unique privilege of tapping into the greatest Mind in the universe. You have the opportunity to so something infinitely wise.

Do you believe God's love is infinite? Then you believe God loves you more than you could possibly love yourself. Your welfare, joy and fulfilment mean more to Him than they do even to you. You can trust a God like that. You can revel in the extravagance of His desires for you.

If you truly believe in the infinity of God's knowledge, love and power, we will never disobey Him. We only disobey when we secretly believe we are smarter than God, that His love for us is inferior, or that He is so weak that our inadequacies can nullify His power.

Satan whispers, 'One little sin won't hurt,' or says about a particular issue, 'Obedience is too frightening/ painful.' He's really saying, 'The God who gave everything for you - even His own Son - doesn't have your best interest at heart. He doesn't know what's best for you. He will command you and then abandon you to your own frailty.'

To disobey our wonderful Lord is to foolishly believe a lie. In any circumstance, the will of God is the one thing you can do that you'll be forever thankful for.

God's will is an exciting manifestation of love. God revealing His will is the Almighty Lord expressing His desire for us to enjoy His very best. And obedience is us receiving that love, delighting and rejoicing in the beauty, perfection and security of God's yearnings for our welfare. Think of it: we need no longer be confounded by the finiteness of our own intelligence; Almighty God loves us so much that He grants us free access to His infinite wisdom and goodness! Obedience is love made real.

2. Is motivated, empowered and controlled by sacrificial, self-denying love

The Christian musician exists to serve. This is not some lofty ideal. It's basic. Fundamental. A servant's heart is essential for a fulfilled life. So much of Jesus' teaching revolves around this. He who loses his life will find it ... if you would be greatest be servant of all ... deny yourself ... It sounds morose. It's actually the secret of a joy-filled life. Love drives a musician to prune every trace of *unnecessary* offence from a performance so that only elements ordained and confirmed by God remain. Don't be surprised if God's leading varies from occasion to occasion. No-one knows the audience like the Lord.

3. Is devoted to prayerful common with god

Bible songs revealed an enormous range of prayers. Virtually every conceivable type of prayer is represented. The songs that the Lord so much approved of that they are included in Scripture, were the works of musicians for whom prayer was as natural as breathing, and more important than eating. The ideal musician understands prayer. For him/her, prayer is not a spiritual sheen added to give a ministry its finishing touch. Prayer is the structural framework around which the entire ministry is formed. You can achieve great worldly success without a word of prayer but Christian musicians are expected to move in the spiritual realm and in that realm you get nowhere without prayer.

Before he made his first album, Keith Green regularly included in his concerts a plea to the audience to pray for the production of the projected album. In addition, prayer teams were formed, praying constantly throughout every studio session. The result was the biggest debut album in the history of Christian recording to that time. He ensured that subsequent albums were also immersed in prayer.

4. Is filled with thankfullness and praise to god

To this general Scripture we can add many that specifically target those who specialise in music. David appointed the Levitical musicians 'to thank and praise the Lord'. This was the very reason for their existence. George Beverly Shea has sung *How great thou art* so many times you'd think he was striving for top billing in the Guinness Book of Records. In just one crusade, he sang this hymn, with choir backing, ninety-nine times. People kept asking for it. He humbly honoured their request.

5. Is Continually Spirit-filled

6. Has a prophetic ministry

Many psalms foretold future events. So did the song of Moses. This obviously makes them prophetic. The essence of prophecy, however, is not prediction, but God speaking through His servant. In prophecy, God frequently speaks in the first person, as He does in many psalms.

Even in inspired songs outside the Psalter, composers with prophetic ministries clearly predominate. Moses, Deborah, David, Isaiah, Habakkuk, and John all contributed to the Bible's songs and had obvious prophetic ministries. Miriam, too, was a prophetess. Moreover, the key Levitical musicians appointed by David - Asaph, Heman and Jeduthum - were all prophets. David placed these three Levites in charge of all the musicians, and the musical leaders came from their descendants. Scripture individually calls each of these three founders a 'seer', in other words, a prophet. Psalm 50, bearing the title 'a Psalm of Asaph,' is prophetic in that it can say 'God says' (cf the familiar prophetic expression, 'thus says the Lord').

When the Lord spoke prophetically to Jehoshaphat, it was through one of the 'sons of Asaph,' presumably a Levitical musician. *Prophets* in 2 Kings 23:2 becomes *Levites* in the parallel passage in 2 Chronicles 34:30, perhaps implying that all Levitical musicians were regarded as prophets. Jeremiah wrote laments that were apparently set to music. Almost every prophet burst into poetry. Of all seventeen prophetic Old Testament books, plus the highly prophetic books of Psalms and Revelation, only tiny Haggai and Malachi contain no poetry. Whether the poems were originally intended to be set to music we cannot always be certain. Music, however, seemed to play a critical role in the prophetic ministry of Elisha and the prophetic bands.

1 Chronicles 25, called by Johann Sebastian Bach 'the true foundation for all God-pleasing music,' describes David's appointment of Levitical musicians. This has to be a key passage for a Biblical understanding of the function

of music. In the span of just five verses, *prophecy* appears once, *prophesied* twice and *seer* once. That's four references in five key verses. We must be careful not to drain *prophecy* of its meaning just because it is used in relation to music. Music is the vehicle of the Spirit. If prophecy is as basic to God's plan for music as Scripture implies, then a brief analysis of its nature is too important to relegate to an appendix. For many years I was very mistaken about the nature of prophecy. Instead of careful analysis of the Scriptures, I was allowing my imagination and experience dictate to me.

Preaching is speaking about God. Prophecy is God speaking. It often foretells the future, not because this is an essential feature of Biblical prophecy, but because the Source of the utterance is the One who knows the future and the darkest secrets buried in the human heart. Godless soldiers blindfolded Jesus, hit him, and mocked, 'Prophesy who hit you.' These brutes were not asking for a Bible lesson! When prophesying, a person is the mouthpiece of the One who cannot be blindfolded. John called the book of Revelation, filled with predictions, a prophecy. *Revelation*'s letters to the seven churches, however, are also prophecy.

Even without the occasional foretelling, they clearly touch a dimension not reached by teaching or preaching. They are personal orders from the Commander and Chief of the church; the piercing words of the One who knows each church with divine knowledge. No wonder Paul said that if newcomers encounter prophecy the secrets of their hearts would be laid bare. This is why, when Jesus started telling the woman at the well things about her that only God could know, it immediately dawned that she was in the presence of a prophet.

The New Testament uses not just the same word to describe Old Testament prophecy and the gift we should be exercising today, but it clearly refers to the same phenomenon. It is not general exhortation, or the expounding of doctrine. It might be, 'Prepare for a famine,' or 'You have five husbands,' or 'I [the Lord] have this against you,' but it is the exact message God wants a certain group of people to hear at that specific time.

In most Christian circles, music is a form of communication either from people to people (such as testimonies and re-hashes of Bible truths) or from people to God (prayer and praise). But before we can begin to imagine our music conforms to the Biblical pattern, we must add a third dimension: from God to people (prophetic music).

Jimmy Owens was 'songwriter-arranger-conductor-producer' of Christian albums. He had made over a hundred when the Lord suddenly showed him he was on 'a colossal ego trip ... trying to build a name for myself in the name of the Lord'. He felt the Lord say that he and his wife should write nothing until they heard from him. One and a half years passed. Then they quickly achieved more for the Lord 'than in all our previous years of ministry combined'. Their secret: 'Hear what the Spirit is saying and let Him say it through you.'

Though the Owens' make no claim to a prophetic ministry, they believe that by being sensitive to the Spirit of God and listening to the ministry of others, they can discern what the Spirit is currently saying to the church. They can then, with the Spirit's empowering and direction, put that message into music. The result is not merely Scriptural truth, but that specific truth which the Spirit knows the church most needs to hear at that time.

Jesus shall reign where'er the sun is one of the greatest of all missionary hymns and yet, marvels mission historian Ruth Tucker, it was written virtually a life-time before the onset of the modern missionary movement. Though more than half a century ahead of its time, Isaac Watts' hymn was so powerful that it stayed in circulation decade after decade until the church finally caught up. How ever did he achieve such a feat? Because his hymn writing was based not on contemporary Christian thought but on the eternal word of God. He was paraphrasing Scripture.

Steve Camp claims most Christian musicians know more about music than about Jesus and they spend more time developing their music than their theology. Camp, who initially focused his music on Christian entertainment, asserts that Christian musicians cannot avoid the grave responsibilities of being teachers merely by labelling themselves Christian entertainers. If the average young person spends more time listening to music than to teachers, parents and pastors, the message in that music assumes great importance.

7. The Bible calls the Levites 'Israel's teachers'.

Billy Graham's personal gift is clearly the spoken word, not music. Yet in a foreword to a book that had nothing to do with music he advised Christians 'to continually be reading and meditating in at least three books: the Bible, the hymnal, and a Christian biography.' But before getting too excited, take a second look at that quote. He said not hearing or singing, but *reading and meditating*. Are your lyrics worthy of this?

Popular songs with questionable theology are said to have 'contributed to the eventual official acceptance of unscriptural practices in the Roman Catholic Church.'

Bishop Wordsworth provides with an astonishing example of what not to do. In his hymn paraphrasing 1 Corinthians 13, he says that neither faith nor hope will remain, only love! One young man, who had written a number of Christian songs, discarded them after a few months at Bible college. The Bible-training had exposed deficiencies in his lyrics.

8. Is Christ-centred

The Bible speaks of songs which focus so much upon God that they are referred to by such expressions as 'the Lord's song'. Animal sacrifice was the focal point of all temple activity. Everything else (music included) served this. Bernard Manning speaks of Charles Wesley's 'obsession with the greatest things', citing as proof the fact that in one on his hymnbooks, one in every nine hymns begins with the name Jesus, Christ or Saviour.

9. Lives a disciplined Life

The Levitical musicians were chosen on the basis of birth, not natural affinity for music. For many of them it must have been a hard slog. And these musicians had to be available for ministry, not only when they felt inspired, but 'day and night'. That meant discipline. Alan J. Lerner had a bit of trouble writing the lyrics to *On a clear day you can see forever*. In fact, it took him three hours a day, seven days a week for eight months. Before he was happy with the result he had written and discarded ninety-one complete sets of lyrics. And he wasn't even writing for the Lord of glory. That's discipline.

Self-discipline is the power factor in a person's life. It is the quality that enables you to maximise your every gift. It means being persistent and consistent; punctual, reliable, committed. Without it you are like someone frantically try to bring life-giving water to a thirsty world, using a bucket with gaping holes. An undisciplined person is his/her own saboteur. This folly left the one-talent man a no-talent man.

There is a law that can be expressed in a formula something like this:

Divine Input X Talent X Discipline = Achievement

Regardless of talent, if discipline equals zero, achievement equals zero. If discipline equals ten, your output is ten times greater, ten times more valuable, than if you had one unit of discipline.

How could your talent move the heart of God? Talent is God's gift to you. Disciplined effort is your gift to God.

Don't think of discipline as fleshly self-effort able to be dispensed with by a spiritual experience. On the contrary, discipline in its purest form is itself the product of a spiritual experience. It is the blending of two of the fruit of the Spirit - patience (better translated perseverance) and self-control.

Without God, however, even the most beautiful quality turns ugly. Leave Him out of the equation and apparent faithfulness becomes a faithless struggle; what should be an expression of love becomes proud self-effort.

Discipline must spring from a heart brimming with thankfulness for the undeserved kindness of God that has cleansed it. Effort must be lovingly, joyously yielded to God. It must not be a vain attempt to win divine or human approval, but a natural response to the realisation that through Christ we already have divine approval - and that's the only approval that matters.

10. Has leadership qualties

Singers tended to lead processions. They might not necessarily have planned the route, but they went out in front and set the pace. Unimpressed? That's because you see the procession as a peace-time ritual. What if that procession were an act of war? You might think twice about leading Jehoshophat's march. God's singers put themselves in the line of fire. If the church and the devil were in some sort of truce it would matter little who stands in front. But each church service should be an advance against dark and hostile forces. Eternal destinies hang in the balance.

The leadership abilities of the temple musicians is obvious from the following Scripture, referring to repairs made to the temple during Josiah's reign:

> '... The Levites - all of whom were expert with musical instruments - had charge of the burden bearers and supervised all the workmen from job to job. ...'

The Levitical musicians were literally foreman material.

Christian musicians are leaders, not performers. They seek not to win the acclaim of spectators, but to bring fellow believers into a greater awareness of the Lord's presence, a deeper love for God, an increased ability to worship, a heightened sensitivity to the Spirit, a more accurate understanding of spiritual truth, and a fuller manifestation of Spirit-led unity. What a privilege!

The psalms place much emphasis upon worshipping God, not just alone, but in congregations. The need for this to be done 'decently and in order' immediately highlights the importance of leadership.

One of the greatest achievements of a good leader is the unification of the body of people, empowering them to pull together in the same direction. Scripture stresses the importance and immense potential of a congregation spiritually moving as one. Music - especially congregational singing - can accomplish this like perhaps nothing else can. When singing, everyone is actively involved in, and focusing on, the same thing. Diverse emotions will be represented in almost any congregation - joy, grief, apathy, solemnity, and so on. Yet even these will begin to merge as the music continues.

Leadership through music is so subtle it often goes unnoticed; yet so powerful it will be acknowledged for all eternity. The original text of Jesus' powerful promise regarding corporate prayer contains the Greek word *symphoneo*.

If the unity achieved when an instrumental or choral group flows together, is an excellent picture of the type of unity Jesus had in mind, why not actually use music to achieve that goal? There is yet another seldom-noticed contribution of music to unity. Noting that most denominational hymnals include the works of writers from very diverse denominations, the hymn book has been called 'the greatest argument for church unity ever printed'.

Writers of congregational songs have the responsibility of assisting large numbers of people to voice their spiritual feelings, enabling them to sing 'with understanding' without the frustration of groping for appropriate words. On the other hand, worship leaders have the even greater responsibility of selecting the exact songs that best meet each person's immediate need to express himself/herself. Since only God knows the exact needs of each person, it is obvious how dependent a song leader is upon divine guidance. Song selection is a huge responsibility. It actually shapes people's communion with the King of kings.

Song leaders have immense power. In seconds they can change the entire mood of a congregation. They can greatly assist, or hinder, the work God's Spirit wishes to do. Like the smell of food luring a nervous church-mouse out of its hole, music can coax hardened, hurting or timid souls to tentatively reach out to the God they desperately need. Yet, at this crucial time, the slightest distraction - just one discordant note - and those tentative creatures will instantly retreat to the dark hole they've been in.

Even self-conscious worshippers may slowly open up to God under the warmth of Spirit-led musicians, who are constantly filling the congregation's hearts with reasons to trust, love and worship their Lord. Yet just one musician's slip - even an inappropriate change of volume or tempo - can almost be like bursting into the privacy of timid lovers, jolting them into awkward self-consciousness. The ever-strengthening link between heaven and earth will have snapped and many people will have to start almost from scratch again.

Whoever has the power to lead a congregation into a greater sensitivity to the Spirit, has the power to destroy that experience. Regrettably, though it may take many musicians to create a perfect atmosphere, it only takes one to shatter it.

'I'm so afraid of power,' confided Keith Green in his private journal. The famous song-writer and recording artist confessed to 'my fleshly desire to rule others. In my heart of hearts I only want serve! ... I want more than anything else to pour myself out for them, for Jesus. But then there's my old nature that wants to control everything ...'

Ideally, only those having such a fear should be entrusted with leadership. In practice, at least one survey has suggested that even in churches, there is a tendency for power to be seized by those who lust for it. That should make us all fear. Christlike leaders are servants, not celebrities. Their task is not so much to bless people as to lead them to the One who can really bless them. Their joy is not in reaching inaccessible heights, but in making those heights accessible to everyone. A leader of God's people must:

1) know where God wants His people to go
2) know how to get there
3) have the courage and faith to take God's people there.

What a spiritually demanding task that is!

Wisdom

Leadership and wisdom are allies. Solomon, for example, sought wisdom in order to effectively lead God's people. He knew that it is through wisdom that 'princes rule, and nobles, even all the judges of the earth'. Another product of his wisdom, however, was one thousand and five songs. Not only does Scripture mention Solomon's songwriting when describing his wisdom, there is evidence that all four people with whom his wisdom is compared might have had musical ability.

Perhaps the bond between wisdom and the ideal musician is greater than is first apparent. According to our western view, wisdom's strongest link would probably be with musical leadership and song-writing. The Hebrew conception of wisdom, however, stretches beyond ours to include artistic skill.

11. Has strong faith

Strong faith is also a prerequisite for being a spiritual leader, as demonstrated when the singers went in front of Jehoshaphat's army, taking the most dangerous position, when approaching three hostile armies of formidable strength. Faith is a vital ingredient is prophesying, and, in fact, in every aspect of the Christian life.

12. Is holy

Of all the peoples on the globe, just one nation was holy unto God. In the midst of this nation was a small minority who stood out as being holier than the rest of God's holy people. Yet even within the Levites, the holiest tribe of the holy nation, was a tiny minority who were holier still. Whereas some Levites lived in secular areas, some in Levitical cities, and some in the holy city, the singers were assigned to the temple itself. Most of God's people occasionally visited the Lord's House and a few ministered in it, but those involved in holy music actually lived there. Even priests could be temporarily unclean, but no-one in that condition could dwell in the temple. To reside in that holy place, would demand a very strict, dedicated life.

2 Chronicles 5:12 tells us the musicians were clothed in white linen. Perhaps it is significant that in Revelation 19:8 linen clothing is explained as being symbolic of righteousness. In 2 Chronicles 20:21 we find an expression that is open to several interpretations, but it may mean that the singers were in 'holy array'. Singing godly songs without living a godly life is futile.

Their songs were from God Himself. Their dedication to sacred music was probably faultless; their musical skills impeccable. But wrong living had nullified their entire ministry. To human ears, the music would sound the same. But to God, what should have been the loveliest strains in the universe, were as hideous as a choir of pneumatic jackhammers. And soon the whole word would know it. The pursuit of holiness may be far from painless but, like salvation and everything else in the spiritual life, it grows from our faith-relationship with the Lord, not self-effort.

13. Shines with unearthlly humility

We have noted that for generations the Levites were little more than labourers and servants of the priests. Even when they entered their musical ministry they were positioned on the east side of the altar, the very side where the ashes and offal were flung. The world and its music industry want 'stars'; Christ and His church want servants. 'Stars' are parasites squandering their talents as they wallow in accolades. Servants are benefactors who roll up their sleeves and get things done.

The world may call egotists 'stars', but they are really black holes, sucking in people's money, self-esteem and talent. Servants are the real stars; suns that brighten, release and empower the lives of those around them. Humble people are spiritually fit; liberated from the excess flab of an inflated ego. They are spiritually perceptive, enjoying heaven's lofty view of reality; seeing things from God's perspective, in contrast to the narrow, gutter level view of an egotist whose eyes can focus on little beyond himself. Egotists are bombed out of their brains by self-delusion.

To many of us humility sounds dull, limp, shrivelled, sickly; pride sounds expansive, vibrant, dazzling, powerful. Nothing could be further from reality. The virtue is so tarnished that we almost need another word. Those endowed with this power are but bold realists who storm to the finish line while egotists are still preening themselves. Humility is a gleaming, high-powered sports car under wraps; pride is a beaten-up wreck under tinsel. Those who humble themselves will be exalted, promises Scripture. This secret weapon operates in numerous natural and supernatural ways. One of them springs from the fact that humble people do not imagine they have 'arrived'. As a result they heed good advice and continue to improve long after the proud have peaked.

Jimmy and Carol Owens' most popular songs, such as *Freely, Freely* from their musical *Come Together,* would never have been written had the Lord not convicted them of the pride that was keeping them from writing such 'simple' songs. There was an enormous cost to the ego for Jimmy to write like that. There's a place for sophisticated and complex music but our Lord reserves a special place for those who humble themselves. Millions of people have been blessed on earth because Jimmy Owens' won his painful battle with pride. Jimmy, however, will be blessed eternally.

14. Has a dynmamic Relationship with god

To follow in the footsteps of 'the sweet psalmist of Israel' we would need more than an abundance of creative musical skill. Even if, in addition to David's musical genius, we had his extensive theological understanding, we would still be hopelessly deficient. We would have to match his beautiful, patient, forgiving spirit, his humility, faith, intense yearning for God, desire for personal holiness and his eagerness to obey the Lord. These are the fruit of a genuine relationship with the living God.

The ideal musician is living proof that the Lord is a mighty, prayer-answering, promise-keeping God. It is noteworthy that the four thousand musicians appointed by David were all aged thirty or over. Consider also the implications of Paul's instruction that a church leader must be what the Good News Bible calls 'mature in the faith'.

15. Has the ideal song

Its every aspect - the writing, arranging, selecting for the occasion, and the performance - is accomplished with a heavy dependence upon the Spirit of God. Both the words and music are enticing and relevant, not just to people in general but to the specific audience on the occasion it is sung. How past generations or out-of-earshot contemporaries would respond is irrelevant.

The words are so well formed and the message so vital that, like Scripture's songs, they would have an effective ministry even without music. The music, too, is so good that it could stand alone. Additionally, tune and words come together as the perfect fit, with, ideally, not one syllable or note seeming a little forced or out of place. Not only does the music - through volume, tempo and so on - not inhibit the words, it highlights the words and adds meaning to them. It arouses within the people a longing to hear the song (and hence the message) over and over. It engenders appropriate emotion, lifting them towards the attitude appropriate to the occasion (thankfulness, praise, joy, awe, repentance etc.), causing people to be more responsive to the lyrics. It seeds the words into the hearers' mind and heart, causing the song and its message to erupt in their minds long after the music has stopped.

The ideal song moves people to respond to God in the way He wants them to respond at that particular time - perhaps to have faith in Him, yield to Him, praise Him, pray to Him, love Him, unburden themselves, appropriate His gifts, or repent. It combines personal experience with Scriptural truth. Some elements of the experience might be foreign to the hearers (it might, for example, be more extreme than what they have personally gone through) but its nature and presentation is so meaningful to the hearers that it touches their own fears, longings, anguish or joy. The Scriptural truth linking it so hits the hearers that they see it as powerful, relevant and life-changing.

It preferably mentions not just 'God' - a word that could mean almost anything to people outside the church - but identifies the true God by focusing upon His only Son, Jesus Christ, the Lord and Saviour of the human race. Above all, the ideal song is God's choice at the exact moment and location in which it is sung. It might even be so divinely tailored to that particular occasion and audience that, like many sermons and most specific prayers, it is never used again.

16. Is committed to christ, not to popularity

Scriptures references to a 'new song' reveal that in the heart of God is a continual yearning for the new. To fulfil this divine longing we must cut loose from the tyranny of old songs and let the fresh winds of the Spirit blow us wherever He wills. Sadly, this will upset traditionalists, just as Jesus and all his Spirit-led followers have always offended those who worship a god frozen in time, instead of Creator God who is forever doing a new thing. However, we must not confuse true spirituality with worldly fashion or with a lust for change. We must be like the Israelites on route to the promised land who moved whenever, and only when, God's cloud moved.

Jesus is 'the same yesterday, today and forever,' but those who would misuse this truth to excuse a retreat into the past must remember that yesterday Jesus was dynamic and controversial. He made a whip and overturned the tables of tradition. And He's the same today. We must cling to Christ. That alone distinguishes a Christian musician, not the fact that Christ's name appears in the music.

Commercial success may demand a commitment to 'the market'. Success in your church may demand a commitment to the status quo. But spiritual success requires fearless commitment to Jesus Christ. The result might be glorious music that few people appreciate.

17. Might be female

The Scriptures amply testify to the significant contribution women can make to both secular and religious music. In fact, Strabo, as a foreign observer of Palestinian music, singled out female, rather than male, singers for his exceptionally high praise. 1 Chronicles 25:5-6 reads as though Heman's daughters, along with his sons, were appointed, '... for song in the house of the Lord, with cymbals, psalteries, and harps, for the service of the house of God.'

This interpretation is supported by many Bible scholars. If correct, it is quite surprising because other temple ministries appear to have been restricted to male Levites. Female singers were amongst the Jewish refugees returning from their Babylonian exile. Some scholars believe they were temple singers. In both Nehemiah and Ezra, temple musicians are grouped with the Levites several verses prior to the reference to female singers.Instead of being included with the temple musicians, the 'male and female singers' are mentioned immediately after 'male and female slaves,' just before a list of the beasts of burden. This suggests that these particular singers were slaves, not temple choristers. The use of musical slaves was no doubt accentuated by the fact that radios and stereos were rare in those days. In addition to entertainment, such slaves may have been in great demand in times of mourning.

Miriam led only her sex in triumphant singing and dancing. In contrast, Judith, the key figure in a Jewish apocryphal book, led both sexes in song and dance. Deborah's musical leadership, as outlined in the book of Judges, probably fell mid-way between these two. She joined Barak in song and is actually mentioned before him, suggesting she may have taken the dominant musical role. The account of Sisera's mother in the last portion of the song has been cited as suggesting feminine authorship. In fact, Bishop Hervey suggested that, relative to Moses and Miriam, the roles were reversed, with Barak leading a male chorus *in response to* Deborah's song.

So it is certain that in Scripture women had important roles in secular and religious music. Whether temple music was included is not quite as clear. If this one barrier to female musicians did exist, however, it surely met the same fate as the temple veil, rent asunder when Jesus died. The only possible restriction would seem to be the New Testament directive that women should not exercise authority over men.

Of many nineteenth-century women could it be said, 'Preachers, theologians and Bible scholars, who would not permit a woman to speak or teach in a worship service, week after week sang her hymns and profited by her ministry.'

18. Is integrated into the body of christ int he exact manner prescribed by god

There is no 'ideal musician'. But there is a way to compensate for our deficiencies. Someone with a music ministry obviously must relate to the other musicians in his group. This, in itself, can provide fertile soil for the fruit of the Spirit to grow. It usually proves to be a wonderful, God-given opportunity for love, patience and self-control to mushroom, as we teeter on the brink of mortal combat, squabbling over musical arrangements and the like!

It was when the trumpeters and singers were in unison, that the cloud of God's glory filled Solomon's new temple. However, a musician also needs to relate properly to people with such diverse ministries as faith, prayer, theological insight, administration, financial support, encouragement, correction, cleaning, welcoming people, and so on. Even those who merely sit in rapt attention have a significant role to play. A musician's contribution to a meeting must blend with every part of the meeting. This involves being in harmony with every other person contributing to the meeting.

But we dare not imagine everything revolves around the music ministry, or even around our particular church. Musicians should look for opportunities to assist other ministries, wherever they are. For example, would a tiny gathering of intercessors be lifted by the mere addition of your singing voice to their feeble attempt to sing?

Using words as a brush, Jesus painted a now-famous masterpiece. On the canvas of our minds, we see two dedicated, God-ordained leaders. One was leaving Jerusalem, probably on his way home after having admirably completed sacred temple ministries. The other was perhaps hurrying towards the holy city to worship and serve the God he loved. An inspiring sight - except they abandoned a fellow countryman, leaving him to squirm in a pool of blood.

The hypocrisy of devout first century Jews is frightening. Their whole lives were dedicated to the study and out-living of God's Word. Their zeal was indisputable. No amount of effort seemed too much for them; no detail too small. How could such committed people see so clearly and be so blind; be so right and yet so wrong? Respected religious leaders murdered their Saviour as an act of religious devotion. The magnitude of God's forgiveness, the expression of His boundless love, is equalled by His power to make us victorious.

Perhaps the Lord has blessed our music even though we are conscious of areas in our lives which we have deliberately not submitted to God. We should note, however, that God's present kindness is intended to lead us to a change of heart. If that doesn't work the Lord has other ways of getting our attention! We are right in putting much emphasis on being in tune musically, but do we put sufficient emphasis upon being in tune with the Lord? And we dare not forget that our relationship with God is inseparably linked to our relationship with people. As John poignantly put it, everyone who loves the Father will love His children.

James exposed the total inconsistency of imagining we can use the same voice to both bless God and slander someone made in the image of God. So do we seek diligently to be in harmony with fellow musicians, or merely in tune with their instruments and voices? And let's not overlook other relationships. Are we, for example, neglecting family responsibilities? Is there something we haven't put right with someone? Is there anyone we haven't forgiven?

Grappling with the issues already raised seems sufficient to keep anyone busy for several life times. Yet, there are still further considerations. (Fortunately, He who dwells within you is exceedingly powerful!) Have you sought God to ensure that the amount and nature of your practice sessions is in full accord with His will for you? Do you give proper priority to being spiritually prepared for your ministry? Prayer makes practice perfect.

Down through the ages, people have noted that almost any trivia can be put to a good tune and people will happily sing it. How far beyond trivia are your songs? We can even love our ministry too much. Our deepest yearning must be to love and exalt the Lord Jesus. Both Isaiah and Amos prophesied the ruin of people who were more devoted to music than they were to the Lord.

The Christian musician's devotion to God should parallel the psalmist's attitude to God's city:

> 'If I forget you, O Jerusalem, let my right hand forget [its musical skill]. If I do not remember you,let my [singing] tongue cleave to the roof of my mouth; If I prefer not Jerusalem above my chief joy.'

Judson Cornwall tells of a talented violinist who surrendered alluring scholarships to follow God's calling. As a missionary, however, he seized opportunities to give Christian concerts. Several times he felt the Lord telling him to abandon his violin altogether. Yet he persisted, arguing that his music would be an asset to his future ministry. Surely it would be irresponsible to discard his obvious talent.

Eventually, God spoke so firmly that he knew no amount of rationalising or bargaining would work. He quit his violin forever. As a result of this obedience, the Lord used that missionary in a powerful way to touch the lives of thousands of people.

Enabling Sprit

God has things in His heart 'He has never given to anybody before because everybody is so busy cloning everybody else,' says Winkie Pratney. To illustrate, he cites the scene he witnessed in a camp where 'God was pouring out His Spirit in incredible ways' upon many teenagers. A girl got up, eyes closed, walked to the piano, sat down and started to play.

Biblical revelation leads us to expect God to at least occasionally endow people with powers beyond their natural abilities. Scriptural instances of supernaturally empowered physical strength, speed, stamina, sight, and speech. To the list of biblical miracles of interest to musicians, we could add divinely bestowed knowledge, wisdom, ability to hear heavenly things, manual dexterity, and artistic skill. These were not native abilities. Some of them occurred just once in a person's life.

Consider the implications if such acts of God were channelled into music. Imagine a flutist playing along with heavenly music she is divinely allowed to hear; a guitarist with supernaturally heightened speed or dexterity; a composer soaring beyond his natural talent under the inspiration of the same God who gave David his psalms, Solomon his wisdom, and Paul his revelations.

If our Lord can give a 'human' voice to an ass, He can give a beautiful singing voice to anyone. The God who taught David's hands 'to war' can instantaneously teach anyone's hands to play an instrument. We are forced to acknowledge the theoretical validity of this. With God all things are possible, and He delights in using unskilled people to put the skilled to shame.

It was mid 1966. Several hundred Pakistanis had gathered in Hyberabad to farewell their beloved Australian missionary. At the end of the meeting, the guest of honour, Rev. Geoffrey Bingham, was asked to close in prayer. He arose to do just that, but instead, he found himself singing.

Somewhat surprised, he sang with transcended ability about Christ suffering on the cross and of the love of the Father and encouraged those present to go on in Christ. Though not sure what his next words would be, his song continued for probably more than ten minutes. An American Episcopal Bishop expressed his amazement, wondering how Rev. Bingham had fit the words into the tune. Both missionaries realised that it was not the usual type of Christian music sung in Pakistan, but the significance escaped them.

In contrast, most of the Pakistanis had tears in their eyes. Not only were they deeply moved by the words, the melody had touched them as well. 'How did you learn our music?' they asked, astonished to hear such music coming from a westerner. They explained that it was the type of music associated with Urdu folk songs which were a thousand years old.

The Spirit of God had not only spoken, He had chosen the perfect melody with which to whisk those words deep into Pakistani hearts. Rev. Bingham is well aware of the tendency for us to unconsciously reproduce tunes we have heard before. Nevertheless, this highly perceptive and intelligent man is convinced that such an explanation of this event is hopelessly inadequate.

Heaven's interest in music extends far beyond song-writing. 'Sometimes, after prayer and fasting, God would anoint me at a practice and show me things on the guitar I'd never done before,' said Stewart Wissell, speaking of his experiences when a member of the gospel group 'Emmanuel.' 'It's as if the Holy Spirit would take control of my mind and hands and put patterns in my guitar playing which I never knew could be done. Even in live concerts this would often happen.'

Mrs. Hall scribbled in the choir loft during her pastor's lengthy prayer. The result was the hymn 'Jesus paid it all'. She showed it to her pastor, who had no difficulty finding a tune. Another church member had written some music and handed it to him. The two matched perfectly. While in Southern Africa, David Pawson wrote a hymn, based on part of the book of Habakkuk. He searched for a suitable tune and could only find one.

Some time later, he visited a church in England. To his amazement, he discovered they had felt led to learn this very tune. They knew nothing about his song. Not having any words, they used to merely hum the melody, in blind obedience to the Spirit's leading. Pastor Pawson had the words the Lord was preparing them for.

Until now, it had apparently been merely an unusual coincidence. But this time, it was a deliberate choice on Brett's part. And everyone knew it.

Brett had a very wide repertoire, including several dozen original songs. Despite this, and knowing that the worn-out hymn had already been ridiculously over-exposed, this young man announced that he felt led of God to sing it yet again! It was Brett's home church. He would have to live with this for a long time. That morning, during his usual time with the Lord, he was reminded that his purpose was not to entertain, but to minister to people, as God's Spirit directed. That clinched it for Brett. He would face the fireworks. There was only one way for him - God's way.

Here was a man God could trust with a snippet of His infinite knowledge. God's direction did not have to make human sense before he would step out in obedience. He had the courage to take up God's challenge. The song completed, Pastor Andrew Evans arose to preach. His text was none other than the parable of the man who built his house upon the rock. So accurately did his sermon fit the song, that Pastor Evans deliberately read verbatim a portion of his typed notes to demonstrate how he and Brett had independently chosen exactly the same theme. It was fitting that Brett be honoured in front of the whole congregation, in whose presence he had risked humiliation.

A life-long dependence

Music which on one occasion assists, will on a similar occasion, hinder. God alone can differentiate. Invitational songs have often been used to bring people to a life-changing decision. But not always. Teenager, George Beverly Shea, came under conviction many times. Each time, however, he would release his pent-up emotions by heartily singing the invitational hymn with the congregation, thus delaying his spiritual pilgrimage.

Background music has sometimes been most helpful, but some people could react so violently to this 'attempt to manipulate emotions' that the music ends up hindering the Spirit's work. At times Billy Graham has chosen not to use music when people in his crusades are making a decision for Christ. No matter how experienced we become in the use of Christian music, we never lose our dependence upon the Spirit's leading.

The Lord whispers His directions to those who sincerely seek Him. But Scripture teaches it is far better to have never received a revelation than to hear and not obey. And why should God even bother to share His secrets with musicians too inflexible or tradition-bound to respond to them? The Bible records times when people sought the Lord's guidance in vain. Knowing they were rebellious, God refused to answer them. So let's rid ourselves of hindrances and enter the exciting realm of Spirit-led ministry.

Divine love is a compelling reason for God valuing our efforts. Here is another: God created our creativity. Our raw natural abilities are as much a product of God's creativity as any music He could ever compose. He could not deny our (consecrated) creative efforts without denying His own creative skill in making us. Some people's claim to divine inspiration produces such mediocrity that it seems an excuse for laziness or, more likely, a failure to see the gap in the 'all of God, none of me' half-truth. Self must die - sinful selfishness, independence, pride and trying to earn heaven's approval. And we must yield everything to Christ, acknowledging that His ways are higher than our's. But to go so far beyond this that we renounce and denigrate our divinely-created mental and physical powers is as unchristian as gnostic heretics who taught that everything physical is of the devil.

Paul's ministry was an astounding mixture of hardship (torture, deprivation, shipwreck) and miracles (healings, earthquake, snakebite survival, blinding of Elymas' eyes). Likewise, your music should be a peculiar mixture of the natural (plain hard work) and the supernatural (divine intervention). The same passage of Scripture that emphasises the prophetic (ie supernatural) side of music, also points to the existence of a training system. During her 'musical visions', Frances Ridley Havergal, for the most part was content merely to marvel at what she was hearing. At times, however, she applied her mind to composing along with the ethereal music, predicting, and in fact *willing* the next sequence.

That our Lord wants us to be submissive but active partners is His work, not mindless robots, is demonstrated in the penning of Scripture. In the original language, the individual style of each human writer is very obvious. It is truly the Word of God, yet the Lord ordained it that each sentence bears the imprint of the human writer. He chose to use, rather than over-ride, the individual personalities of the writers. If this is so for Scripture, which is more God-inspired than anything we could produce, it will be true for even our most Spirit-filled music.

A man and a woman in love long for a union, the natural result of which is offspring that are neither entirely the man's, nor the woman's, but bear the unmistakable marks of both. That union, Scripture boldly declares, has a spiritual parallel. Though this initially shocks our impure minds, it rings true. The human desire to express love in this manner was placed within us by the One who fashioned us in His image. The inexhaustible creativity of God longs, through our union with Him, to birth within us unique and wondrous things, bearing the image, not just of one partner, but of both Him and us.

A musician and an instrument unite to produce sounds which neither would produce without the other. We are living instruments fashioned by the divine Instrument Maker with greater sophistication than any man-made instrument, having our own creativity. Like an instrument maker with his cherished instrument, our Maker longs to blend His ability with ours to produce unique sounds to bless the world. So, both to express His unfathomable love for us and to display His own genius in creating us, the omnipotent Lord treasures our contribution. But because that same love yearns for intimacy with us and that same creativity forever craves new expression, the Almighty longs to couple His supernatural ability with our natural effort to birth something as unique and as precious as is a child to its loving parents. The product of this supernatural union will be in one sense human, in another sense divine; an earthly song glowing with heavenly glory.

Let's clarify the often misunderstood role of human effort. As a proud attempt to earn salvation, good works are abhorrent. Wrong attitudes turn good works sour. As an expression of loving submission to God, however, sweat is beautiful. For the Spirit-filled Christian in divine submission, human exertion and divine enabling are not opponents but allies. View inspiration and effort not as an incompatible mix of oil and water but as bricks and mortar. They merge to build a monument of love for the glory of God - glory that His father-heart longs to share with us.

Electronic breakthroughs have irrevocably changed the scene for Christian musicians. As never before, earth's best music is available to almost everyone. This is good, to the extent that it motivates us to raise our standards. If it means people can be more effectively ministered to, it is marvellous. Yet it is a tragedy if it causes any of us to feel so out-classed that we fail to pursue our God-given ministry. Even such big names as Andraé Crouch have been sorely tempted to quit, feeling they have nothing to contribute. We need to stubbornly resist such temptations.

Prior to this century, deliberately teaching a congregation a song, was more powerful than performed music in engraving a message upon human minds. As they went about their daily work, they could not be followed by a choir. Only their memories could go with them. Now, recordings are almost as portable, and certainly more reliable than, memories. And people can hear recorded music over and over, learning songs without conscious effort. In effect, this has increased the power of performed music. Regrettably, these electronic developments have caused a corresponding increase in competition from secular music.

Do we produce music to make money, or to seriously challenge worldly music in the battle for minds? That catchy jingle from the television commercial and that godless song on the radio constantly threatens to push godly music out of Christian minds. How much money are we going to demand from our brothers and sisters before permitting them access to a viable alternative to ungodly music? There are no universal rules.

Bible-believers know that God is forever taking His people from strength to strength and from glory to glory. In the midst of a decaying world, 'the people who know their God will be strong and do exploits.'The path of the just is as a shining light, that shines more and more unto the perfect day.' The darker this world gets, the brighter God's people will shine.

With such truths jumping for joy in minds, it's hard to imagine the quality of godly music fizzling out as we approach this planet's greatest hour. Surely we won't be bereft of the best and be left with drab, inferior music with which to herald our King's coming. How fitting for mortal music to triumphantly attain its highest glory as the climax of the ages hastens towards us.

Is your Lord calling you to be part of this - to yield yourself to Him so that He can inspire you to hitherto unimagined heights of musical excellence? Let's shed the deadweights of doubt, conformity and mediocrity, and soar with our Lord to new heights, to the praise of his glory.

6

Modernity in Traditional Music

It was modern times that invented the very concept of traditional music, as we know it today. The term has evolved over the years: we have moved successively from country to popular, from popular to folk, then from folk to traditional. At the beginning of the nineties, the traditional music movement was caught up by another musical wave which has its origins in England: the "world-music" phenomenon.

As part of the identity of each region and as a universal artistic language, traditional music lies at the heart of European stakes. For, indeed, if its deep roots in a localized culture, in a historical tradition, enable it to contribute to the blossoming of cultural diversity, its plasticity renders it capable of nourishing the richest of dialogues between the various cultures. It therefore forms one of the cultural areas that is best adapted to achieving the objectives set out in the Treaty on European Union, in other words, to contribute "to the blossoming of the cultures of the Member States with respect for their national and regional diversity, while bringing the common cultural heritage to the fore" and to the creation of an "increasingly closer union between the peoples of Europe".

Developing co-operation at a European level in this area seems all the more necessary to us since European cultural diversity (and therefore the vitality of traditional music) is increasingly under threat from the growing rule of economism (which transforms any culture into saleable goods) and its corollary, cultural standardization.

In France the traditional music and dance domain is little-known. Let us judge its importance through these few figures:

— 5,000,000 records and cassettes sold in one year (through ten or so specialized labels, and several tens of private productions).

— 2,500,000 annual spectators.

— 10,000 annual stagings (from the cafe-concert, to the City of Paris Theatre show, via Occitan dance and Breton "fest-noz").

— 2,500 associations, spread throughout the land (from the village hall folk group to the folk-rock band, via "country", or immigrant community associations, contributing to the maintenance of social cohesion and cultural vitality.

— 2,500 professional musicians (800 groups), and 400 accompanying jobs.

— Several tens of thousands of amateur musicians, and several hundreds of thousands of dancers.

— A turnover generated of 700 million francs.

— In total, a sector chosen by 11% of the public, i.e. in the forefront of the cultural domain (survey by the French Culture ministry on culture enthusiasts).

A sector, furthermore, in the process of genuine growth: carried on the crest of the wave of the so-called "world" musicians, and by the increasing need of the public to put down roots, today it must respond to strong demand (whether it be in the area of education or distribution, support for research or for creativity), without having the means to react in a satisfactory manner.

Paradoxically, however, despite being the breeding ground for musical diversity, cheerfully exploited by all other musical forms, its success remains muted: little disseminated by the broadcasting media (no radio or television programme being specifically dedicated to it), it does indeed benefit from state institutional recognition which, however, struggles to be translated into hard cash: for example, it is the recipient of a budget granted by the French Culture ministry which is the equivalent of 1% of the budget dedicated to the Paris 1 Opera house alone. No doubt the specific history of the development of the French nation plays a certain role in this paradox ... in the land of "Enlightenment", a taste for traditions is always suspect. And the champions of official culture, typically Parisian, have always pigeon-holed the defenders of popular culture, provincial by nature, under the obscurantist label! It is therefore not unhelpful to carry out a historical account of this field, as well as of the various interest movements in terms of traditional music.

The diversity of the terms used to qualify "traditional popular music" reveals a complex history and a variety of ideologies: folklore, ethnic music, traditional, popular, folk-music, world-music, are all terms that bear the mark of the times in which they were born. Even if popular cultures were never really absent from learned culture, they took on renewed vigour with the arrival of romanticism. Furthermore, popular environments in their "original primitiveness" were at the heart of the concerns, sources of inspiration and objects of research.

In France, this movement appeared late and imitated German romantics who had already broken away from French classicism. Just like Herder's "naturpoesie" ideal, the XIX century was to abound in a wealth of literary production which contributed to the creation of regional stereotypes, that are still relevant today. At the same time, research became more organized: the publication of collections of songs, sometimes largely altered by their authors, delivered the treasures of "popular myth" to a wide public.

From 1852, the date of the FORTOUL decree that organized a vast collection of popular works from all over France, to the birth of recorded archives, numerous debates took place concerning the true nature of these collections. The musical material, thus gathered together, gave birth at the beginning of this century, to a specific musical genre in charge of " maintaining " traditions; it was the golden age of folk groups that asserted the identity of their territory, a link between the past and the present. Closer to us, in the 1970's, a new generation of researchers-musicians gave new life to the collections and to this music. Sometimes inspired by American folk songs, the folk movement brought together a young population, more interested in new musical sensations than in authenticity.

Finally, modern distribution methods and the explosion of the record industry at the time, authorized hitherto unheard of sound combinations and unexpected encounters. Even if world-music sometimes appears as a new humanism that avoids the crystallization of identities, it may also seem dangerous to others, since it levels out specific characteristics and leads to cultural standardization. Thus, traditional music has always managed to survive through the ages, thanks to its prodigious vitality. Jean-

François Dutertre, Director of the TMIC (Traditional Music Information Centre) / CIMT (Centre d'Information des Musiques Traditionnelles) is now going to show us how much they are at the heart of modernity.

From Folk to World Music

After having been confined for a long time to the confidentiality of scientific studies or to the regional practices of folk groups, traditional music came very much back into fashion from the 1970's onwards and was pushed to the fore of the artistic scene. Alongside particularly lively amateur playing, it developed a professional industry that brought together artists and groups, show and label producers.

Combined today with other popular forms, under the "world-music" label, it benefits from the burst of interest for this heterogeneous ensemble of musical expression that is characteristic of the 1990's. It is now classified along with "modern music" in the same way as jazz, rock or popular song. This proximity with decidedly contemporary musical genres means that traditional music has been endowed with an unexpected modern character.

Traditional Music and Modernity

It may seem strange to accord to traditional music a recognized degree of topicality and even more so to associate it with modernity. Topicality defines a form that is appropriate to its period. Modernity identifies inventive research, which, although situated in the continuation of the previous forms, claims to be innovative, or even in contradiction with or in revolt against previous approaches. The term traditional, on the other hand, refers to a concept that is deliberately anchored in the past. It is developed around an inheritance and therefore around a heritage that is scrupulously passed on — or at least in the illusion of it being scrupulously passed on. However, it was modern times that invented the very concept of traditional music, as we know it today.

The term has evolved over the years: we have moved successively from country to popular, from popular to folk, then from folk to traditional. Each of these terms covers an episode in cultural history and follows the dictates of the specific concerns of the period that uses them. Initially strictly limited to ancient popular expressions, the term used during each period has grown today into a more heterogeneous concept. It now includes popular oral traditions, but also learned traditions from beyond the Occident — and as much the native traditions as the non native expression from other countries, transported to a different social context by the constraints of immigration.

The Folk Movement

At the end of the 1960's, in the wake of the American folk song, French youth discovered its own traditional music. At the time Paris was the dwelling place of numerous American musicians, often at odds with their country due to their opposition to the Vietnam war. They served as a vehicle for an entire repertoire of traditional and political songs, the protest-songs, which were the work of a school of young singers from whence emerged Bob Dylan, Tom Paxton and Phil Ochs. All of them were influenced by their elders in the political struggle, singers who grew up with American socialism, such as Cisco Houston and Pete Seeger — grouped together around the emblematic figure of Woody Guthrie. Campuses trembled at the sound of the subversive texts denouncing the "masters of war". They had their Madonna in Joan Baez, whose warm voice interpreted both the ancient British ballads found in Kentucky and Dylan's most recent verses. The political struggle soon merged with the rediscovery of traditional song. In France, at the time, the movement benefited from an exceptional social context.

Traditional song was first perceived as popular. Its content was of little importance, what counted was to show the recall of an authentic art belonging to the people. This popular form of expression was even more highly regarded since it came from all areas of France and therefore stood in opposition to centralizing "bourgeois" culture. Furthermore, its rural origins reflected the myth of Nature, the movement where people returned to the countryside and the emergence of the ecological trend.

The return to nature and sexual freedom resided together in it with the traditional instruments brought into keeping with the style of the day and the ancient ballads sung around the fire. The general atmosphere of libertarian protest spread to the music. Learning took place through lending one's ear in the warm atmosphere of the "workshops" and training courses. Emphasis was placed on how easy it was to access and to implement: at last it was a true popular practice that had rid itself of the models of learned music and its inevitable notation. Preference was given to group work where the musical arrangements were the result of unwritten collective creation.

The public was encouraged to intervene directly in concerts by taking part in them, or even by dancing and their immediate reaction also determined how the show was put together. The anti-concert idea was predominant, thus linking the folk movement to contemporary theatre research at the time — let us remember the work carried out by the Living Theatre — as well as to the trend of complete shows, happenings, that mix music, theatre plastic arts, light shows, dance and cinema.

THE INSTITUTION'S CARD

At the beginning of the 1980's, the public began to desert the movement and turned towards other forms of music. Concert halls became empty and less records were sold. Musical associations reacted to the situation, which led to the appearance, amongst others, of a movement organized mainly around collecting and broadcasting musical traditions from Central France, "Les Musiciens Routiniers/ The Routine Musicians". The movement started in Lyon, expanded and became a federation. It was later responsible for a detailed study of traditions revolving around bagpipes and violins and for the creation of the Modal magazine.

The period was characterized by work that led to an increased awareness of the sector and its institutionalization. Indeed, the State finally took an interest in the sector. Meetings held in Ris-Orangis in 1981 led to the creation of an advisory Commission within the Ministry of Culture (Directorate of Music and Dance). The Commission included musical associations — and in particular the large regional associations, such as Dastum for Brittany, the UPCP for Poitou-Charentes or the Conservatoire of the Langue d'Oc region in Toulouse — musicians and researchers. A post for an inspector in charge of regional music was created. From this time onwards, the sector was therefore recognized by the authorities and disposed of a representative at the Ministry of Culture.

In 1985, the Commission led to the foundation of the Federation of Traditional Music Associations (FTMA that has today become the FTMDA, due to the essential addition of dance) as well as to the creation of traditional music centres in the regions. The latter came into existence by relying on structures that already existed and were labelled by the Ministry and signed an "objectives agreement" with the State. Research, training and distribution are all part of the regional centres' programme of activities. The creation, in 1992, of the Traditional Music Information Centre completes the picture. Little by little, the network was built up on French territory, directed according to a north-west / south-west axis and determined by the regions that had kept up a strong practice of traditional music and dance. The most urban regions have also seen a fast development of musical practices. The Rhône-Alpes region, but in particular the Ile de France (Paris region) have the strongest concentrations of artists devoted to world-music and intense distribution, thanks to both the large cultural facilities and the smaller places. It may be said that this is the result of a deliberate policy "of territorial development" through a network that is unique in Europe and that continues to pursue its actions today.

The World-music Wave

But at the beginning of the nineties, the traditional music movement was caught up by another musical wave which has its origins in England: the "world-music" phenomenon. The movement originally masked an economic concept, a marketing operation led by record companies that were determined to open up and protect a new market. Today, traditional music is to be found under the "world music" label, a notion that is even more heterogeneous than all of those that have been defined previously. This centrifugal current carries along in a jumble, ethnic and traditional music, learned traditional music from outside Europe, genres derived from traditional forms, popular urban music from five continents, light music and song coloured by local traditions ... all of this musical imbroglio arranged according to geographical origin.

Traditional music however forms the core of this wave, and remains a source that is still intact and where all of these genres can come to find inspiration. The "world-music" phenomenon carries with it the apology of "interbreeding". A mixture of styles and genres repertoires and forms, in the image of a society that dreams of ridding itself of its conflicts through the merger of cultures. Yet traditional music remains strongly impregnated with the theme of identity.

Drowned in the anonymity of large towns, people from the same community often use their traditional music and dance to perpetuate, in order to hold back the centrifugal movement of the community. It is very tempting to withdraw into the awakened dream, to cut oneself off from social and economic reality, or even to awaken old hostile feelings. Although it is a wonderful tool for achieving social cohesion, traditional music may also turn out to be a factor that aggravates the feeling of isolation instead of serving as a lever for integration into the host community. We will not forget that the appearance of the first folk groups in large French towns is linked to the development of regional "solidarity", the associations for helping people from the same province.

The risk of shutting oneself off that we underlined above, has as its counterpart that of diluting traditional culture into a servile adaptation of the musical forms imposed by the market. Certain promoters of world-music seem occasionally to succumb to the temptation of recovering all the richness of traditional world music in order to exploit it in their interest and force it into the musical format of light western music. Erasing the harsh tones of its scales, and planing down the roughness of the instruments and the voices by wrapping them in a harmonious layer very different from their initial function, very often they do nothing more than recreate another model that is just as insipid and standardized.

Light music is continually in search of new genres in order to make them available to the market. This thirst for novelty periodically seizes one or other of the artistic expressions of Western culture. In order to produce, the latter constantly requires new sources and material. It often searches for them outside its field. In the past, the outside world was able to situate itself in its own peoples.

Today, the whole world is forced to contribute, or robbed, in other words. A world-wide standard imposed by western production is emerging, but at the same time "local" musical forms (as described in the awful jargon of the "majors") succeeds in re-emerging and diverts this imposed standardization in their interest.

Useless Regrets

There is no point regretting this movement that now carries traditional music along in its wake in the initial meaning of the word. In the same way as the folk movement plunged into the folk song trend, traditional music can but deliberately launch itself into this new adventure. Even though this appellation masks heterogeneous forms, "world-music" nevertheless proposes a first approach to cultural multiplicity. Today we can no longer stick firmly to our own roots and show disinterest or hostility to other cultures or other musical genres. Curiosity is becoming the main quality necessary for traditional music players and is joined along the way by that of supporters of other aesthetics. New forms are in gestation. This germination is without a doubt the sign of a real intense life, a determination to impose itself as "topical".

Putting Modernity to Good Use

It does not therefore matter that we note, once again, that traditional music appears at the front of the stage as soon as a modern cultural object is under construction. But the essential contribution that it makes to contemporary creation is of no interest, unless it operates and respects its original authentic forms. This is where modernity lies. Contenting oneself with the standardization that we mentioned previously leads to the ephemeral — whereas a creative act is built up in time and resists against time.

Modernity is not about reducing a traditional melody to the even temperament of a synthesizer or to a scale of chords in keeping with the treaties of harmony or a binary rhythm that is a sign of modernity. The modernity of traditional music lies in the very heart of the forms and lessons that it offers us. The extraordinary variety of its rhythms, from the African polyrhythms to the asynchronous rhythms of central Europe has the power to shatter our controlled classical beat.

The universally known modality, its thousand-year-old systems with an unrivalled number of combinations can give free rein to the uniformity of our two unique styles. The sumptuous richness of the popular polyphonies from beyond the west, from the Corsican paghjella to the learned counterpoints of the pygmies, has the power to shatter this learned harmony, which, not so very long ago, lived under the illusion that polyphony was the distinctive privilege and mark of European "classical music".

The unexpected side of the multiple temperaments and musical scales have the strength to finally twist the predictable even temperament that imprisons all our instruments. Traditional music now has its place amongst "topical music" and its presence, alongside jazz or rock, gives an insight into the demands of those who play and the understanding that is predominant today.

Although traditional music brings with it age-old inheritances and archaic traits, it is still considered as a unique source of revival of artistic forms and practices. At the same time, it appears as the clearest demonstration of each culture's identity without necessarily relinquishing what is universal. And it is precisely this anchorage in the past and this investment in the present that gives it its resolutely modern character.

Policy in Favour of Traditional Music

Traditional music, a testimony to its era. If it is the case that traditional music lies at the heart of current cultural and political European debate, as these contributions will have convinced you, it is because they reflect, in their own way, the crisis which is affecting our civilization, a crisis which is, above all, a crisis of meaning. The solution to this crisis is therefore no doubt of a cultural nature (or even "religious" in the initial sense of the term — "that which binds together", — for the loss of meaning is, first and foremost, a loss of bonding). (Re)endowment of meaning, firstly involves the (re)discovery of the links with one's memory, one's history, not denying one's special characteristics under the pretext of increasing globalization, but rather updating them in their role as tools for dialogue and exchange.

It does not involve opposition to the various heritages with which we have been invested (family, local, regional, national, European, ...), but rather the acceptance of their complementarity and harmony, turning them into tools which "bridge" the diverse cultures which nourish us, thereby living our "Creolité" (borrowing a word from Raphael Confiant) as a source of richness, and not as a handicap. At the service of these objectives, traditional music has an essential role to play. Music from the memory, cultural expression, deeply rooted, assign a place for all in terms of a specific history, or region.

A universal artistic language, its aesthetics, spreading beyond the single framework which witnessed its birth, render dialogue possible with different musical traditions from elsewhere in the world, thus linking each to other histories, other lands. Endowed with a flexibility which has enabled it to span the centuries, in a state of permanent rebirth, it induces a form of cultural action which can serve as an example, being founded on the fruitful reconciliation of values perceived to be contradictory.

An organization by way of example. Thus, in France, we have tried to structure a development policy for this sector, with the assistance of the Minister of Culture, and the support of the regional centres, forming a network within our Federation. The eleven regional centres created as a result of this policy (in Aquitaine, Auvergne, Berry, Brittany, Ile de France, Languedoc-Roussillon, Limousin, Midi-Pyrenees, Poitou-Charentes, Provence-Alpes-Cote d'Azur, Rhône-Alpes), and the associations of traditional music and dance under the umbrella of FAMDT, are making every effort to tackle all areas simultaneously: conservation, research, education, distribution and creativity, bringing about co-operation between professionals, amateurs and institutions, under constant quality constraints.

This approach, with the public in mind, contributes to the provision of resources for, and to the improvement of a broader application ; open to other musical genres, it serves as a tool for the removal of barriers, and for the initiation of meetings. It furthermore plays an important role not only in the major urban centres (Paris, Lyons, Toulouse, Rennes, ...), but also in the rural environment, looking to establish its place in terms of overall "national development".

With strong links to local culture, it permits the valorization of local cultural identity, at the same time as favouring openness, marrying self assertiveness and dialogue with others, leading to an encounter between Music From Here and Music From There. Both cosmopolitan and with individual identity, we believe that this approach inscribes itself within the ideal of cultural democracy.

Proposals for a European Policy

With the benefit of this experience behind us, unique in Europe, of the networking, structuring and development of this sector, we propose the setting up of a co-operation agreement in this domain which, we believe, corresponds fully with the objectives of the European Union. This project necessitates an initial phase: the carrying out of a status report in each of the European countries, and the concerted presentation of these status reports, enabling exchange and debate on the structures and tools best suited for close co-operation. It will be the subject of the European Conference on Traditional Dance and Music which our federation is looking to organize in Autumn 1997, in partnership with the various organizations of other European states. This conference will therefore have the goal of:

— issuing a status report on the situation in each European state,

— proposing directions for co-operation in terms of the following themes: research documentation, education, distribution of live events, information, publications, dance,

— achieving the setting up of a European network for co-operation in the traditional music and dance domains.

The network could then propose the drawing up of a development plan, utilizing a number of selected places/ organizations (mirroring the French regional centres), in accordance with the following thematic approach;

— research and documentation (inventory of researchers and information gatherers, and of the archives put together, digitalization programme of documentary works, ...),

— education (initial, professional or further, encouragement towards the breaking down of barriers, ...),

— support for the creation and distribution of live events,

— support for written, sound or audio-visual publications,

— the implementation of communication tools utilizing the new technologies.

At the risk of becoming tedious, we must emphasize the extent to which we are convinced that the challenge represented by the development of this sector goes far beyond strict musical interests. At the close of this millennium, in a world which is losing its bearings, to deny the need of each individual or social grouping to put down firm roots would be pointless, and would on the contrary only lead to the reinforcement of the temptation to withdraw into a particular identity, occasionally leading to the worst of excesses, even to ethnic cleansing.

Valorizing each individual's cultural identity, whilst at the same time revealing his share of the universal and his capacity for dialogue with others, such is the formidable challenge facing the concerted development of traditional music and dance, within a European co-operation network. For universality is not to be looked for through the negation of singularities, but is embodied in their expression. It is thus a question of "each digging his personal well, thereby attaining the water table which is common to all".

Traditional Music and Copyright

Copyright, as defined by the Berne Convention, means the set of rights in rem and in personam conferred on the creators of literary and artistic works. Neighbouring rights are the rights allied to copyright which guarantee that certain classes of persons of enterprises contributing to a cultural act can derive an income from their activities.

Copyright is an intellectual property right, meaning that it can be bought or sold like any other form of property. The first owner of a copyright is the creator of a literary or artistic work. The owner of copyright in a work has the exclusive right to do, or to authorise anyone else to do certain things with the whole or any substantial part of the work. These things are called the acts restricted by copyright and they are as follows:

— To copy the work

— To issue copies to the public

— To lend or rent copies to the public

— To perform, play or show the work in public

— To broadcast the work or include it in a cable programme service

— To make an adaptation of the work or do any of the above in relation to an adaptation

The standard set in adjudicating originality is very low. "Original" here means only that the work has its origin in the creator. There is no requirement that the work be different from all that has come before. It need only embody a minimum level of creativity and owe its origin to the author or composer claiming copyright. Copyright in a literary, dramatic, musical, or artistic work lasts until the end of the seventieth year after the death of the author.

There is already a measure of European Community-wide "harmonisation" as a result of directives on copyright and neighbouring rights applied throughout the European Market (e.g..EC Directive 93/98), and these will herald major changes in the music industry and other cultural industries in the European Union. These moves towards greater harmonisation serve to emphasize the importance of copyright and neighbouring rights, and to consolidate their position within Europe:

Copyright and Neighbouring rights form the foundation of intellectual creativity and the propagation of culture. Protection of these rights guarantees the maintenance and development of creativity and cultural diversity to the benefit of authors, of performers, of cultural industries, of consumers and ultimately of society at large. Because of the recognition of copyright's role and economic importance, however, "copyright law has been dragged out of its slightly eccentric legal resting-place to become and issue of international conflict, a new locus for debates over political access and monopoly power".

Copyright in the arts as we know it today is based on a narrowly-defined, text-based concept of the "literary or artistic work" as it has developed since the enactment of the Statute of Anne in 1709, which has at its core particular philosophical premises relating to authorship, creativity, originality, individualism, and intellectual property; most of which received their elaboration during the Romantic Movement. This elaboration of the work-concept and the resultant premises of copyright are well suited to the processes of commodification within a capitalist system.

However, traditional culture, and traditional music and song in particular, comes into conflict with this conceptual framework in two fundamental ways:

a) In the everyday practice of these cultural expressions tunes or songs are conceived of as the consensus of practices, with the emphasis on process, variation, and individual contributions over time, alongside the recognition of the contribution of creative individuals in adding to a corpus of communally practiced and disseminated repertoire.

b) The key to understanding transmission in traditional musical expression, the perpetuation of these forms at amateur and community level, is the concept of Community Economy, a system of reciprocal exchange which privileges participation, the "doing of the doing", and generosity of distribution; none of which conform readily to the concepts of Market Economy, private property, commodification, and copyright.

As a result of this divergence at a conceptual and practical level, traditional cultures find themselves with a problem. Many musicians from traditional cultures are partaking of the fruits of a burgeoning music industry that considers traditional forms of music marketable commodities on the

"World Music" scene, thereby unknowingly working within two fundamentally contradictory, it not at least paradoxical worldviews. The hegemonic nature of the capitalistic ethos, its inherent ability to predominate and penetrate at all levels of culture, and the natural attractions of a full-time career in the music industry for musicians who love what they do, combine to increasingly commodify the musical expressions of traditional culture, making them available for financial exploitation.

If the advancing commodification of traditional culture is allowed to go unhindered, without adequate and sympathetic official protection for the originating non-market community system, then the transmission process itself, as a vital scene of community cohesion and humanising personal development, will itself be placed under threat.

The Philosophical Bass of Copyright

Authorship

At the centre of the copyright paradigm is the 'author", the "creator", as a distinct and discrete entity. In earliest times "Creator" was a name of Divine privilege, the human creative process finding its expression in ideas of craft and craftsmanship. The notion that the writer or composer is a special participant in the production process, indeed the only one worthy of attention, is a relatively recent one, "a by-product of the Romantic notion [18 th - 19 th centuries] that significant writers break altogether with tradition to create something utterly new, unique - in a word, 'original' ". Incorporated in this more recent formulation of authorship are assumptions founded on an individualism that developed in the seventeenth century, replete with a conception of the individual as the proprietor of his own person or capacities, which became one of the major influences on related ideas of originality and creativity as they took hold on the literary, legal, and public imaginations through the "cult of the artist".

The Work

An acceptance of the "author" or "creator" as a discrete, autonomous individual is usually coupled with the acceptance of a concept of the autonomous "work", a term signifying the abstraction that receives physical manifestation in a particular "copy" or "copies". This notion is.first and foremost of text-bound provenance, but the acceptance of perceived musical aesthetic autonomies took hold in the Western Art or Classical music tradition in the late eighteenth or early nineteenth centuries:

> The work-concept of music not only provided musicians with a theoretical equivalent to the tangible and highly valued objects of painting and sculpture, it served to conceal music's social and performative aspects by diverting attention away from musical processes to musical outcomes conceived as autonomous objects.

Together with "authorship", the formulation of the work-concept consolidated the power and influence of Romanticism in the development of societal structures, to the point that it became taken for granted as the only valid explanation for creative realities, and therefore the only possible foundation for legal philosophy: The view of the musical world the romantic aesthetic originally provided has continued, since 1800, to be the dominant view. This view is so entrenched in contemporary thought that its constitutive concepts are taken for granted. We have before us in fact a clear case of conceptual imperialism.

The Basic Inadequacies of Copyright

a) *Collectivity of Creativity; Organic Nature of Creative Systems*

In recent times, cultural theorists such as Michel Foucault and Roland Barthes, and legal theorists such as James Boyle and Peter Jaszi, have uncovered many of the shaky foundations that have supported the construct of autonomous "authorship", deconstructing the assumptions of originality and individualism to reveal the collaborative and collective nature of cultural production. But whereas cultural and legal theorists have signalled a need for a complete reassessment of "authorship", "originality", and copyright, there has been little or no response at a practical legislative level, with the consequences that such a failure to address this problem entails.

"The 'authorship' concept, although highly visible in contemporary copyright law, usually appears as a focus of consensus rather than debate. 'Authorship', as deployed in texts and in cultural understandings, has been anything but a stable, inert foundation for the structure of copyright doctrine. Rather, the ideologically charged concept has been an active shaping and destabilizing force in the erection of that structure".

The recent groundbreaking, interdisciplinary Bellagio Declaration stated clearly:

"In contemporary usage an 'author' is the sole creator of unique works of art, the originality of which warrants their protection under laws of intellectual property known as 'copyright' or 'author's rights'. So firmly established is this notion that it persists and flourishes even in the face of contrary experience. For on reflection it is evident that our creative practices are always derivative, generally collective, and increasingly corporate or collaborative. Yet we continue to think of 'genuine' authorship as solitary and originary, and may even imagine that the value we assign it is timeless and universal".

Musicologist Charles Seeger once wrote:

"It is well known that conscious and unconscious appropriation, borrowing, adapting, plagiarizing, and plain stealing are variously, and always have been, part and parcel of the process of artistic creation. The attempt to make sense out of copyright laws reaches its limit in folk song. For here is the illustration par excellence of the Law of Plagiarism. The folk-song is, by definition, and as far as we can tell, by reality, entirely a product of plagiarism".

Taken to extreme logical conclusions this recognition of collaborative production provokes extreme, uncompromising responses, which call for the eradication of all intellectual property regimes:

"Copyright is theft because it claims ownership of a common cultural heritage. It loots ideas, images and sounds from the naturally free-flowing cultural milieu. To copyright something is to deny sources. Copyright presents as the property of one, that which is taken from the lives of many. Authors imperialize their influences when their work is copyrighted". Simon Frith marries the assault on "authorship" with a critique of the fixation that musical copyright implies in trying to explain many of the problems relating to intellectual property, e.g. sampling, that currently beset the music industry:

"Until recently it was taken for granted that 'music' (a particular organisation of sound) was constituted as something fixed, something authored, and something that exists as property. These assumptions reflect the two sides of the bourgeois ideology of art, its simultaneous stress on individual creativity and individual ownership, on the Romantic-capitalist ideology which has survived both the rise of the mass media and the development of electronic means of cultural reproduction.

During the last two hundred years, though, the contradictions involved in this account of art have become harder and harder to manage - hence the huge elaboration of legal and institutional mechanisms to contain them, to sustain the belief that a work of art expresses an individual sensibility (even when collectively produced, as in the cinema, television and recorded music), and to keep in balance the theory of intellectual property (something abstract, 'owned' by its creator) and the practice of the intellectual commodity (creatively realised in a material object, something to be 'owned' by its consumer)".

b) Recombination and the Nature of the Musical Work in Traditional Music

Keeping these things in mind, it is no surprise that the musical application of copyright, born of the Western Art tradition, has been found to be almost entirely inadequate when faced with traditional musics in particular, as has been recognised by the World Intellectual Property Organisation:." It seems that copyright law may not be the right, or certainly the only, means for protecting expressions of folklore. This is because, whereas an expression of folklore is the result of an impersonal, continuous and slow process of creative activity exercised in a given community by consecutive imitation, works protected by copyright must, traditionally, bear a mark of individual originality. Traditional creations of a community, such as the so-called folk tales, folk songs, folk music, folk dances, folk designs or patterns, may often not fit into the notion of literary and artistic works. Copyright is author-centric and, in the case of folklore, an author - at least in way in which the notion of 'author' is conceived in the field of copyright - is absent".

Traditional songs and tunes seem to conform more to a model of a "consensus of practices". As Ciaran Carson has written of Irish traditional music, "The same tune is never the same tune twice. A traditional tune printed in a book is not the tune; it is a description of one of its many possible shapes". It is interesting to now note that even in the Western Art tradition the idea of tangible fixation of a "work" that copyright requires is now deemed inadequate:

"Musical works enjoy a very obscure mode of existence; they are 'ontological mutants'. Works cannot, in any straightforward sense, be physical, mental, or ideal objects. They do not exist as concrete, physical objects; they do not exist as private ideas existing in the mind of a composer, a performer, or a listener; neither do they exist in the eternally existing world of ideal, uncreated forms. They are not identical, furthermore, to any one of their performances. Performances take place in real time; their parts exist simultaneously. Neither are works identical to their scores".

In traditional music there is the added issue of the continual reworking of available material, or "recombination" that takes place within the traditional musical system. As folklorist W.F.H. Nicolaisen has written, variation in folklore is creative because it is the result of, "deliberate, intentional, and therefore far from accidental, changes and choices introduced by the individual folk artist whose creative genius is not content with mere imitative repetition in the process of appropriating a variant of a tale (or song) as his or her own personal version. Far from being at odds with each other, creativity and tradition, individual and community, together produce vital variability thus keeping alive the very items that their integrated forces help to shape".

At no point, moreover, is it to be denied that creative individuals contribute new tunes and songs to be played or sung:

"The personality of the artist is often an important factor in folklore expressions, and individual contributions to the development and maintenance of such expressions may represent a creative source of enrichment of inherited folklore if they are recognized and adopted by the community as expressions corresponding to its traditional artistic expectations".

But an acceptance of creativity in traditional systems, or what we might call composition, does not automatically mean that we must subscribe to the philosophical, concept-laden frameworks of "composer" and "work" that have been passed down in the Western Art or Classical music tradition. Ethnomusicologist Colin Quigley, writing of French Newfoundland traditional fiddler Emile Benoit, makes clear that Emile's highly developed compositional skills were part and parcel of traditional expression:

"Emile's musical knowledge and skill were fairly typical of his musical peers. Creation of new strains and entire tunes is not uncommon or atypical, and most musicians have a few such pieces in their repertoires. Emile's intense level of commitment to the continuing search for creative musical expression, however, transformed his musical abilities into a powerful tool for composition. As an unusually prolific composer, he was not at odds with his tradition. Rather, he internalized its essential characteristics and actualized its inherent potential as a generative system of musical expression".

Creative activity in traditional contexts must be assessed within its contexts of production and consumption, and cannot be understood as an autonomous realm, as copyright would encourage us to do. As a result, "the law is not so much systematically hostile to works that do not fit the individualistic model of Romantic 'authorship' as it is uncomprehending of them. Such works are marginalized or become literally invisible within the prevailing ideological framework of discourse in copyright".

Copyright as an Instrument of Commodification Within Capitalism

At this stage in history it is almost impossible to separate intellectual property from its role as an instrument of commodification within capitalist systems:

"In capitalist economies, one function of the market is to assure the public distribution of commodities, but the discipline of the market extends to the private attributes of individuals (personality, emotion, sexuality, artistic self-expression) only to the extent that these can be effectively 'commodified'".

In fact, their development throughout history has been concurrent. The appearance in the eighteenth century of things of the mind as transferable articles of property matured simultaneously with the capitalist system. It could be argued that the application of intellectual property in any circumstance assumes the a priori application of capitalism, where the production and distribution of goods depend on invested private cultural capital and profit making. If this is the case, then unlimited participation in a capitalist system, which seeks by its nature the furthermost penetration of the market, and the unbounded acceptance of intellectual property as a legal solution, impose an unnecessarily individualist vision.

Ecologist Vandana Shiva has written that:. "The first restriction of Intellectual Property Rights is the shift from common rights to private rights. This excludes all kinds of knowledge, ideas, and innovations that take place in the 'intellectual commons'. The second restriction of Intellectual Property Rights is that they are recognised only when knowledge and innovation generate profits, not when they meet social needs. This immediately excludes all sectors that produce and innovate outside the industrial mode of organization of production. Profits and capital accumulation are recognised as the only ends to which creativity should be put".

This brings us back to an earlier point in relation to copyright. In clarification of what actually happens when copyright is vested in an individual, copyright and related rights give the holder sole and exclusive power to authorise or prohibit the use and reproduction of the whole or any substantial part of works and other protected matter. This is possessive individualism in practice. This degree of control, if applied to traditional music and song, bestows rights on an individual which they would not previously have had within the traditional practice of musical transmission, and which would in fact run contrary to the welfare of the transmission process. Even when dealing with the relatively unproblematic literary copyright the issue of restriction as a threat to the sensitivity to creative processes arises:

"Authorship is possible only when future authors have the ability to borrow from those who have created before them. If too much of each work is reserved as private property through copyright, future would-be authors will find it impossible to create. Society would presumably suffer from the decreased production of creative works. Proper construction of our copyright law therefore depends on striking a socially acceptable balance between the interests of authors and the public".

Community Economy

Some of the characteristics of a Community Economy are as follows:

a) Innovations are Product and Property of a Group

We have already seen how recombination and collective innovations provide the core of traditional music practices. It is as a result of reciprocal practices that the corpus of traditional music and song is perceived as a common pool of material, the product of a group rather than of individuals, the whole of which emerges as a continually developing consensus of practices and expectations that defines a community.

"But group pooling does not always imply open access or equality of shares. Social rules may sustain power differences, and distribution of resources may depend upon age, gender, or kinship differences. Particulars aside, a community does not allocate shares by calculating the marginal efforts and yields of individuals. Of course, community sectors today are increasingly dominated by market principles, but even within the competitive market itself communal practices are encountered. Pure gifts, charity and altruism remain important in market economy, even if they do no more than indicate the suspension of self-interest and an ephemeral commitment to community".

b) Innovations Emerge Through Practices as Ends in Themselves

In the commercial realm goods circulate through trade. One of the vital keys to understanding traditional musical forms is in the predominance of participation as an end in itself, as the means whereby circulation of knowledge, in this case musical knowledge, takes place. "Based on the commensality of its participants, the community economy emphasizes qualities such as sharing and reliance upon others. An economy of trust and fostering, these qualities extend to all who make up the community".

Variation, recombination, and even new compositions primarily serve to feed the system of participation rather than draw overt attention to individual contributions. "The aim is to sustain or maintain a way of living; and this is understood in a total sense: well-being in the community is defined in terms of participation and social continuity as opposed to individual acquisition". Although hierarchies of talent and status undoubtedly evolve over time, nevertheless traditional forms invite musical interaction at all levels of ability, making the musical practice a means to an end of social interaction and community cohesion, a domain of gift. This stands in marked contrast to a market economy, where intellectual property rights connote that the property has value as a means to accumulate more wealth or money.

c) Material Processes are Cyclical or Self Contained

In traditional communities music was constantly reinvested through performance into the cyclical process of transmission. This still occurs, but problems have manifested themselves through the participation of outside agencies with no sense of the reciprocation required by the musical community; e.g. the use of traditional material by record companies and non-traditional groups. The reluctance of traditional composers to copyright their tunes, thus leaving their work vulnerable to piracy, stems from a complex web of social relationships and a recognition of a "tradition" that incorporates past, present, and future generations.

Erroneous copyrighting of these tunes and songs means that neither the original composers nor traditional music communities will benefit from royalties, and amateur traditional musicians may eventually be deprived of the free use of the music. In many cases individuals have personally appropriated traditional tunes or songs by way of registration; a peculiar version of "first-come-first-served" and "what they don't know won't hurt them". No one is suggesting that traditional cultures can survive in cocoons, but as Stephen Brush states in relation to the application of intellectual property in biodiversity and genetic engineering:

"Common heritage does not mean that a person who seeks to obtain genetic resources has no obligation to those who provide them. On the contrary, common heritage implies a reciprocity between the collector of genetic resources and the producer. The reciprocity is that collective knowledge flows in both directions".

Public Domain

The term "public domain' is often used in relation to traditional music and song, but, in much the same way as the terms "author" and "work", "public domain" at the present time finds itself under threat. John Frow, of the University of Queensland, has written that:

"The concept of public domain has a precise application in modern legal systems, where it forms the cornerstone of copyright law and indeed of Intellectual Property doctrine generally. Yet the concept is a purely residual one: rather than being itself a set of specific rights, the public domain is that space, that possibility of access, which is left over after all other rights have been defined and distributed. It has had a shadowy legal presence through common-law principles such as fair use but its lack of positive doctrinal elaboration leaves it vulnerable to erosion. It is a concept which is in many ways in crisis".

The use of the term often leads to confusion in traditional music, implying anonymous or unknown authorship, meanings which are often attributed wrongly to the word "traditional" itself. As has been shown, however, "traditional" implies the presence of a community economy, in which authorship is certainly not a central concern. The concept of public domain, in the sense of unlimited access to all who wish to participate in the community economy, is such a given - for newly composed material as well as for the musical heritage that has been passed down through the generations - that its use as a term would seem superfluous. Composers in traditional communities allow their material to be subsumed into the traditional participatory processes in return for the very participation that begot their efforts in the first place. This fluidity of musical practice across complexly layered communities makes intellectual property rights difficult to assign and equity hard to achieve.

The conceptualization of the public domain as "that space, that possibility of access, which is left over after all other rights have been defined and distributed" (above), is once more a product of a copyright-bound worldview that does not allow for an alternative reality; the product of a world view that can ultimately be traced back to Platonic and Cartesian mind/body dichotomies. Continual and unexamined application of such concepts leads to further misunderstanding of the issues at stake. It leads us to persist in our understanding of the stuff of life as products and not process. As Stephen Gudeman has written in the context of biodiversity:

"The expression, 'intellectual property rights', with its emphasis on the mind, connotes abstraction, decontextualization, formalization, and the use of written information. Through the concept of intellectual property rights we deploy widely accepted Western assumptions. We assume that innovations as products or processes have a technical essence that can be identified; once distinguished, this core can be abstracted from its context of use, converted to a written form, transported home, and tested in a laboratory. The implication is that local knowledge, if it is valid knowledge, can be restated within a scientific and general language that we possess. If local knowledge cannot be fitted to this discourse, it must be faulty".

Intellectual Property as a Threat to Community Life

The continued application of the principles of intellectual property within community economies carries within it the threat of breakdown of a human community whose relationships are expressed through and maintained by creative expression and resources. Community economies still exist as realities, despite the blurring of community boundaries and the imposition of market principles, and despite the assumption that communitas is merely a fanciful ideological reconstruction of the Sixties Folk Revival. "Vernacular cultures have not been wholly subsumed into mass commodity culture, despite - in some respects because of - the threat of a universalization of the marketplace. The two react against each other, colliding into and at certain points galvanizing each other in a continual process of tension and contradiction".

Recognition of the place of community economy within traditional culture, and recognition that copyright and intellectual property is not going to go away, makes it tempting to just accept that intellectual property is the lesser evil. But again, unchanged application of intellectual property rights carries profound implications, as Stephen Gudeman rightly points out:

"In my view, the use of intellectual property rights on an international scale to compensate nonmarket economies not only raises problematic issues but presents a paradox. Some people would use the legal and monetary entitlements afforded by intellectual property rights to protect and foster the local knowledge and innovations of a folk in order to secure global equity and help them preserve community identity. But if intellectual property rights is a property and component of Western capitalism, then abetting its acceptance elsewhere must lead to economic transformation or adoption of the market form exactly among those people whom it is said to protect. Here we need to distinguish carefully between using intellectual property rights to protect innovations within a market economy and using them between economies".

We have to be careful that our actions do not simply reproduce a long history of transforming all aspects of pre-industrial forms of community economy into post-industrial models of capitalist market economies, for in doing that we subvert the humanising ingredients of the mix. "The argument for extending the market's logic to community economies is not an argument for achieving greater efficiency within the market, but often a justification for market penetration and private engrossment. Extending an intellectual property rights system to a community commons is a way of parsing and converting it to the market form, where it may be used for individual gain. This subverts the trust and mutuality of which the commons is an expression". It is a common problem for all traditional musics as they strain under the weight of the growing penetration of the market economy and intellectual property.

As Sheryle Mills has concluded, "Western Law has evolved in tandem with Western Music, focusing primarily on the protection of individual property rights and financial profits. Thus, traditional music and Western law clash at the most fundamental level". There has to be a realisation that the world-view of economics is not an all-encompassing, universal truth, as is commonly assumed. Michael Pickering and Tony Green, in their article "Towards a Cartography of the Vernacular Milieu", have written:

"The threat of capitalist development in the modern world is the subsumption of all social life into the marketplace. This universalisation of the market is, as Braverman has put it, 'one of the keys to all recent social history'. It is not only material and service needs which are threatened by this development; 'emotional patterns of life' also become increasingly 'channelled through the market' and 'relationships between individuals and social groups' tend 'not to take place directly, as co-operative human encounters but through the market as relations of purchase and sale'".

The enclosure of the traditional transmission process by commercial concerns is jettisoning essential elements of community economy that maintain transmission in fluid motion, and is directly related to the decline of community level participatory forms of musical expression. The musical community economy, which has long contained the seeds of its regeneration, now invites with open arms the seeds of its possible destruction.

That the world of Homo Economicus is a significant, dominant, and oft times beneficial way of looking at the world at the end of the twentieth century there can be no doubt. But to suggest that there is no alternative, or to suggest that certain valuable aspects of traditional culture have no right to exist contemporaneously on their own terms is going too far down the evolutionist trail. Even the famed economist John Maynard Keynes warned us not to "overestimate the importance of the economic problem, or sacrifice to its supposed necessities other matters of greater and more permanent significance".

In recent years there has been a general recognition of crisis in Legal, Economic, Scientific and similarly mechanistic systems in the light of their inadequacy to deal with an organic and highly complex reality. Certain elements of the market economy in the form of intellectual property have come into contact with a largely incompatible traditional counterpart. A certain part of the body traditional is rejecting the transplant. That is not to ignore the question of overlapping practices or even the full-blooded participation of some traditional musicians in the capitalistics of the music industry. Neither is it to ignore the gift-bounded processes at all levels of the Music Business, or indeed any capitalist system. Polarisation in absolutes only produces oversimplification and distortion.

Perceptual Similarity Measures for Music

Large music repositories require intelligent interfaces to interact with their contents. One critical building block for these interfaces is automatically calculating the perceived similarity of music. Applications which can be built upon such similarity measures include enabling users to find new pieces similar to a given piece, making recommendations of new pieces based on a model of the user's musical taste, automatically organizing and visualizing music collections according to similarity, or creating playlists. However, perceived similarity is an ill-defined concept and depends on various factors such as instruments, timbre, melody, rhythm, lyrics, style, and many more. Furthermore, the importance of each factor varies with the context.

Unfortunately, there is no ground truth for music similarity. Nevertheless, developing similarity measures is an emerging research field with a main focus on applications. Although several approaches have been published, little attention was given to comparing their performances. Each publication contains performance results for the respective approach, but they are very difficult to compare. One of the main reasons is that no common test data collection is available. Most pieces in digital music collections are proprietary which prohibits sharing them. Recently, an effort was made to build a copyright-cleared music database for research purposes.

However, it is not clear if this rather small collection will be able to establish itself as a common database for evaluations. Another problem encounter when trying to evaluate similarity measures is that conducting the necessary large-scale listening test is very costly.

Similarity Measures

There are five similarity measures. Each of these measures focuses on different aspects of music and uses different techniques to describe them.

Logan and Salomon (LS)

The feature extraction chosen in LS is based on Mel Frequency Cepstrum Coefficients. MFCCs have been applied successfully in speech processing, and their application to all audio types seems straight forward. LS describe music in terms of spectral envelopes each of which is characterised by 19 MFCCs and thus with relatively high detail. The average loudness, in particular the first MFCC is ignored. As an effect of removing the average loudness of each time frame it is quite impossible to locate beats. Another observation is that compared to the other representations MFCC 19* has the highest texture resolution on the frequency axis, thus, details in the spectrum are captured which the other measures ignore.

A piece of music is summarized by 16 typical spectral envelopes which are determined using k-means clustering. The high number of typical envelopes allows a detailed description of the piece. The main characteristics are that the spectral envelopes are mostly flat beyond 10 Mel and below 10 Mel most of them depict a strong increase in loudness, due to the strong bass beats.

To compute the distance between two pieces a highly efficient technique developed for image retrieval is applied which is based on linear programming, namely, the Earth Mover's Distance. For the Mel-scale, the implementation of the Auditory Toolbox where the first centre frequency of the Mel scale is located at 200Hz and the last, i.e., the 40th, around 6.4kHz. The 3 highest frequency bands were not used because their centre frequencies are beyond 5.5kHz and used 11kHz audio as input. For the EMD used the implementation provided by Rubner.

Aucouturier and Pachet (AP)

Like LS the feature extraction chosen in AP is based on MFCCs. However, the main difference is that significantly fewer coefficients are used, namely only the first 8. Furthermore, the average loudness is not removed. Unlike MFCC 19* the location of the strong beats can easily be identified. Another difference is that compared to MFCC 19* the texture on the frequency axis is much smoother.

Unlike LS, scaling the maximum level of an audio signal to a different value would significantly change AP's representation. However, such problems can be circumvented by normalizing the audio signal prior to computing the AP representation. To summarize the spectral envelopes of a piece of music the same idea applied in LS is used but with different techniques. A Gaussian Mixture Model is used instead of k-means. Instead of 16 only 3 typical spectral envelopes are used. However, the diagonal covariance of the GMM offers additional flexibility. Furthermore, since the spectrum envelopes are represented with less details also fewer typical envelopes are necessary to describe the variations.

Spectrum Histograms (SH)

The spectrum histograms (SH) are a drastically simplified approach to summarizing the spectral shape. The idea is to obtain the same results as AP but with a simpler model. Unlike LS and AP the SH are based on a Sone/Bark representation of the audio signal. The main differences is that the Bark scale covers also lower frequencies. Although only 20 Bark-bands are used, i.e., almost half of the number used in the MFCC representation, 2 bands have their centre frequencies below 200Hz. In addition, a model of the outer and middle ear is applied to simulate the unequal perception of loudness at different frequencies. Furthermore, spectral masking is applied which substitutes the smoothing of the DCT. Finally, instead of using dB-SPL the Sone values are computed.

The SH summarize a piece of music by counting how many times a loudness level was reached or exceeded in the frequency bands. The values are stored in a 2-dimensional histogram which has 20 rows for the Bark-bands and 50 columns for the loudness resolution. The sum of the histogram is normalized to 1. In accordance with AP and LS the SH frequently reaches a high relative strength in the low Bark-bands. The spectrum is rather flat otherwise.

Two SHs are compared by interpreting them as 1000-dimen-sional vectors in an Euclidean space. Combined with a PCA compression this approach is many times faster than AP or LS.

Periodicity Histograms (PH)

Periodicity histograms were originally presented in the context of beat tracking. A similar approach was developed to classify genres. Details of the differences between the similarity measure use and these two approaches can be found in. The idea is to describe (only) periodically reoccurring beats regardless of their frequency. The features are extracted by further processing the Sone/Bark representation. First, a half wave rectified difference filter is applied on each Bark-band to emphasize percussive sounds. Then the signal is sequenced into 12-second segments which are further processed individually. Each sequence is weighted using a Hann window before a comb filter bank is applied to each Bark-band with a 5bpm resolution in the range from 40 to 240bpm. Then a resonance model is applied to the amplitudes obtained from the comb filter.

To emphasize peaks at specific periods a full wave rectified difference filter is used before summing up the amplitudes for each periodicity over all bands. The 12-second representations are summarized using a 2-dimensional histogram with 40 equally spaced columns representing different frequencies (bpm) and 50 rows representing strength levels. The histogram counts for each periodicity how many times a level equal to or greater than a specific value was reached. The distance between two PHs is computed the same way as between two SHs.

Fluctuation Patterns (FP)

One of the main differences between the FPs and the PHs is that the FPs use a simple FFT instead of the computationally more expensive comb-filter to find periodicities in the Bark-bands.

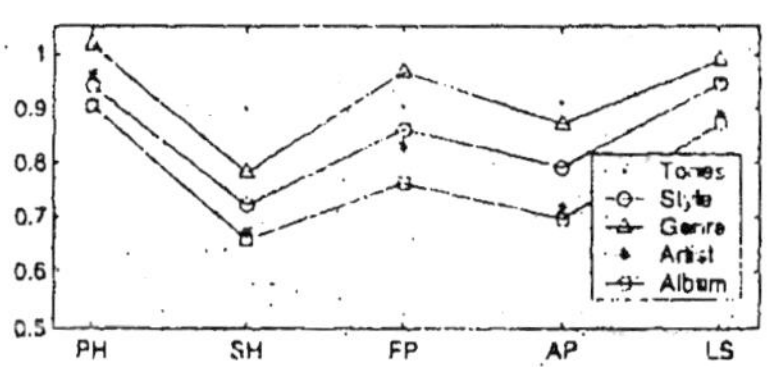

Figure 1. Results of the quantitative evaluation. The vertical axis represents the ratio between average distances within a group versus the average distances in the whole collection.

Furthermore, while the PHs use a resonance model which has a maximum at about 120bpm the FPs use a fluctuation model which has a peak at 4Hz (240bpm). The biggest difference, however, is that the FPs include information on the spectrum while the PHs disregard this information.

Large Scale Evaluation

To conduct a quantitative evaluation, a collection of 314 CDs by 177 use different artists or groups with a total of 270 hours of music and 3961 tracks (excluding tracks with less than 25-second length). The collection covers a broad range of musical taste with a main focus on popular and alternative music. To evaluate the similarity measures, group the pieces of music by album (or single), artist (or group), genre, style, and "tones". The last three were obtained for each artist from All Music Guide. The AMG genres are a very rough categorization.

The following AMG genres are represented in the collection where the number in the brackets indicates the number of artists in the genre: Folk (1), Celtic (1), Newage (1), Reggae (1), Classical (1), World (2), Jazz (9), Rap (12), Latin (17), Electronica (18), and Rock (112). The AMG styles include, for example, Third Wave Ska Revival (2), Blue-Eyed Soul (3), British Invasion (4), College Rock (8), Psychedelic (9), Brazilian Pop (9), Trip-Hop (11), Pop/Rock (28), Alternative Pop/Rock (47), and many more. In total there are over 200 different style descriptors which apply to the music collection.

The AMG tones describe more general attributes of music. For example, for Michael Jackson AMG lists the following tones: Energetic, Passionate, Sentimental, Rousing, Joyous, Confident, Exuberant, Stylish, Earnest, and Party/Celebratory. In total 127 different tones are assigned to the 177 artists in the collection. The evaluation was conducted as follows. For each measure the average distance between all pieces was computed. This average distance was then compared to the average distance within the groups (artist, genre, etc.). The resulting ratios are depicted in Figure 1 and in Table 1. A ratio of one means that the distance between arbitrary pieces and members within a group are about the same. The lower the ratio the better the members of a group are distinguished from other pieces.

The most surprising result is that the simple SHs outperform all other measures. The PHs perform worst. Perhaps periodicity characteristics are not as important as spectral characteristics or maybe the particular PH measure used is not well suited as similarity measure. AP performed better than FP which performed better than LS. Best results were obtained on the level of individual albums followed closely by artists. The worst results were obtained for genres. The performance on AMG tones is practically independent of the measure used.

Table 1: Results of the quantitative evaluation.

	PH	SH	FP	AP	LS
Tones	0.92	0.90	0.90	0.91	0.96
Style	0.94	0.72	0.86	0.79	0.95
Genre	1.02	0.78	0.97	0.87	0.99
Artist	0.96	0.67	0.83	0.72	0.89
Album	0.90	0.66	0.76	0.70	0.87

In LS some results were published with respect to the average distance in the collection versus the average distance within albums. The published numbers (0.48 for all average, 0.21 for album average using 4 MFCCs) suggest a ratio below 0.5 which is far better than the results. Perhaps there are significant difference in the implementations of the LS similarity measure, e.g., a different Mel scale covering also low frequencies. Perhaps this enormous difference can also be explained by the fact that two completely different collections were used.

In AP some results describing the average distance between all pieces. The resulting ratio of 0.99 is significantly higher than the value of 0.87 which we have obtained for AP. Again this might depend on different implementations or more likely on different genre structures in the database.

In general using genre or similar descriptors to evaluate similarity measures is problematic. First of all, no standardized tax-onomies exist. Furthermore, the different taxonomies used are inconsistent with overlapping genres. The number and types of genres used influence the classification results. For example, it is easy to automatically classify pieces of music into one of the three genres Rock, Classical, and Electronica. However, distinguishing between Hard Rock and Metal is more difficult.

Furthermore, also the use of the album information to evaluate similarity measures is problematic. In particular, it is likely that all tracks on the same CD have undergone the same normalization, dynamics compression, and equalization. Thus, a similarity measure which measures these production characteristics would outperform others.

So far the numbers obtained from the quantitative evaluation are not too useful. One way to study the results in more detail is to look at extreme cases. In particular, looking at the artists/albums which are very homogeneous or very in homogeneous. For example, the group Daft Punk (2 CDs in the collection) has the largest average distances between its pieces according to the PH. This is quite intuitive since the pieces by Daft Punk have very strong beats and the different beat patterns in their recordings have a strong impact on the PH.

PH, SH, and FP have the most homogeneous artist in common, namely, Brad Mehldau, a jazz pianist (1 CD with 7 tracks in the collection). The most inhomogeneous artist in terms of SH and AP is Placebo. The most inhomogeneous artist in terms of LS is Goldfrapp.

On the level of individual CDs a Daft Punk single, namely Around The World, is the most inhomogeneous in terms of PH. The most homogeneous in terms of PH is a single by Mariah Carey, namely One Sweet Day. Another observation is that SH and LS both consider a different album of France Battiato to be most in homogeneous and LS and AP both consider a different album of Bad Religion as most homogeneous. Although some insights into the measures can be gained when analysing the results of the evaluation it is difficult to directly use these insights to improve the measures. To understand why PH has performed so poorly and why SH so well it is necessary to study the measures on a different level.

Small Scale Evaluation

For the qualitative evaluation we can use a very small collection of only 120 sequences each 10 seconds long. Each sequence was manually selected with the intention to cover a broad and well balanced spectrum of music. Furthermore, from some pieces 2 or 3 sequences were selected which were either very similar or very different. With these duplicates is possible to easily evaluate if similar pieces are mapped together, and to test whether a similarity measure is sensitive, for example, to effects of a dynamic compression.

Obviously such a small collection cannot contain all different varieties of music. However, the main advantages are that it is very easy to make a complete evaluation (the whole set can be listened to in 20 minutes). Furthermore, adapting parameters of the similarity measures and evaluating the results can be done nearly in real time, and it is also easier to judge the similarity between two pieces if they are only 10 seconds long because it is not necessary to remember what the piece sounded like 3 minutes ago.

As a main tool to evaluate such small collections we can use the Self-Organizing Map. The SOM maps similar pieces close to each other on a 2-dimensional visualization space where the cluster structure can be visualized using smoothed data histograms. One main benefit of the SOM is that general properties of a similarity measure can easily be studied by visualizing the code-book (i.e., a collection of typical patterns in the data set).

In general AP patterns which have a stronger contribution in the lower Mel-bands and weaker contribution in the higher bands tend to be less noisy (e.g. Classical or Jazz).

On the other hand, horizontal lines indicate quite noisy pieces. This is particularly true if it is a very sharp line, which means that there is not much variation in the loudness. If the line is blurred and horizontal it represents music with strong beats: the maximum loudness level in all bands is reached regularly, but in between beats the loudness level is significantly reduced. Using a SOM it generally only takes a very short time to get a general impression on how well the measure performs. Moreover, it is usually not very difficult to find cases in the collection where the similarity measure has failed.

Bibliography

Adler, Israel, ed. Hebrew Writings Concerning Music. RISM. Munich: G. Henle, 1975.

Avenary, Hanoch. "Contacts Between Church and Synagogue Music." In Proceedings of the World Congress on Jewish Music, ed.Judith Cohen. Tel Aviv: Th e Institute for the Translation of Hebrew Literature (Naidat Press), 1978.

Barry, William A S.J., & William J. Connolly S.J., *The Practice of Spiritual Direction*. New York: HarperCollins, ©no year given.

Basart, Ann. "Music and the Holocaust: A Selective Bibliography." Cum notis variorum, 101 (April, 1986), pp. 1-30.

Blank, Rebecca M. *Do Justice: Linking Christian Faith and Modern Economic Life*. Cleveland, Ohio: United Church Press, 1992.

Cohen, Judith, ed. Proceedings of the World Congress on Jewish Music. The Institute for the Translation of Hebrew Literature. Tel Aviv: Naidat Press, 1978.

Conroy, Maureen, R.S.M. *Experiencing God's Tremendous Love: Entering Into Relational Prayer*. New Jersey: Upper Room Spiritual Center, ©1996

Cusson, Giles, S.J.. *The Spiritual Exercises Made in Everyday Life*. St. Louis: Institute of Jesuit Resources, 1989.

Dougherty, Rose Mary, S.S.N.D. *Group Spiritual Direction: Community for Discernment*. New York: Paulist Press, 1995.

Eisenstein, Judith Kaplan. Heritage of Music: The Music of the Jewish People. New York: Union of American Hebrew Congregations, 1973.

Gerson-Kiwi, Edith. "On the Musical Sources of the Judaeo-Spanish Romance." The Musical Quarterly 50 (1964): 31-43.

Herzog, Avigdor. "Metrical Aspects of Samaritan Music." In Proceedings of the World Congress on Jewish Music, ed. Judith Cohen. Tel Aviv: The Institute for the Translation of Hebrew Literature (Naidat Press), 1978.

Jacobson, Joshua. "Choral Music for Chanukah." Choral Journal XXXI (2 1990): 19-28.

Katz, Israel J. "The "Myth" of the Sephardic Musical Legacy from Spain." In The Fifth World Congress of Jewish Studies in Jerusalem, edited by Avigdor Shinan, World Union of Jewish Studies, 237-243, Year.

Index